P9-DGF-422

COAST TO COAST:
HOCKEY IN CANADA TO THE SECOND WORLD WAR

As an institution that helps bind Canadians to an imagined community, hockey has long been associated with an essential Canadian identity. However, this reductionism ignores the ways Canadians consume hockey differently based on their socio-economic background, gender, ethnicity, and location. Moreover, Canadian culture is not static, and hockey's place in it has evolved and changed.

In *Coast to Coast*, a wide range of contributors examine the historical development of hockey across Canada, in both rural and urban settings, to ask how ideas about hockey have changed. Conceptually broad, the essays explore identity formation by investigating what hockey meant to Canadians from the nineteenth century to the Second World War, as well as the role of government, entrepreneurs, and voluntary associations in supporting and promoting the game. *Coast to Coast* is an intriguing look at the development of a national sport, a must-read for hockey fans and historians alike.

JOHN CHI-KIT WONG is an assistant professor in the College of Education at Washington State University.

Coast to Coast

Hockey in Canada to the Second World War

Edited by John Chi-Kit Wong

UNIVERSITY OF TORONTO PRESS
Toronto Buffalo London

© University of Toronto Press 2009
Toronto Buffalo London
www.utppublishing.com
Printed in the U.S.A.

Reprinted 2015

ISBN 978-0-8020-9778-1 (cloth)
ISBN 978-0-8020-9532-9 (paper)

∞

Printed on acid-free, 100% post-consumer recycled paper.

Library and Archives Canada Cataloguing in Publication

Coast to coast : hockey in Canada to the Second World War / edited by
John Chi-Kit Wong.

Includes bibliographical references and index.
ISBN 978-0-8020-9778-1 (bound). – ISBN 978-0-8020-9532-9 (pbk.)

1. Hockey – Canada – History – 19th century.   2. Hockey – Canada –
History – 20th century.   3. Hockey – Social aspects – Canada – History.
I. Wong, John Chi-Kit, 1955–

GV848.4.C3W66 2009   796.9620971   C2009-901789-X

University of Toronto Press acknowledges the financial assistance to its
publishing program of the Canada Council for the Arts and the Ontario
Arts Council.

University of Toronto Press acknowledges the financial support for its
publishing activities of the Government of Canada through the Book
Publishing Industry Development Program (BPIDP).

Contents

Proem

In their seminal work on hockey and culture, *Hockey Night in Canada: Sport, Identities and Cultural Politics* (1993), Richard Gruneau and David Whitson lamented 'the ambivalence of Canadian academics towards hockey.'[1] They point as evidence to the scarcity of academic work on an activity that is so closely tied to what it means to be Canadian. In the intervening years, the difficulty of finding scholarly work on hockey has lessened. A number of theses, dissertations, and articles have examined the sport through a variety of lenses.[2] Moreover, scholarly interest increased to such an extent that Dr Colin Howell at Saint Mary's University in Nova Scotia was able to organize the first conference on the study of hockey in 2001, gathering presenters whose work spanned many disciplines.[3] As a sign of changing times, a third conference focusing on women's place in hockey was held at Saint Mary's in conjunction with the women's world hockey championship, in March 2004. Despite these exciting developments in the study of hockey, scholarly book-length treatment of the subject remains rare, even though there are plenty of books about hockey for sale in Canadian book stores.[4] Indeed, the idea for this project came in March 2003, when I met with University of Toronto Press editor Len Husband to discuss my first book on hockey (*Lords of the Rinks*). We both agreed that there should be more scholarly studies on such an important institution. This book makes a modest contribution towards correcting this situation.

As an institution that helps to bind Canadians to an imagined community, hockey has long been equated with the Canadian identity – 'the Canadian Specific,'[5] 'the game of our lives.'[6] Indeed, it is no surprise that the Canadian Broadcasting Corporation's national television network, responsible for contributing to a shared national consciousness and identity, produced a ten-episode epic documentary, *Hockey: A People's History*, that traces the history of a sport that, the CBC argues, has 'shaped a nation' and 'woven itself into our cultural language and fabric.'[7] This identification of hockey with being Canadian seems to be accepted almost unquestioningly by Canadians and foreigners alike. Given the devotion of the Canadian people and media to the sport, hockey, according to some, is and must be naturally and uniquely Canadian – a kind of Canadian exceptionalism that views hockey as 'a natural Canadian cultural resource ... developed almost magically out of an exposure to ice, snow, and open spaces' and 'an essence that exists outside of the influences of social structure and history.'[8] Yet, this reductionism ignores the different ways Canadians consume hockey based on their socio-economic background, gender, ethnicity, and location. Moreover, the essentialist nature of this view implies an unchanging conceptualization of hockey's place in a monolithic Canadian identity and culture.

Following their acclaimed work on hockey and culture, Whitson and Gruneau released their second book on hockey, *Artificial Ice: Hockey, Culture, and Commerce*, in 2006 – an edited volume assessing the state of hockey in the early twenty-first century. Certainly, many Canadians accept hockey as an important part of their identity today, in part because of what one of the book's contributors, Brian Wilson, called a 'selective memory' of a nostalgic past.[9] But what in fact happened in bygone years? Has hockey always been both the signifier and signified of the Canadian people or did identity formation emerge and develop momentum with the formalization of the sport in Canada in the nineteenth century? If so, how and why did hockey become a signifier of Canadianness? If not, how was hockey presented to, and how did it represent, different groups of Canadians at different times? This book attempts to answer some of these historical questions by examining what hockey meant to Canadians from the late nineteenth century to the Second World War.

Noted American filmmaker Woody Allen was once rumoured to have lamented that a project's final product rarely resembles the idea that started it. In my search for contributors to this book, the issue of hockey's presentation and representation of different groups in different regions of Canada called logically for a scope as inclusive and expansive as possible. Despite increased interest in studying hockey, it turned out to be quite a difficult task to locate historians who would take on the breadth of inquiry that the project, as originally conceived, demanded. Readers will find that certain regions of Canada and certain people's experiences are missing, most regrettably those of the French-speaking and the indigenous populations. Hopefully, that misfortune will provide an opportunity for another volume at another time. Still, the contributors to this project represent some of the brightest of Canada's new generation of historians, some of whom, despite being in the early stage of their careers, have already published in top-tier journals and won prestigious awards.

As the title suggests, *Coast to Coast* includes hockey histories from different regions of the country in order to examine if hockey served as a common denominator in the creation of a Canadian identity or if it allowed for expressions of differences. The seven chapters follow roughly the historical development of hockey in Canada, moving from east to west.[10] Since the object of this book is to examine hockey broadly, the investigation, unlike in many hockey books, does not privilege the dominant hockey organization, the National Hockey League (NHL), whose franchises are located in large urban centres. Instead, these will take readers across Canada, into communities large and small, and study both amateur or professional hockey. In the course of this trip, readers will find that hockey did have a special place in the formation of Canadian culture and identity. At the same time, there is no denying that different groups of Canadians in different parts of the country also appropriated hockey to promote their own interests. Hence, at least up until the Second World War, hockey was a negotiated space in the formation and re-formation of identity and culture.

For hockey to be associated with being Canadian, the sport must resonate with a majority of people in a number of ways. At the very least, it must be perceived as advancing certain social perspectives and cultural values. In this sense, hockey carries capital with the public at large. Pierre Bourdieu identifies two important forms of capital, symbolic and cultural, in the production of culture. Symbolic capital comes from the 'degree of accumulated prestige, celebrity, consecration or honour and is founded on a dialectic of knowledge (*connaissance*) and recognition (*reconnaissance*).'[11] During the late nineteenth century, social reformers in North America attempted to build a progressive society using various measures to reduce existing class antagonism, assimilate immigrants and aborigines, promulgate and reinforce proper behaviour, and define citizenship. Sport in general and hockey in particular became part of this social engineering scheme and underwent a process of modernization. For those sports that resisted modernization, such as pedestrianism and blood sports, social and legal censures drove them underground or out of existence. The sports that did modernize invariably developed governing structures that defended their existence and promoted their social usefulness in establishing a progressive society. Advocates trumpeted modern sports' potential and contribution towards building character, instilling the importance of teamwork and self-sacrifice, inculcating a work ethic, and promoting fairness. Within this rationale of modern sports' utilitarian function, modernized hockey became accepted as a legitimate institution.[12]

Yet, conflicts and tensions existed in the legitimizing process that made hockey as maker and representative of Canadian values – a kind of cultural capital, 'a form of knowledge, an internalized code or a cognitive acquisition which equips the social agent with empathy towards, appreciation for or competence in deciphering cultural relations and cultural artefacts.'[13] While social reformers tried to impose their values through sports, different segments of society did not necessarily adopt the same values without question. Some accepted the reformers' efforts gleefully and redistributed these values enthusiastically. Others adapted sports to their own circumstances. There were, of course, those who rejected the impositions outright. Hence, hockey's accumulation of cultural capital in Canadian society has never been value-free, nor was the process staid. As an institution, then, hockey served to define who was Canadian and who was less (or not) Canadian. Indeed, the sport became the battleground for the conceptualization of class, gender roles, ethnicity, amateurism/professionalism, race, and a host of other social issues that forged the 'Canadian' identity. The chapters in this book will delve into some of these issues.[14]

Dan MacDonald begins this study with an examination of community hockey leagues in industrial Cape Breton during the interwar years. He argues that these locally organized leagues, though long neglected by history, were meaningful institutions – the zero weather game – to their participants and supporters. The community leagues became contested ground for larger issues concerning amateurism and professionalism, regionalism, civic boosterism, and class relations.

In neighbouring Quebec, Matthew Barlow investigates hockey and the Irish community in the city of Montreal. Through the successful Shamrock hockey club, around the turn of the twentieth century, the Irish middle class in Montreal constructed an identity based on class and masculinity – rather than their ethno-religious heritage – that helped them move into the dominant Anglo-Protestant circle. Barlow contextualizes this construction of a middle-class Irish identity within the changing view on masculinity of the larger society in the late nineteenth century. Yet, he is careful to point out that identity could be different things to the different stakeholders of the Shamrock club. While the larger hockey community associated the Shamrock players with class and masculinity, ethnicity and religion were still important to the players and some of their supporters.

As cultural capital, hockey faced an important test during the Second World War. In examining the Canadian government's policy on the sport's place in the war effort, J. Andrew Ross argues that hockey, at least as represented by the NHL, had less cultural capital than might have been expected. Despite Ottawa's initial blessing, the continuation of NHL hockey during the Second World War was a continuous process of negotiation and contestation, both within Canada and without after the United States entered the conflict. Even as the NHL positioned itself and its brand of hockey as a morale booster for the home front, government policymakers were divided in their opinions of hockey's importance and over the exemptions that the NHL sought for its players.

The debate on hockey and its usefulness in time of war hints at the gendered nature of the sport. In examining the history of the Ladies Ontario Hockey Association (LOHA), Carly Adams reveals the difficulties women encountered in organizing and maintaining their own league. Like hockey organizations in Cape Breton, the LOHA operated at the community level. Unlike its counterparts for men in Cape Breton and elsewhere, however, the LOHA faced different and unique obstacles in terms of control, administration, and, perhaps most importantly, the negotiated (and often contested) femininity of its participants. This fascinating history reminds us that early women's hockey was on the outside looking in even as the media was proclaiming hockey Canada's 'national' pastime from the turn of the twentieth century.

The marginalization of women in hockey for much of the sport's existence has, in large part, much to do with the physical, aggressive, and often violent aspect of the game, which contradicts deep-rooted notions of femininity. Even for men, however, physical aggression in hockey matches was not accepted without question. Through their examination of the 1907 hockey season, Stacy Lorenz and Geraint Osborne explore the meaning of violence in the construction of and differentiation between 'respectable' and 'rough' masculinity as media, fans, players, and, at times, the law struggled to legitimize the level of physical play. The authors conclude that hockey violence embodied middle-class and working-class ideals of manhood in establishing a culture of high tolerance for physical aggression in the sport.

Robert Kossuth takes a path seldom travelled in the writing of hockey history when he inquires into hockey's place in rural southern Alberta. He questions the assumption that hockey, first formalized and popularized as a middle-class, urban, male activity in Central Canada, was a homogeneous experience across the country. Kossuth discovers that hockey's popularity was uneven in small towns across southern Alberta during the interwar years. The requisite investments for a hockey team, especially in terms of facilities, made the game unaffordable for many of the smaller communities. Moreover, Kossuth's findings corroborat Adams's assertion that women were largely marginalized in this 'Canadian' game. Even those communities that managed to assemble a team found the question of professionalism dogging them, just as it did teams in Cape Breton and in the large urban centres in Canada.

Although hockey thrived in urban areas, Vancouver was an exception, at least until 1911, mostly because of its mild winters. It was daring entrepreneurship that promoted and instilled a hockey culture in the city, according to John Wong's chapter on the Vancouver Millionaires. As part of the Patrick family initiative, Frank Patrick developed a hockey market on the West Coast. While his primary motive was undoubtedly profit, Patrick also brought Vancouverites into the hockey culture by challenging the Central Canadian monopoly in elite-level professional hockey and, at the same time, differentiating his undertaking as dissimilar from that of the East.

This journey of hockey through the Canadian landscape shows that hockey, as the national pastime, defined 'Canadian' as white, male, aggressive, and middle class before the Second World War. To some degree, the sport also provided a crucible for competing social perspectives. Hence, hockey was a showcase as well as laboratory of the Canadian identity.

NOTES

1 Richard Gruneau and David Whitson, *Hockey Night in Canada: Sport, Identities and Cultural Politics* (Toronto: Garamond Press, 1993), 4.
2 For samples of dissertations and theses, see Daniel Scott Mason, 'The Origins and Development of the International Hockey League and Its Effects on the Sport of Professional Ice Hockey in North America' (MA thesis,

University of British Columbia, 1994); Michel Vigneault, 'La Naissance d'Un Sport Organisé au Canada: Le Hockey à Montreal, 1875–1917' (PhD diss., Université Laval, 2001); Julie A. Stevens, 'The Canadian Hockey Association Merger: An Analysis of Institutional Change' (PhD diss., University of Alberta, Spring 2001); Kerry Noonan, 'The Discourse of Hockey in Canada: Mythologization, Institutionalization, and Cultural Dissemination' (MA thesis, Carlton University, January 2002); and Helen Patricia Hughes-Fuller, 'The Good Old Game: Hockey, Nostalgia, Identity' (PhD diss., University of Alberta, 2002). *Sport History Review*, the former *Canadian Journal of History of Sport*, recently devoted a special issue, 'Hockey and History' (May 2006), entirely to hockey.

3 Presentations can be found in Colin Howell, ed., *Putting It on Ice*, 2 vols. (Halifax: Gorsebrook Research Institute, 2002). A sample of the presentations at another conference, in 2005 at Bridgewater, Massachusetts, were published in the special issue of *Sport History Review* mentioned in note 2.

4 Recent scholarly treatments include Nancy Theberge, *Higher Goals: Women's Ice Hockey and the Politics of Gender* (Albany: State University of New York Press, 2000); Michael A. Robidoux, *Men at Play: A Working Understanding of Professional Hockey* (Montreal: McGill-Queen's University Press, 2001); John Chi-Kit Wong, *Lords of the Rinks: The Emergence of the National Hockey League, 1875–1936* (Toronto: University of Toronto Press, 2005); and David Whitson and Richard Gruneau, eds, *Artificial Ice: Hockey, Culture, and Commerce* (Peterborough, ON: Broadview Press, 2006).

5 Attributed to Al Purdy; cited in Gruneau and Whitson, *Hockey Night in Canada*, 3.

6 Peter Gzowski, *The Game of Our Lives* (Markham, ON: Paperjacks, 1983).

7 http://www.cbc.ca/hockeyhistory/about.html (accessed 12 November 2006).

8 Gruneau and Whitson, *Hockey Night in Canada*, 25.

9 Brian Wilson, 'Selective Memory in a Global Culture: Reconsidering Links between Youth, Hockey, and Canadian Identity,' in Whitson and Gruneau, eds, *Artificial Ice*, 53–70.

10 By no means, however, is this book an endorsement or legitimation of a particular place as the 'birthplace' of hockey. For the controversy of the 'birthplace' of hockey, see, for example, Garth Vaughan, *The Puck Starts Here: The Origin of Canada's Great Winter Game Ice Hockey* (Fredericton: Goose Lane Editions and Four East Publications, 1996); J.W. Fitsell, *Hockey's Captains, Colonels and Kings* (Erin, ON: Boston Mills Press, 1987); and Michel Vigneault, 'Out of the Mists of Memory: Montreal's Hockey History, 1875–1910,' in *Total Hockey*, ed. Dan Diamond (New York: Total

Sports, 1998), 10–14. See also the report on the origins of hockey by the Society for International Hockey Research, available at http://www .sihrhockey.org/origins_report.cfm.

11 Randall Johnson, 'Editor's Introduction: Pierre Bourdieu on Art, Literature and Culture,' in Pierre Bourdieu, *The Field of Cultural Production: Essays on Art and Literature*, ed. and intro. Randal Johnson (New York: Columbia University Press, 1993), 7. For more of Bourdieu's view on culture production and reproduction, see Pierre Bourdieu, *Distinction: A Social Critique of the Judgement of Taste*, trans. by Richard Nice (Cambridge, MA: Harvard University Press, 1984).

12 For the modernization of sports, see Allen Guttmann, *From Ritual to Record: The Nature of Modern Sports* (New York: Columbia University Press, 1978) and Mel Adelman, *A Sporting Time: New York City and the Rise of Modern Athletics, 1820–70* (Urbana: University of Illinois Press, 1986). See Arthur S. Link, *Progressivism* (Arlington Heights, IL: Harlan Davidson, Inc., 1983) for a review of the Progressive movement. For modern sports' utility in this movement, see Mark Dyreson, 'The Emergence of Consumer Culture and the Transformation of Physical Culture: American Sport in the 1920s,' *Journal of Sport History* (Winter, 1990): 261–8.

13 Johnson, 'Editor's Introduction,' 7.

14 On cultural capital as instrument of inclusion and exclusion, see Michelle Lamont and Annette Lareau, 'Cultural Capital: Allusions, Gaps, and Glissandos in Recent Theoretical Developments,' *Sociological Theory* 6 (1988): 153–68; and Paul DiMaggio, 'Cultural Capital and School Success: The Impact of Status Culture Participation on the Grades of U.S. High School Students,' *American Sociological Review* 47 (1982): 189–201. For cultural capital in sport, see Carl Stempel, 'Adult Participation Sports as Cultural Capital,' *International Review for the Sociology of Sport* 40 (2005): 411–32; and Joanne Kay and Suzanne Laberge, 'Mapping the Field of "AR": Adventure Racing and Bourdieu's Concept of Field,' *Sociology of Sport Journal* 19 (2002): 25–46.

COAST TO COAST:
HOCKEY IN CANADA TO THE SECOND WORLD WAR

1 'Class, Community, and Commercialism': Hockey in Industrial Cape Breton, 1917–1937

DANIEL MACDONALD

The National Hockey League (NHL) occupies a solid mental space in the consciousness of the Canadian public. As a hyper-capitalist, mega-metropolitan sports cartel, which is not without its labour difficulties, it has been naturalized as the premiere hockey league in North America and probably the entire world. On Saturday nights from October to June in Canada, millions tune their televisions simultaneously to the Canadian Broadcasting Corporation (CBC) during the hockey season to watch oversized and unnaturally strong men skate swiftly, pass precisely, and score smartly. In all likelihood, some will engage in fisticuffs. The success of the league was not always certain, however. As Bruce Kidd has noted, the NHL limped along after its inception in 1917 with only three teams, and John Wong has suggested that by the early 1920s it was a 'small regional business.' Furthermore, its uncertain reception by the public was due to the fact the NHL was just one of many commercial hockey leagues operating at that time.[1] In industrial Cape Breton, the *Sydney Daily Post* covered the inaugural NHL match in Montreal in a somewhat half-hearted fashion that suggested the new organization's beginnings were indeed localized. And such regional support for hockey also occurred in Cape Breton. Less than a month later, one thousand people turned out at the local Arena Rink to see their own hockey season opening match featuring Sydney and North Sydney.[2]

As a particular zone of study, the 'zero weather game' can be defined as the site of local community hockey in the pre-1937 industrial trapezium of Cape Breton: Sydney, North Sydney, Glace Bay, and New Waterford. Hockey matches were held in open-air arenas that were subject to natural weather conditions. They often made for an unpredictable and occasionally uncomfortable evening, with often only a roof overhead protecting participants from the elements. The history of the Cape Breton game was marked by two periods and one theme. In the first period, 'Containment and Exclusivity,' lasting from the late teens to 1928, hockey in Cape Breton operated as an extremely open-ended and democratic sport in terms of athletic access. Slowly, however, the game was transformed. What was once petty commercial recreation in an open-air rink with limited costs had become rationalized, exclusive, and, with the new artificial ice rink, part of the emergent sports entertainment nexus. Consent for the evolving game was continuously won through class accommodation, regional discontent, and nationalist imagery. Ideologies, competing and sometimes complementary, such as antimodernism and amateurism, commercialism and professionalism, worked to legitimate the advancement of the game. Perhaps more than anything else, the logic of competition came to define and characterize many of the debates of the local game.

The second period can be characterized as 'Negotiating the Working Class Position.' Occurring from about 1928 until 1937, it was marked by the emergence and existence of two leagues vying for spectators. The first was an unsuccessful provincial loop that did not last long, and the second a local commercial league for workers in the area. The latter league was the site of a corporate welfare workers' circuit transformed into a commercially driven sporting meritocracy called senior men's hockey. The concomitant increased emphasis on the logic of competition helped expunge local players from the second league. In response, workers founded another community league of their own. The overarching theme that brings the two periods together is 'The "Building" of Consent.' The rationalization for a new hockey facility culminated in the construction of the Sydney Forum, which boasted artificial ice and other amenities. The new rink would symbolize both the deep cleavage between capitalist modernity and the zero weather game of open-air rinks as well as the local communities' ability to function and be competitive in Canada's emerging sporting edifice. On a practical level, the struggle for a local artificial ice rink has been a story of community and commercial accommodation that culminated in the development of a hybrid model of sport which served the interests of both community and commerce, but succumbed to neither.

Most people are aware of the large market share the NHL has carved out for itself, but what of community or small town leagues? How did the 'other' leagues, in this case the community leagues in industrial Cape Breton, survive simultaneously with the NHL? How did these leagues operate during the decades of the 1920s and the 1930s? How did they change by the end of the period? What were the effects of operating hockey games in open-air arenas? What justified the building of an arena capable of supplying artificial ice? Judging by the plethora of books related to the NHL compared to those about small-town leagues, there is, I would suggest, an imbalance in historical output and historical knowledge. This chapter reintroduces to the historical record an 'other' sport tradition in the form of community hockey that has, generally, failed to excite hockey scholars in the existing literature.

Almost without exception, when a story of community hockey is written, which is usually by sportswriters and not academic historians, it is done in a romantic and often popular manner. For Ken Dryden and Roy MacGregor, hockey is Canada's communal paste. 'The land,' they write, 'separates and disconnects place from place, person from person. What links it all together seems so hopelessly overmatched [while hockey] is a giant point of contact.'[3] Hockey is seen to provide communal stories, dreams, and even a national mythology for civic-minded people. Similarly, sportswriter and television broadcaster Scott Russell has highlighted Al MacInnis, former big-league defenceman and son of a Cape Breton coal miner, in order to introduce community-oriented hockey traditions described by one tournament organizer in these terms: 'They come here to see others they have missed all year. Hockey is the way the community gathers itself again.'[4] Against the uncertainty of modernity and industry, hockey has been portrayed as a humanizing, cathartic force. Cape Breton sportswriter Russ Doyle has recently reminisced that 'for years there was nothing for the miner or steelworker after work besides hockey and baseball and that's why the [steel] mill and mines brought in the players.'[5] Doyle's hyperbole begs the reader to underestimate the healthy sport and leisure culture that has developed in industrial Cape Breton and overrate the magnitude of local hockey. The idea of community hockey is not adequately developed in such popular works. Time and again, it is romanticized in terms of innocent and charming pond hockey with often folkish and unreal players.[6] The CBC's annual *Hockey Day in Canada* celebrates just such an essentialist understanding. This chapter will hopefully serve as a modest correction.

The Uncertainty of the Early Game

Just after the turn of the twentieth century, hockey in industrial Cape

Breton reflected the ever-present tension that existed between the forces of amateurism and professionalism. For the most part, the existing leagues could be termed semi-professional, with amateurs and professionals playing together. This arrangement stood in direct contrast to the professional-amateur war between 1902 and 1907. In 1908 the local Cape Breton hockey league featured teams such as the Northside Victorias, the Glace Bay Hockey Club, the Sydney Hockey Club,[7] and the Sydney Nationals. The mixing of 'home-brews,' or local players, and professionals was common practice.[8] Local teams competed for the league's Cruise Cup, although leagues per se tended to be transitory due to financial insecurity and the out-migration of labour. Often players were brought in from Halifax to replace Cape Breton hockey players who left the island in search of work.[9] In 1910 the entire North Sydney Victorias team – also called the Northside, being based north of the larger metropolitan area of Sydney – was imported. That year only a few league games were played before President James G. Lithgow of the Maritime Provincial Amateur Athletic Association suspended the league for violating the rules of amateurism. The all-or-nothing amateur code meant little to out-of-work transient hockey players looking to sell their labour. Local players from Cape Breton Island resented mainland (Nova Scotia) intervention. Walter Warren, a clerk for the Dominion Iron and Steel Corporation (DISCO) and player for the Sydney team, has recalled about hockey in the 1910s that Cape Breton received much unsolicited legislation from amateur sport authorities in Halifax.[10] The league subsequently folded and most of the North Sydney players left for steady employment in the mines of the nickel belt in Cobalt, Ontario. The Sydney Nationals and Glace Bay clubs were left to play out the season in a series of exhibition games.

Hockey leagues in the pre-1914 era operated irregularly with some adopting new rules, professional or amateur, while others thought new facilities would enhance the game's attractiveness. Certainty, whether it was financial or athletic, was a luxury afforded no one in this period. The adoption of strict league rules offered short-term assurance that organization and conformity would translate into league survival. In 1911 the Sydney Nationals, North Sydney Victorias, and Glace Bay devised a league that adopted nationally established notions of amateurism. The league, which consisted mainly of local talent and was dominated by the team from North Sydney, was unsuccessful and did not operate for more than one season. Others found that, as a product, hockey warranted a new venue to show off its athletic wares and that league certainty could be achieved by hiring professional players from out of town. In 1912 the Rosslyn Rink in Sydney was sold and the Sydney Arena constructed soon thereafter. Both were open-air facilities, but only the arena was used for *competitive* hockey, which gave it a stamp of sporting modernity, whereas the Rosslyn Rink was used for *recreational* skating. From then until the First World War the local, professional-only hockey operated out of the Arena.[11]

Containment and Exclusivity

Despite the pre-war reorganization of the rinks that favoured the Arena for its commercial possibilities, the post-1917 hockey seasons in industrial Cape Breton began on a decidedly amateur note. There were various leagues in the Sydney area some were operated by men and some by women.[12] Andrew Holman has noticed a similar phenomenon in Rossland, British Columbia, where 'men and women, workers and capitalists' played the game.[13] According to the press in Cape Breton, it appeared that sport, especially hockey, was extremely democratic and almost anyone could play. This would change as the game was machined in later decades into a white, male, urban game played by skilled, at times professional, hockey players in the industrial areas.

This narrowing process is best explained by sport historian Colin D. Howell, who has suggested that at the turn of the twentieth century sport in Canada followed the code of the 'true sportsman' or the 'gentleman,' which meant two, often explicit, things. Those who followed this code were embracing a creed of exclusivity based on gender and class. Working-class athletes could ill afford to follow such a concept, even if they were granted the opportunity to do so, because of a simple lack of financial resources. Moreover, the celebration of the 'manly' athlete, which was entertained more by middle- than working-class men, 'left little ideological space for women.'[14] By the First World War, the masculinization of sport had taken on a decidedly nationalistic theme. Sport was thought of as a saving grace for young middle-class boys and unemployed veterans. Representatives of the national sports body, the Amateur Athletic Union of Canada (AAUC), whose members were almost all English-speaking, middle-class males, preached sport for all – meaning all males.[15] It seems to follow that sports in Canada after the turn of the century were characteristically bourgeois and masculine. Urban sports in Cape Breton were no different.

In addition to masculine gentrification, sport went through the process of being re-imagined. For purposes of national identity, sport has been used time and again to elucidate that which is difficult to articulate, especially when it comes to nation-building. In his study on the prevalence and spread of nationalism, Benedict Anderson has suggested that nations, as communities, 'are to be distinguished, not by their falsity/genuineness, but by the style in which they are imagined.'[16] He contends that although most people of even the smallest nation will never come to meet each other, they will, to a certain degree, share a similar mental space about the nation. It is in this space that sport resides to solidify and suggest the communion of the nation. 'Cultural institutions,' such as sporting events and the underlying sporting bureaucracy, 'act as unifying cultural enthusiasms [and] help construct the nation as a coherent identity.'[17]

To the imagination of many, the practices of sport and nation-building can take on very real significance. During and after the First World War, sport's connection to the nation became more lucid, even celebrated. Consider the following passage from a Cape Breton newspaper just a few short years after the war. The sportswriter sought to understand the spirit of Canada and its citizens through sport. Hockey, as it were, revealed the very 'essence' of the nation. It seemed to percolate biologically from Canadian blood:

> Hockey, the king of speed games, is Canada's national sport. The pace of it, the speed and thrill of it appeals to the youth of Canada. No other boys in the world could ever play hockey quite as Canadian youngsters do, hockey has developed to suit the temperament which expresses itself most completely in this game. It is the spirit of Vimy Ridge and Festubert which crops out strongest in a fast rush down the ice with the puck. The vigor, stamina, fearlessness and self restraint [and] manliness demanded by the game are natural, because the Canadian came first and hockey developed as his characteristic sport.[18]

As Anderson has suggested, it would be fruitless to guess whether there are truths or falsehoods in such a statement. It is only worthwhile to note the 'style' in which the nation's game is imagined.[19] In this case, war and military might were translated into hockey supremacy. This is the style in which Canada and hockey were imagined, and this message, nationalistic in scope, was delivered to local Cape Breton audiences.

The grafting of nationalism to sport is not without its complexity.

Anderson reminds us that 'all communities larger than primordial villages of face-to-face contact (and perhaps even these) are imagined.'[20] Regions are also communities, and should be treated as such, since they are imagined into being. In Cape Breton hockey occasionally offered a platform for local boosterism and the official regionalism espoused by Maritime Rights advocates.[21] An example of this phenomenon took place in 1921 during a dispute about the amateur status of two hockey players from the local area. Jimmy Wilkie of Sydney and Harvey Richardson of North Sydney were suspended from the amateur ranks and placed under investigation by the AAUC. This incident prompted the *Sydney Post*'s sportswriter to condemn the pan-Canadian athletic union for neglecting the Maritimes. To him provincial and regional authority was being ignored. When placed in the context of other grievances, such as Maritime underdevelopment, deindustrialization, and growing outside control of local industries, sport became a site for regional struggle. It was time for the Maritimes to develop its own athletic union so disputes could be handled regionally and not in places such as Winnipeg.[22] Interestingly enough, the *Sydney Post* writer was attempting to carve out a regionalist position for the Maritimes within a larger national framework. This awkwardly nationalist stance was a recurrent theme in Maritime sports during the interwar years. It was not until 1927 that the Maritime Amateur Hockey Association (MAHA) was affiliated with the Canadian Amateur Hockey Association (CAHA). Until then, there was little contact between the two hockey bodies.[23] Feelings of regional alienation further fuelled the history of protest that characterized the 1920s. David Frank has suggested that during this time 'important groups of Maritimers failed to accept the decline of the region with equanimity and mounted a struggle against underdevelopment.'[24] It is important to note that this neo-nationalist position was found not only in economic circles, but in social and cultural circles as well.

Part of the re-imagining of sport in general and hockey in particular had been the recurring debates concerning amateurism and professionalism. The bulk of these debates concerning hockey took place in the early 1920s and tapered off by the 1930s. A self-assured article in the *Sydney Post* in 1921, reflecting confidence in the abilities of Cape Breton hockey players, talked about the athlete-labourers – ones who played sports in return for a comfortable job secured for them by club management – who were, in fact, professional 'in the guise of the simon-pure brand.'[25] These players would legally receive amateur cards and could therefore play amateur hockey, benefiting, if not directly, from their athletic prowess. Their profession was to play hockey rather than attend to their official employment. Apparently, this practice was rampant in many parts of the country, but Cape Breton hockey had been 'singularly free from such tactics and as a result the clubs competing will probably end the season in the black.'[26] While the latter was probably untrue, club finances were of special importance when the perennial issue of using imported versus local players came into play, and dogged local professional leagues more than the amateur ones in the following years.

In spite of the media's confidence in the abilities of local players, the practice of using imported players continued in Cape Breton throughout the 1920s and 1930s. The position of the proponents of this practice was simple: they believed paying customers wanted to see fast, entertaining hockey, and with that in mind, the fastest and most skilled players must be found to provide such entertainment. The *Sydney Post* sportswriter concurred, suggesting that local teams should have been commended for 'going *out* after the best.'[27] 'Out,' in this case, meant that team managers searched beyond the Island for talented players. Despite efforts made to keep home brews on Cape Breton teams, such as holding tryouts for locals and beginning the 1923 Cape Breton County Professional Hockey League schedule with only home brews, one can see the erosion of support, at least in the press, for local players.[28]

For local players, playing in Cape Breton was at times controversial. After a dispute involving amateur athletes in Cape Breton, all local athletes (hockey players included) and team officials were barred from the Maritime Provinces Branch of the Amateur Athletic Union (MPBAAU) of Canada.[29] It is not at all surprising that some athletes from Cape Breton accepted remuneration for their athletic endeavours when one considers the economic situation and class war that was waging in Cape Breton in the early 1920s. In the local coal industry alone, the first half of the decade saw no fewer than fifty-eight strikes in the Sydney coal fields over issues such as union affiliation, the functioning of pit committees, fines and suspensions, and work assignments.[30] The disastrous effects of deindustrialization and capitalist reorganization in Cape Breton's urban area in the 1920s and 1930s prompted many young hockey players from the area to accept payment for playing the game. The drawback to turning professional for Cape Breton athletes who sought employment, said an anonymous sportswriter in December 1922, reflected the harsh reality of the common slogan 'once a pro, always a pro.' 'Where are these [local] boys going to fit when they go to college in a year or two?' The writer further suggested that the banished athletes 'will not be able to take part in any events simply because they erred in their youth because they saw the chance to earn a few dollars in sport.'[31] One cannot help but notice the writer's sympathy for young players' actions in the face of an antiquated and unsympathetic rule that punished people for selling their athletic labour. There is, however, a tacit condemnation of selling athletic labour in referring to their actions as an error. With locals accepting money for playing, the home-brew-versus-import issue became even more complicated, as some professionals were allowed to compete with amateurs.

Shortly thereafter those hockey promoters in favour of professionalism got together and formed a fully professional league that featured an emphasis on imports, with home-brews given a chance to try out. Teams were from urban areas such as Sydney, Glace Bay, and North Sydney. Although home-brews were given a chance in the new league, the local news suggested that 'if any of the clubs feel that they [home-brews] do not muster up to the strength of [imports] ... then they can be replaced by faster company.'[32] Interestingly the ethos of professionalism, competitiveness, and, ultimately, meritocracy continually fractured the importance placed on the local player who played for the local team. The emphasis was clearly placed on winning, and looking beyond Cape Breton for players was fast becoming 'common sense.' 'If the home brews fail to live up to expectations they will have to give way to better men and, judging by the spirit that has dominated the league so far, the Cape Breton teams are likely to go to any length to secure the coveted championship.'[33] Seeking players outside the local area was justified to create a winning senior team. In Cape Breton skilled players were increasingly associated with imports who often made local athletes look second-rate. This development marked an interesting shift in community allegiance from local players to the local team, and was not confined to hockey, as local professional baseball leagues underwent a similar transition in the 1930s. There were even thoughts, albeit fanciful, that National Hockey League players could be persuaded to join the Cape Breton County Professional Hockey League.[34] This has been referred to as a 'cultural riddle' by Bruce Kidd, who has suggested that athletes often act as community surrogates.[35]

The interests of local Cape Breton promoters and their drive to establish a professional league were complex. There was, on the one hand, the drive to win and establish a league that resembled the capitalistic National Hockey League. Hopes of increased revenues prompted them to recruit fast skaters and provide heightened entertainment. On the other hand, however, was it reasonable to assume that local communities in industrial Cape Breton could sustain a professional hockey league? At a meeting just days after the professional league was suggested, North Sydney revealed it was unable to secure imports for its team, although Sydney and Glace Bay were successful. League officials at the meeting suggested that a more affluent town be allowed to join the hockey loop. They turned to Stellarton and New Glasgow as possible candidates. Although these two towns did not suffer a class war that garnered national attention[36] and could afford imports, they were uninterested. Without the new towns, the league would be a bust for the 1922–3 season.[37] By 17 January 1923 a date still had not been set for the opening of the professional league schedule. The league finally went through a four-week, unsuccessful, season with teams from Sydney, North Sydney, and Glace Bay.[38] The games appeared lacklustre at best and failed to arouse community support.

While the professional enterprise did not fare well in the early interwar years, the amateur leagues in Cape Breton and the Maritimes were much more successful by comparison. One explanation for this success was the adjustments made in the import rule by the amateur leagues to counter the anticipated fan support for the more skilled out-of-town players in the professional league. The 1924–5 Maritime Hockey Rules allowed that an athlete 'living in a town where ... no organized league hockey is played, may play with a team playing organized hockey in one of the two nearest towns of his choice.'[39] While this rule affected resident Maritime professional players relatively little because many of the talented players had migrated to New England to play professionally there, it opened the door for movement of players among the amateur clubs. Yet, the loosening of player movement did not receive endorsement from the two powerful amateur sport governing bodies in Canada, the AAUC and the Ontario Hockey Association, as they complained bitterly about a depletion of players.[40]

Although out-migration of hockey players in central Canada elicited a hostile reaction from the AAUC, little, if any, angst appeared in the Maritimes. The *Sydney Post* exclaimed with pride that the 'Maritime Provinces are continuing to make good in the great national pastime which has made wonderful progress in New England.'[41] The reason for this was twofold. First, the region had had a strong historical relationship with the northeastern United States, such that 'the boundary did not separate, but connect[ed] them,' as Holman has argued of borderlands communities.[42] The second was that out-migration from the Maritime provinces had reached the state of psycho-social common sense. It was a generational response to the dissatisfaction with local social and economic conditions. This survival strategy ensured that many Maritime labourers, in this case hockey players, were geographically dispersed. During the 1920s the Maritime provinces' population grew less than 1 per cent. Politically, the Maritime Rights Movement, composed mostly of Maritime capitalists, attempted to combat the region's shrinking parliamentary representation and influence, supraregional control of local industries, and consequent deindustrialization.[43] It has been estimated by demographers that 122,000 Maritimers left the region during the 1920s, the largest single exodus experienced by the provinces in a single decade.[44] That is why the *Sydney Post* boasted of athletes such as Ajax Campbell a hockey player from Cape Breton who became a success in Boston, Massachusetts. A large player at well over two hundred pounds, Campbell, had been playing with the Boston Amateur Athletic Association and studying at medical school. He graduated in the spring of 1924 and was slated for an appointment at the Boston City Hospital.[45] Ajax Campbell exploited sport and out-migration to its full emancipatory potential, as he likely paid his way through university by playing hockey for the Boston team.

Despite the press's approval of hometown boys who made good in the United States, hockey interloping and residency rules remained contentious issues between regional sporting bodies. The MPBAAU and the MAHA sparred over jurisdictional control over hockey. In 1923 the newly developed MAHA was given sole control over hockey in the region by the MPBAAU. However, by 1926 this control extended only to the formal organization of the game and not to the athletes. Since the athlete was at the centre of the residence clause, the MPBAAU claimed full control. According to J. Gordon Quigley, secretary treasurer of the MPBAAU, cities and towns were to develop their own athletes and resist importing them from elsewhere. In this way, local clubs, such as those from Cape Breton, would remain amateur and free of ringers and the lure of professionalism while developing a civic infrastructure for sport.

Quigley's advice seemed practical, but tended to favour larger metropolitan areas. In addition, his recommendation carried with it a message about the usefulness of sport. 'In other words,' he suggested, 'sport should be for sport's sake and not so much for the prize at the end

of the race.'[46] The prize of which Quigley spoke was economic remuneration provided for athletic labour. This intermingling of civic duty
and morality by amateur hockey promoters reflected a bigger issue
concerning class and capitalism. As an antimodernist impulse that in-
fused much of the cultural production within Nova Scotia and around
the world during the interwar period, the diatribe against pay for play
was intended to make sport culturally innocuous and fanciful and,
above all, to keep amateur athletes in the Maritimes pure, safe from
the disenchantment of capitalism and those who profited from sport.
Among those to be avoided were capitalistic team owners who operated for profit and working-class people who sold their athletic labour.
Throughout the 1920s the MPBAAU defeated successive resolutions
designed to provide compensation for workers who lost wages during
athletic activities.[47] This denial of what became known as broken-time
payments was to level the playing field by exorcising amateur sport
of its professional element. The MPBAAU was not alone in its opposition to broken-time payment. Amateur sporting organizations like the
AAUC and the MAHA also took a hard-line position and continued to
refuse such payments for athletes.

Amateurism, supposedly, promoted equality of opportunity for all
participants, regardless of their background, to demonstrate their own
abilities and eliminated the possibility of buying victory or defeat. Amateur officials argued that if athletes descended into the realm of professionalism, sport would become too utilitarian and the idea of play
for play's sake, as Quigley mentioned, and its accompanying catharsis
would eventually suffer. It would seem that promoters of amateurism
strove to instil a sense of spirituality within sport. This sentiment of
anti-commercialism was not confined to sport or to Nova Scotia or even
the Maritimes. 'Practically everywhere in the interwar world we find
great refusals of capitalism's "disenchantment of the world" and an
intellectual search for something more real, authentic and essential.'[48]
On the surface, it would appear there was something strangely naive
about the middle-class assumption that by removing the profit motive
from sport, or at least from the athlete, class differences would dissolve
and equality would abound in the face of good-natured recreation. In
reality, it was an unworkable assumption and accomplished nothing.[49]
Bruce Kidd has sensibly suggested that stringent amateurism ideologues defined professionalism primarily as a 'moral issue, not a practical one' and reflected the conservative mindset of most Canadians at
the time.[50]

Kidd's assessment may in fact be true; but no matter how hegemonic conservatism was in Canada at the time, refusing broken-time payments for athletes served bourgeois ends and helped reify existing class divisions.[51] The attempt to drive a wedge between the material and sporting worlds often created an unaffordable position for labourer athletes, forcing them to choose between becoming athletic labourers or professionals. At the most basic level, for working-class athletes in Cape Breton during the interwar years of substantial regional deindustrialization and economic depression, involvement in sport carried a price. An amateur hockey player had to pay club dues (a portion of which went to parental bodies such as the MPBAAU and the MAHA), purchase a uniform and equipment, pay for travel and accommodations, and incur lost wages. These costs could be offset by broken-time payments, if approved by the amateur governing bodies, without stigmatizing those athletes who could least afford to take time off work; but this course was constantly refused by sport bureaucrats.

The penalties for infringing on basic amateur by-laws were often severe if not hysterical. In a case involving mainland Nova Scotia players, the punishment was indeed stern. The MPBAAU's new president, S.F. Doyle, and his secretary treasurer, J.G. Quigley, suspended all the playing members of the Dartmouth Amateur Athletic Association for transgressing the residence rule. As a tactic to isolate the guilty party, Doyle and Quigley warned all clubs and players under the auspices of the MPBAAU 'against playing with or against any player or players representing the Dartmouth AAA in either league or exhibition games. Such action will render them liable to suspension.'[52]

Transgressions of the amateur code could often be used by teams attempting to negotiate better competitive positions in local leagues. In 1927 the Sydney amateur hockey team from the Cape Breton County League protested the use of Dr Stephen (Duke) Isaac by the Glace Bay team. The Sydney club claimed that Dr Isaac was actually a resident of Sydney, but had his practice in Glace Bay. At issue here was the interpretation of the rules by those who did not submit to or take refuge in a legislated blanket meaning or rule that might be considered objectively binding. Instead, they interpreted according to their own meaning, thereby creating their own authentic ends. Glace Bay interpreted the residence clause as being flexible enough to include not only town residents, but resident employees. Sydney waited until the season was half-over and Glace Bay was a sufficient threat before invoking a narrow interpretation of the by-law. During the interwar years, the

Caledonia rugby team from Cape Breton also manipulated the amateur code on several occasions in order to obtain an advantage on the field. Time and again, clubs, often with professional athletes of their own, would protest the use of professional players against them.[53] In spite of anti-democratic ideologies that guided hockey during the 1920s, local players continued to struggle for representation. The examples above suggest that some aspects of professionalism and amateurism were not simply prescriptive in terms of ideology, but contingent and at times manipulated by players or clubs to suit their purposes. In the next period the hockey in Cape Breton would achieve a modest stability as two important leagues develop.

Negotiating the Working-class Position

In 1928 there were two premier hockey leagues in operation in the Sydney area of Cape Breton. The first was the Antigonish and Pictou County (APC) league, which had teams from across Nova Scotia. Sydney represented Cape Breton interests, while New Glasgow, Stellarton, and Antigonish came from the mainland. The other league was the more localized Commercial Hockey League, which was supported by local businesses from Sydney and surrounding area. The Cape Breton representative in the mainland APC league (also known from time to time as the Antigonish, Pictou, and Cape Breton league) was the Sydney Amateur Athletic Club. The team was something of an all-star cast from the Sydney area, as it had been an amalgamation of the local St Thomas and other urban teams. The St Thomas Club brought players such as Dr Duke McIsaac, a former Glace Bay player, (Big) Alex McDonald, Mark Bates, Charlie Campbell, and Joe Wrigg to join with former Sydney team members Tommy Young, Gus McLean, Billy Snow, and Eric Dunn to form the core of the new Sydney Amateur Athletic Club.[54]

Because of the all-star composition of the team, media and fans had high hopes for the amalgamated club at the beginning of the season. The *Sydney Post* considered the team a 'formidable aggregation ... that will get results.'[55] Sydney opened the season with a 4–1 victory over Antigonish in front of twelve hundred people at the Arena rink in Sydney. Controversy, however, followed not long after, as the MAHA cancelled the amateur cards of Alex McDonald and Charlie Campbell. Local fans were upset and the press suspected the move was 'inspired by interests in New Glasgow who have opposed the entry of the Sydney team all along.'[56]

Amidst public cries of mistreatment, President A.L. Mercer of the Sydney club and several others travelled to Halifax and met with MAHA officials. At the meeting Mercer et al. convinced those necessary that both McDonald and Campbell were legitimate amateur hockey players.[57] Just days later, the MAHA reinstated McDonald and Campbell. In their next game after the reinstatement, Sydney and New Glasgow roughed it up. Sydney was dealt the mightier blows, as the team was 'badly crippled' by the mainland players.[58] Hyperbole aside, injuries ranged from Bill Snow's blackened eye to Mark Bates's more serious knee injury received from a low check. The doctor's examination, revealed that his knee cap was fractured and some ligaments torn. The Sydney team complained that its players had been on the receiving end of 'dirty tactics' doled out by New Glasgow.[59] Despite these injuries, the Sydney team went on to a relatively successful season with several wins; but did not represent a serious challenge to the league championship. The league, meantime, had a difficult time maintaining a stable membership.

The second and more stable loop in the Sydney area, the Commercial Hockey League, usually had six teams: the Sydney Post (newspaper), Telephone Company, Druggists (local pharmacy), Christies (named after league president Christie Stevenson), BESCO (British Empire Steel Corporation – a steel and coal conglomerate that employed thousands in the local area), and Cape Breton Electric clubs. From the start, the league was seen as second rate in comparison with the APC loop. With six local teams from the Sydney area, the entire league saw action on game nights with three scheduled matches. Unfortunately, games were often played after the APC matches. Hence, Commercial games often lasted late into the night on badly scored ice.[60]

During the late 1920s and early 1930s, the Commercial League was a consistent feature of working-class sport and leisure. The league was not-for-profit, and admission costs for games were to help 'defray playing expenses of the clubs.'[61] The most successful teams of the late 1920s were the squad from the *Sydney Post* and the pharmaceutical seven called the Druggists. Although the league never achieved the attendance figures of the sporadic APC, hundreds of fans consistently patronized its games, in part because the Commercial League represented local businesses and therefore drew crowds locally. On the other hand, the thousands that attended Sydney's APC contingent spoke to the 'for-profit' nature of the league that required it to draw paying patrons from the entire Sydney community and the surrounding area. In other words, the 'for-profit' APC league cast a wider net as surrogates representing an entire metropolitan area.

Despite lower attendance numbers, the Commercial League was the premier loop in Cape Breton by about 1931 when the APC folded, probably due to the unstable finances of its teams.[62] By this point, newer teams in the Commercial League included the Glace Bay Co-operative, the Whitney Pier YMCA, and the Seals. In 1933 the Commercial League was reorganized. The new league managed to incorporate the former APC players (many of whom were amateurs in name only) and enhanced the league's attendance numbers. More than a thousand people now regularly attended what was to become 'Senior B' hockey games. By the opening of the Sydney Forum in 1937, Senior B hockey continued to operate, but a another Commercial League was created to accommodate the working-class players of Sydney who failed to make the Senior B league. Senior B became too competitive for most local players. The new league consisted of teams such as Superior Chain Stores, a hardware store team, a combined team representing the newspaper merger of the *Sydney Post* and *Sydney Record* called the Sydney Post-Record, a Canada Packers team, a Canadian National Railway team, and one from David's Market.[63] It was clearly a less talented league, though it did offer a haven for labourer hockey players.

The new Commercial League reflected a type of corporate welfare. Local working-class players played for and represented the organization that employed them. The teams competed for the Merchant's trophy donated by four Sydney capitalists: league president Christie Stevenson, F.A. De Young, Fred Merchant, and George Hault. Christie Stevenson was owner and operator of Christies Sweet Shop on Bentinck Street. F.A. De Young operated a confectionary on George Street that sold retail produce, dairy products, and poultry. Fred Merchant sold a variety of dry goods, clothing, and housewares from his two shops, in Glace Bay and Sydney, while George Hault operated a local jewellery and a grocery store.[64] In her study of female softball, historian Joan Sangster criticizes sport organized under this type of paternalistic employer–employee relationship. 'Paternalism,' writes Sangster, 'was to preserve managerial authority and to satisfy a patrician sense of philanthropy.' Furthermore, often 'cloaked in a rationale of obligation, duty or honour, paternalism essentially justified, extended or at most modified existing power relationships.'[65] For Sangster, the company softball (or, in the present case, hockey) team was a tool for expressing managerial authority.

Contemporaries were not unaware of this class-based power relationship. Local labour poet and sportswriter Dawn Fraser, in his *Maritime Labour Herald* essay entitled 'A Communist Football Team,' provided a forthright and unsubtle view on working-class sport in 1922. Fraser wrote that corporation sports should be organized along class lines to ensure workers were reminded of the need for social reform. To organize sports along corporate lines pitted workers against workers and compromised class solidarity. 'Loyalty is created to the [employer],' so 'why not organize a Communist team ... to uphold the Communist Revolution on the playing field?'[66] Fraser continued: 'It is foolishness to organize sports along a slave basis. The human work animals in the [workplace] become so accustomed to looking upon themselves as slaves ... they actually go out and fight on the field of sport in the name of the slave [workplace] in which they wear their slave collar.'[67] A BESCO employee from Sydney Mines put the issue of the corporate sports club rather starkly, 'The only club that is going to do the Nova Scotia miner any good is the club in his hand.'[68] Other local people, however, actually supported corporate welfarism in the form of sport clubs, which suggests that local views pertaining to corporate sports were mixed.[69]

Though thoughtful and worthy of careful reflection, Joan Sangster's comments ultimately fall short of substantial historical application because of her emphasis on social control. For Sangster, sport is seen solely as a pacifying force with no emancipatory possibility. The sport solution is a means to an end, a weapon used to discipline the female workforce.[70] In this case, the subjugation is more subtle than forceful, which is duly noted, but how had workers really created sport? Had they created it for Westclox? Had they used it to re-create themselves in spite of the company? Was it both or neither? Beyond utilitarianism and the one-dimensional social-control thesis, it is probable that the workers fostered notions of opposition and collective self-worth such as teamwork, discipline, and solidarity in addition to the other more nefarious aspects of corporate sports of which Sangster wrote.[71] Dawn Fraser made similar criticisms on corporate-sponsored sports grounded in Comintern rhetoric. Yet he saw sport's potential only in terms of class struggle when he advocated organizing sports along Communist lines. In terms of cultural production, Fraser seemed to have taken a chapter from the *Communist Manifesto* in expressing his philosophy of sport. He extended Karl Marx's maxim that 'the history of all hitherto existing society is the history of class struggle' to the field of play, because 'freeman and slave, patrician and plebeian, lord and serf, guildmaster and journeyman, in a word oppressor and oppressed, stood in constant opposition to one another, carried on uninterrupted, now hidden, now open fight, a fight that has each time ended, either in a revolutionary re-constitution of society at large or in the common ruin of the contending classes.'[72] Far from being nihilistic, Fraser believed that capitalism had reached its apex and was in certain crisis as a result of the contending classes. Hence, sport could be used as a crucial site for this struggle to take place for, as Marx suggested, the reconstitution society at large. Since class warfare existed in society, sport should not be an exception to this rule and so Fraser advocated class conflict, for the sake of reform, on the field of play. The founding of a new Commercial League, in fact a working-class league, demonstrated the ability of local workers to craft their own leisure as they saw fit. Moreover, it highlights the limitations of competitive sport, which limits accessibility and is fundamentally anti-democratic. Other instances of class antagonism, however, did not exist in the APC or the Commercial leagues, the connection between nationalist imagery and the sport itself.

After the First World War Canada had emerged as a successful hock-ey nation. Hockey carried an imaginatively communal mythology and was symbolically national in weight. In 1920 the Winnipeg Falcons were successful in the world championships in Antwerp, and in 1924 the Toronto Granites won the first Winter Olympic gold medal in hock-ey.[73] Locally, the press suggested hockey was the natural outgrowth of being Canadian and argued that 'the vigor, stamina, fearlessness, and self-restraint manliness demanded by the game are natural, because the Canadian came first and hockey developed as his characteristic sport.'[74] Note the word 'natural' and its implications of hockey being instinctive, intuitive, deterministic, and even biologically appropriate for Canadians, as opposed to its being invented, fabricated, or socially constructed. In this context hockey did little to dramatize class inequal-ity and even less to foster oppositional thinking.

According to Morrow and Wamsley, 'Implicit in the idea of nation-hood is the understanding that Canada and Canadians have often sought to establish a national identity in distinction to other nations, especially the United States.'[75] Hockey was seen as 'essentially' Cana-dian and the myth/symbol complex it buoyed up went far to denigrate alternatives such as baseball and rugby, largely seen as pastimes of the United States and Britain respectively, not to mention the alternative thinking found in the writings of Dawn Fraser that was drawn from a foreign ideology. Ironically, the politics of the Maritime Rights Movement served as an important ingredient to the national mythology of hockey. The most visible expression of this movement in terms of hockey was the debacle over the selection of the 1936 Olympic hockey team, which featured not one member of the 1935 Allan Cup–winning team from Halifax.[76] This incident is interesting because it highlights the dominant regionalist position of the time, which was to negotiate an improved place for the Maritimes within the nation rather than without it. Interestingly, hockey emerged as both a common ground that served to neutralize domestic dissent through a national mythology that promoted a seemingly organic connection to the game and, paradoxically, a place for contest when it came to mounting albeit limited regional resistance and articulating working-class concerns about the anti-democratic nature of competitive sport.

The 'Building' of Consent

Most hockey games from the 1920s and 1930s relied solely on the weather for favourable ice conditions for hockey players and fans alike. If the weather was warm, fans would be more comfortable, but the ice would quickly become wet and heavy, causing travel on it for a skater or puck to become very slow and plodding. If it were too cold, the ice would become extremely fast and crisp. In addition, the puck would move quickly over it and become bouncy and unpredictable. Bruce Kidd suggests that since rink managers relied on the $0°$ or below weather to freeze the ice, 'arenas were kept unheated and could almost be as cold and uncomfortable as the out-of-doors.'[77] Once too cold, however, the temperature could chase away those who came to watch as these conditions did not make for an enjoyable situation.[78]

This predicament was quite common for rinks across Canada. In fact, weather interfered with the 'highest' levels of the game. The 1920 Stanley Cup finals were bedevilled by Mother Nature. It was unusually warm during the opening three games of the post-season finals between Seattle and Ottawa, which created slushy conditions with large pools of water. As a result, even the fastest rush was slow and passing plays were made difficult. The remaining games of the series were transferred to Toronto.[79] Thanks to such conditions, throughout Canada in the 1920s and 1930s, many towns and cities expressed their need for an enclosed arena.[80]

On countless occasions before 1937, the senior leagues of Cape

Breton hockey played with a sense of unpredictability and uncertainty due to the weather. In a 1921 match featuring Sydney and North Sydney, an unexpected cold snap created desirable ice conditions. As the *Sydney Post* noted: 'The ice was in excellent condition, the frost of yesterday at the right time to prepare an ideal sheet.'[81] The natural ice arenas in Cape Breton ensured a short, unpredictable season. Consider this December 1924 comment on the upcoming season: 'It's hard to get action on the *zero weather game*, when the thermometer hangs several points above freezing. Still we haven't missed a winter yet, not in the life of the oldest inhabitant at any rate, and before many days, Jonathan Q. Frost will be in our midst for a more or less protracted stay and the puck chasers will have plenty of chances to get action' (emphasis mine).[82]

The pitfalls of natural ice kept the seasons, and consequently revenues, noticeably short and uneven.[83] This problem led Christie Stevenson, already noted president of the Commercial League, to speak out in favour of constructing an artificial-ice arena for hockey in Sydney in 1930 to counter the uncertainty of the weather for proper ice-making: 'Should we have an artificial ice rink? Well, I should say so. It is undoubtedly the solution to our hockey problem. Due to the *uncertainty* of Cape Breton weather, the hockey season here is usually only eight or ten weeks at the most, while other centres have six to eight weeks longer, either because of prolonged cold spells, or the presence of artificial ice in one or more rinks depending on the size of the city' (emphasis mine).[84] He went on to point out that in a longer, unbroken season, which could start as early as November and extend to the end of March, players in the local area could be practising longer and developing advanced hockey skills. In a few years, these same local players could contend for the Maritime championship. If that was not enough of an incentive, Stevenson emphasized the economic versatility of such a rink, which could be used for a variety of events such as 'auto shows, exhibitions, prize fights, community banquets [and as a] reception hall for distinguished visitors.'[85] 'The rink would not only be a rink,' he went on to say, 'but a profitable investment all year round.'[86] The commercial flexibility of the rink was championed not only by Stevenson, but also by a delegation of 'leading businessmen' who met with Sydney city council to encourage the municipalities' participation in the development of an artificial ice rink.[87] The community-corporate proposal was encouraged by the council, but they stopped short of promising actual funding.

Stevenson, the local shop owner, appeared to be right on track with like-minded visionary capitalists of the National Hockey League during the 1920s and 1930s, for it was within this period that such edifices as the Montreal Forum, New York's Madison Square Garden, the Boston Garden, Chicago Stadium, the Detroit Olympia as well as Toronto's Maple Leaf Gardens were constructed.[88] The building of new hockey arenas was part of a sporting paradigm shift that echoed larger trends in society such as the growth of a consumer culture, a process encouraged by various forms of mass media.[89] Sport was increasingly being seen as a commodity fit for the marketplace. It is within this world of consumer capitalism, with auto shows, exhibitions, and prize fights, that Stevenson legitimized the construction of a new arena in Sydney.

Almost immediately, another prominent local merchant, Don J. Buckley, came out in support of building an artificial-ice rink in Sydney,[90] in his plan a community arena comparable to one in the relatively similar sized city of Oshawa, Ontario.[90] The plan called for a $75,000 building complete with ice-making equipment designed to host 5000 people, 3750 seated and 1250 standing. The ice plant would cost an additional $30,000, which brought the total to $105,000. Like Stevenson, Buckley noted that the arena could be used as a multi-sport facility that would benefit young people who had recently lost their local YMCA to a fire. Interestingly, Buckley's rink project was civic in nature, as opposed to the previous corporate community scheme offered to the city council. That is, it was his plan to have the city pay the bill and also enjoy the profits, both social and financial. Should there be any losses, they would also be incurred by the city.[91]

Alan Metcalfe has suggested that many rink proposals were 'rooted in the idea of community and only by community involvement [could] financial resources be raised.'[92] Almost six weeks later, Buckley proposed, with the help of the local contractors Chappells Ltd, to erect a pared-down structure: a $100,000 building with a capacity of 4000, 2900 seated and 1100 standing. By this time, however, Buckley was attempting to secure private financial backing and certain concessions from the city to build the arena.[93] By 1935 the artificial rink still had not been built, as the city had rejected the idea. That January, mild weather caused the cancellation of many local games.[94]

In 1936 an article from New York appeared in the *Sydney Post-Record* suggesting that the game of hockey had reached global status. The reasoning attributed to the growth of the game was the invention of artificial ice. The ice was made by flushing sub-zero brine (very salty or ocean water) through pipes hidden in concrete flooring. Steel filings used to conduct the cold studded the concrete. It then became possible to make at least an inch of ice in places such as Madison Square Garden – or any local arena, if one were to be built. This global-local justification, it was suggested, would bring Cape Breton into step with the sporting fashion of metropolitan cities such as New York. In addition, such rinks were capable of hosting a multiplicity of events, just as Christie Stevenson had suggested six years earlier. The process was simple: running hot brine through the same pipes would melt the ice, which could then be swept away in little time, leaving a hall with a large concrete focal point able to host dancers, boxers, wrestlers, and basketball players.[95] The article was a strong reminder that the Sydney area could make much use of a new rink capable of producing and reproducing ice and concrete surfaces with relative ease. Still, that year, the Cape Breton Hockey League playoffs were scheduled to take place from 15 February to 2 March, 'if weather conditions permit[ted].'[96]

Finally, on 6 January 1937, the new civic facility, the Sydney Forum, was officially opened as '[a] sport-starved Cape Breton public licked its chops.'[97] It was suggested that people from all over the city and the county would turn out to see the new 'ice palace.'[98] Indeed, 3000 fans turned out to witness the opening hockey game, which featured local working-class teams. The telephone company squad defeated the Sun Oil Company (Sunoco) team in a heavy-checking game, 1–0; and the goalies were outstanding, stopping 28 and 23 shots respectively. Telephone defenceman Kenzie MacNeil scored the only goal, in the second period.

The facility was a modest triumph for civic concerns in that it was owned by the city, but it would also serve commercial purposes by hosting various sports, leisure, and entertainment events that would help to pay for the cost of its construction. It was thus a physical manifestation of the local hybrid development of community-capitalist sport, which succumbed to neither interest in totality during the interwar period. Interestingly, after the rink's completion it was not heralded solely in the language of finance, accumulation, or investment, the logic under which it was conceived. Instead, it was touted as a 'monument to community progress and enterprise,'[99] an enunciation of the connection of sport, community, and capitalism that was solidified during the interwar period. Drawing on work from Harry Braverman, Bruce Kidd has suggested that because of the universal transformative qualities of capitalism, cultural production came to be taken over by entrepreneurs.[100] This is correct, but in Cape Breton during the interwar period the civic component of sport was enough to challenge full market sport. In other words, local merchants promoted the *building* of consent, but did not own it. Some power to define community sport was left at a local level, in resistance to the universalist logic of capitalist sport, such as that found in the National Hockey League.

Located on the corner of George and Falmouth Streets, just behind the Joy Supermarket and adjacent to the Dominion Coal Company Yard, the rink was a product of local construction company J.W. Stephens.[101] Stephens took out a large advertisement in the *Sydney Post-Record* thanking the rink committee for the business and 'therefore set out to justify the confidence of our good workmanship that had been shown by these men.'[102] The press considered the rink to be 'one of the finest buildings of its size in the Maritimes.'[103] With outside dimensions measuring 140 feet wide by 205 feet long, a regulation-sized ice surface (85 by 190 feet), and a vertical apex of 48 feet, the imposing structure contrasted sharply with the small city's 1937 horizon. The entire project took just over four months to build and cost slightly in excess of $60,000, well under previous estimates.

Interestingly, the press noted that the construction of the rink was a source of steady employment for Sydney's workers. In the midst of the economic hardship of Cape Breton in the 1930s, the arena construction was a 'welcome outlet for the absorption of hundreds of Sydney's jobless citizens who otherwise would have been contented remaining on relief lines last summer and fall.'[104] Of semi-fire-proof fabrication, the Forum was complete with a gondola (a replica of that found in Maple Leaf Gardens), electric clock (donated by the Imperial Tobacco Company), excellent press facilities, heated dressing rooms, canteen, band balcony, and basement. It was a testament not only to the hybrid community-capitalist development of local sport, but also to the community's working-class labour, all of which signalled the end of the zero-weather game and forever changed organized community hockey in industrial Cape Breton.

Conclusion

In the post 1937-era, local hockey continued down its community-capitalist path. The Forum became not only a competitive sports entertainment complex, but it also hosted, as was hoped, a menagerie of civic events, concerts, dances, recreational skating, beer festivals, and so on. Before 1937 the hockey seasons usually lasted eight to ten games from

January to February or as long as the ice remained naturally frozen at the local Arena rink; now, with artificial ice, they ran from November to March, with about forty to sixty games. Hundreds and sometimes thousands attended games in the new facility to witness *competitive* hockey, while the natural ice at the Sydney Arena, a casualty of heavily financed sport, was used for *recreational* skating only, just as the Rosslyn rink had been when the Sydney Arena was built in 1912. The issue of home-brews versus imports continued to bedevil local hockey as well as those of salary limits, player swapping, and increased admission charges. By the 1940s a feeder system developed in Cape Breton and minor hockey became quite popular. Senior amateur teams such as the Glace Bay Miners, North Sydney Victorias, and Sydney Millionaires challenged for the Allan Cup each year. In the 1950s it became increasingly difficult to sustain local professional and amateur senior hockey teams. While much of the rest of the country was experiencing the 'fabulous fifties,' with spectacular growth in the construction, staple, and service industries,[105] Sydney and Glace Bay remained an economically challenged area despite the steel and coal industries. Attendances dropped while the rules for importing players loosened, resulting in a top-heavy pro league. Teams began fund-raising and selling club shares before eventually folding. The 1960s brought an official end to senior pro hockey in Cape Breton (until the arrival of the Edmonton Oiler farm team in the 1980s). The fans demanded sophisticated hockey and teams responded with more imports; but that was unaffordable and brought on continued salary crises. Ultimately, by the late 1960s, fans became so disappointed and disillusioned by the inability of the local leagues to operate smoothly that they stopped coming, bringing a close to pro hockey in Cape Breton.

This chapter has examined the development of small-town hockey and the overlapping of community and commercial interests in Cape Breton. Bruce Kidd made an overly rigorous assessment when he set the two in opposition to one another in his groundbreaking *The Struggle for Canadian Sport*. The fact is, the tentacles of capitalism have penetrated sport at all levels, including professional and amateur hockey, but this development has been modified by those with civic welfare in mind. In the immediate years after the First World War, access to hockey became narrowed as the ideologues continuously redefined amateur and professional athletic guidelines. The game was reformed and became increasingly competitive, which prompted local players to interpret rules to suit their needs and even devise a league of their own.

A symbol of the game's viability in Cape Breton was the construction of a new rink with artificial ice. The new Sydney Forum was marketed not only as a rink, but as a multiple-sport facility capable of hosting year-round events. The end of the zero-weather game came gradually as the progressive, competitive, sports entertainment industry won favour. In the process, hockey was continually transformed, and with it the community changed to accommodate new rules and regulations. In the process, the competitive open-air game came to an end.

NOTES

1 John Wong, *Lords of the Rinks: The Emergence of the National Hockey League, 1875–1936* (Toronto: University of Toronto Press, 2005), 71. Bruce Kidd, *The Struggle for Canadian Sport* (Toronto: University of Toronto Press, 1996), 185.
2 *Sydney Daily Post*, 18 January 1918, 8.
3 Ken Dryden and Roy MacGregor, *Home Game: Hockey and Life and Canada* (McClelland and Stewart 1989), 18–19.
4 Scott Russell, *Ice Time: The Unsung Heroes of Canadian Hockey* (Canada: Penguin Canada, 2001), 54.
5 Bill Boyd, *Hockey Towns: Stories of Small Town Hockey in Canada* (Canada: Doubleday, 1998), 138.
6 See Garth Vaughn, *The Puck Starts Here: The Origin of Canada's Great Winter Game – Ice Hockey* (Fredericton, NB: Goose Lane, 1996) and Martin Jones, *Hockey's Home: Halifax-Dartmouth, the Origin of Canada's Game* (Canada: Nimbus Publishing Co., 2002). Vaughn and Jones make some insightful comments about the origins of the game: both locate the birthplace of hockey as Nova Scotia (Vaughn suggests Windsor and Jones Halifax/Dartmouth) and use a breadth of sources to back up their opposing views. Their weaknesses lie in the treatment of the game, which is ultimately celebratory and lacking in rigorous historical, social analysis.
7 Though mentioned as a competing team, this club disappeared from the historical record, suggesting it had either folded or was unsuccessful.
8 Cape Breton University, Beaton Institute of Cape Breton Studies, MG12-61, MG14, 'History of the Cape Breton Hockey League,' in W.W. Warren papers, 1894–1912, 1.
9 MG12-61, MG14, 2. Interestingly, it would seem that out-migration from the Island facilitated the rise of professionalism in the local area. This theme is more evident later in the chapter.
10 MG12-61, MG14, 3. Information about Walter Warren can be found in local

directories: *McAlpine's Nova Scotia Directories, 1908* (Halifax: McAlpine's Publishing Co., 1908) 1281; *McAlpine's City Directory for Sydney and Cape Breton County, 1918–1919* (Halifax : McAlpine's Publishing Co., 1908), 204; *McAlpine's Sydney City Directory, Volume IV, 1923* (Halifax: Royal Print & Litho Co. Ltd, 1923), 174; *The City Directory of Cape Breton* (Halifax: Might Directories Atlantic Ltd, 1928) 141.

11 MG12-61, MG14, 3.

12 For the Sydney and Glace Bay women's teams and the play-by-play action, see the *Sydney Post*, 10 February 1921, 8, and 11 February 1921, 8. See also New Glasgow's 'lady' team, ibid., 15 February 1921, 8.

13 Andrew C. Holman, 'Playing in the Neutral Zone: Meanings and Uses of Ice Hockey in Canada-U.S. Borderlands, 1895–1915,' *American Review of Canadian Studies* 34, 3 (Spring 2004): 40.

14 Colin D. Howell, *Blood, Sweat, and Cheers: Sport and the Making of Modern Canada* (Toronto: University of Toronto, 2001), 5.

15 Kidd, *The Struggle for Canadian Sport*, 46–8.

16 Benedict Anderson, *Imagined Communities: Reflections on the Origin and Spread of Nationalism* (London: Verso, 1983), 6.

17 Howell, *Blood, Sweat, and Cheers*, 129. Kidd suggests something similar in that 'sports create broad communities of language and cultural experience'; *The Struggle for Canadian Sport*, 27.

18 *Sydney Post*, 26 February 1921, 10.

19 Anderson, *Imagined Communities*, 6.

20 Ibid.

21 For Maritime Rights, see Ernest Forbes, 'The Origins of the Maritime Rights Movement,' in Ernest Forbes, ed., *Challenging the Regional Stereotype: Essays on the 20th Century Maritimes* (Fredericton, NB: Acadiensis Press, 1989). The movement was a conservative, neo-nationalist vision that sought to address the ills of the region in terms of shrinking parliamentary representation, deindustrialization, and growing outside control of Maritime industries. The cultural side to this neo-nationalism is best found in Ian McKay, *Quest of the Folk: Antimodernism and Cultural Selection in Twentieth Century Nova Scotia* (Montreal: McGill-Queen's University Press, 1994); the ten-year reassessment of this powerful work in *Acadiensis* 35, 1 (Autumn 2005): 132–57 by various authors. See also Gwendolyn Davies, *Myth and Milieu: Atlantic Literature and Culture 1918–1939* (Fredericton: Acadiensis Press, 1993).

22 *Sydney Post*, 8 February 1921, 8. Holman has suggested, quite rightfully, that 'hockey was one of many ingredients in the formation of a regional identity.' 'Playing in the Neutral Zone,' 37.

23 Ronald Lappage, 'Sport between the Wars,' in Don Morrow et al., eds, *A Concise History of Sport in Canada*, 90. The *Sydney Post* cited the amalgamation of the MAHA with its national counterpart, the AHA, as occurring in 1928. See *Sydney Post*, 17 January 1928, 8.

24 David Frank, 'The 1920s: Class and Region, Resistance and Accommodation,' in E.R. Forbes and D.A. Muise, eds, *The Atlantic Provinces in Confederation* (Toronto: University of Toronto Press; Fredericton: Acadiensis Press, 1993), 236.

25 *Sydney Post*, 21 February 1921, 8.

26 Ibid.

27 *Sydney Post*, 6 December 1922, 10.

28 *Sydney Post*, 18 December 1922, 10; 21 December 1922, 10.

29 *Sydney Post*, 7 December 1922, read: 'Every town in the Maritime provinces have their amateur organizations and send delegates to meetings who have a voice in the proceedings. All but Cape Breton' (14). Apparently the avowedly nationalist A.W. Covey, the 'czar' of the MPBAAU, took the dispute extremely serious and outlawed Cape Breton from all proceedings. For a saccharine biographical sketch of Covey, see *The Sydney Post*, 24 November 1924, 10.

30 For extensive treatments of the class struggle during this period in industrial Cape Breton see Don MacGillivray, 'Industrial Unrest in Cape Breton, 1919–1925,' MA thesis (University of New Brunswick, 1971); David Frank, 'Coal Masters and Coal Miners: The 1922 Strike and the Roots of Class Conflict in the Cape Breton Coal Industry,' MA thesis (Dalhousie University, 1974); David Frank, 'Class Conflict in the Coal Industry: Cape Breton 1922,' in G.S. Kealey and P. Warrian, eds., *Essays in Canadian Working Class History* (Toronto 1976); and David Frank, 'The Cape Breton Coal Miners 1919–1925,' PhD thesis (Dalhousie, 1979). For a thorough discussion of the use and frequency of the state militia during the 1920s, see Don MacGillivray, 'Military Aid to the Civil Power: The Cape Breton Experience in the 1920's,' *Acadiensis* 3, 2 (Spring 1974): 45–64. For a gender/class revision/synthesis see Stephen Penfold, '"Have You No Manhood in You?": Gender and Class in the Cape Breton Coal Towns, 1920–1926,' *Acadiensis* 23, 2 (Spring 1994): 21–49.

31 *Sydney Post*, 7 December 1922, 8.

32 *Sydney Post*, 18 December 1922, 8.

33 Ibid.

34 Those looking to recruit NHL players to local leagues in Cape Breton were never successful, although in 1922 Toronto St Pats defenceman Bill Stuart was said to be 'dissatisfied' with the NHL and planned to move to

Amherst, Nova Scotia, and play professional hockey. Stuart planned to work at the local freight shed to supplement his hockey income; the two combined matched his income at 'the big show.' See *Sydney Post*, 6 December 1922, 8.

35 Kidd, *The Struggle for Canadian Sport*, 267. This theme of representational sport is developed further by Nancy Bouchier in *For the Love of the Game: Amateur Sport in Small Town Ontario, 1838–1895* (Montreal-Kingston: McGill-Queen's University Press, 2003), 3–4, 42, 67, and 137.

36 One quarter of Canada's armed forces was employed in defence of the British Empire Steel Corporation which employed over ten thousand local men in the steel and coal industries, who struck over fifty times in the 1920s. David Frank, 'Class Conflict in the Coal Industry: Cape Breton, 1922,' in Ian McKay, ed., *The Challenge of Modernity: A Reader on Post-Confederation Canada* (Toronto: McGraw-Hill Ryerson Ltd, 1992), 258; also see chapter 6 his *J.B. McLachlan, a Biography: The Story of a Legendary Labour Leader and the Cape Breton Coal Miners* (Toronto: James Lorimer & Co. Ltd, 1999).

37 *Sydney Post*, 21 December 1922, 10; 22 December 1922, 10.

38 *Sydney Post*, 18 January 1923, 8; 20 January 1923, 12; 1 February 1923, 8; 13 February 1923, 10; 15 February 1923, 10.

39 *Sydney Post*, 20 December 1924, 10.

40 *Sydney Post*, 6 February 1924, 8; 7 February 1924, 8; 8 February 1924, 8. This trend had also been national in scope, with the 'greatest exodus' of Canadian hockey players being found in one of the eastern divisions of the United States Amateur Hockey Association. Although the players were amateurs, it was rumoured they were being paid for playing hockey.

41 *Sydney Post*, 6 February 1924, 8.

42 Holman, 'Playing in the Neutral Zone,' 37.

43 Forbes, 'The Origins of the Maritime Rights Movement'; see also John Reid, 'The 1920s: Decade of Struggle,' in McKay, *The Challenge of Modernity*, 246–55, and Frank, *The 1920s*, 234.

44 Frank, *The 1920s*, 234; see also Patricia Thornton, 'The Problem of Out-Migration from Atlantic Canada 1871–1921: A New Look,' *Acadiensis* 15, 1 (Autumn 1985): 3–34. Thornton's article should be retitled 'The Solution of Out-Migration' to reflect the social mindset of out-migrants, who saw their sojourning as an answer to their social and economic circumstances. See also A.A. MacKenzie, 'Cape Breton and the Western Harvest Excursions 1890–1928,' in Ken Donovan, ed., *Cape Breton at 200: Historical Essays in Honour of the Island's Bicentennial 1785–1985* (Sydney, NS: University College of Cape Breton Press, 1985), 71–84.

45 *Sydney Post*, 6 February 1924, 8. See also *Sydney Record*, 27 October 1923, 8, for other reports of out-migrating hockey players.

46 *Halifax Herald*, 21 December 1925, 8.
47 For an example of this prohibitive legislation see *Sydney Record*, 21 October 1922, 8.
48 McKay, *Quest of the Folk*, 37. See also MacDonald, *Gridiron and Coal*, 66.
49 Don Morrow, 'A Case Study in Amateur Conflict: The Athletic War in Canada, 1906–8,' *British Journal of Sport History* 3, 2 (1986): 190; Alan Metcalfe, *Canada Learns to Play: The Emergence of Organized Sport, 1807–1914* (Toronto: McClelland and Stewart, 1987), 132.
50 Kidd, *The Struggle for Canadian Sport*, 35.
51 It should also be noted that the idea of a nation being *conservative* and deriving its morality from this collective mindset seems problematic and reductive. On the issue of moral reform Mariana Valverde has suggested that morality in Canada was not one-dimensional. It was deeply rooted in the construction a white Protestant Canada, sexuality, immigration, prostitution, class, gender, and other things. Surely these concerns did not simply come from conservatism. Valverde, *The Age of Light, Soap, and Water: Moral Reform in English Canada, 1885–1925* (Toronto: University of Toronto Press, 2008).
52 *Halifax Herald*, 13 January 1926, 8.
53 For some examples of Caledonia's rule interpretations see Daniel MacDonald, 'Gridiron and Coal: The Making of Rugby Football in Industrial Cape Breton,' unpublished MA thesis (St Mary's University, 2001), 68–71. See also Neil Hooper, 'A History of the Caledonia Amateur Athletic Club,' unpublished MA thesis (University of New Brunswick, 1987).
54 *Sydney Post*, 4 January 1928, 8.
55 *Sydney Post*, 6 January 1928, 8.
56 *Sydney Post*, 11 January 1928, 8.
57 *Sydney Post*, 24 January 1928, 8.
58 *Sydney Post*, 30 January 1928, 8.
59 Ibid.
60 For example, the 14 January 1928 edition of the *Sydney Post* reported that a late afternoon APC game was played before a crowd of 1200 on 'perfect ice' (8). Much later that same evening the Commercial League played its three games on the arena's 'heavy ice,' which was often warm, inconsistent, and generally unfit for play.
61 *Sydney Post*, 13 January 1927, 12.
62 *Sydney Post*, 6 January 1931, 8. As with the APC league games, attendance figures for Commercial League games were usually offered in the local press after the analysis of the game.
63 *Sydney Post-Record*, 28 January 1937, 8.
64 *The City Directories of Cape Breton including: Official City Catalogues of Syd-*

ney, North Sydney, Sydney Mines, Glace Bay, Dominion, New Waterford, Louis-burg 1928, 40, 55, 104, 144; *The Mercantile Agency Reference Book, Containing Ratings of Merchants, Manufacturers and Traders Generally Throughout the Dominion of Canada, Newfoundland, etc. with an appendix containing Banking towns, Bankers, Banks, etc.* (Canada: R.G. Dun and Co., 1928).

65 Joan Sangster, 'The Softball Solution: Female Workers, Male Managers and the operation of Paternalism at Westclox, 1923–1960,' *Labour/Le Travail* 32 (Fall 1993): 169. See also Ronald Melcher's more charitable assessment of workplace sports, 'Sports in the Workplace,' in Jean Harvey and Hart Cantelon, eds, *Not Just a Game: Essays in Canadian Sport Sociology* (Ottawa: University of Ottawa Press, 1988), 51–67.

66 *Maritime Labor Herald*, 30 September 1922, 5.

67 Ibid.

68 *Sydney Record*, 5 December 1927, n.p.

69 In the *Glace Bay Gazette*, an unidentified person suggested that BESCO be more involved in corporate sports. 'I think the officials of the Company should take more of an interest in trying to promote sport.' Quoted from Don MacGillivray, 'Industrial Unrest in Cape Breton 1919–1925,' unpublished MA thesis (University of New Brunswick, 1971), 129.

70 Sangster's assessment is much like that of Althusserian Marxist scholar Jean-Marie Brohm, who thinks sport is an opiate for the masses. See his arguably classic and clever, yet thoroughly depressing, text *Sport: A Prison of Measured Time* (London: Pluto, 1989).

71 MacDonald, *Gridiron and Coal*, 16.

72 Karl Marx, 'Manifesto of the Communist Party,' in *The Marx Engels Reader*, ed. Robert Tucker, 2nd ed. (New York: Norton, 1978), 473–4.

73 Don Morrow and Kevin Wamsley, *Sport in Canada: A History* (Canada: Oxford University Press, 2005), 201.

74 *Sydney Post*, 26 February 1921, 8.

75 Morrow and Wamsley, *Sport in Canada*, 202.

76 For this incident see *Sydney Post-Record*, 7 January 1936, 9; Mark Savoie, 'Broken Time and Broken Hearts: The Maritimes and the Selection of Canada's 1936 Olympic Hockey Team,' *Sport History Review* 31, 2 (November 2000): 120–38; and John Wong, 'Sport Networks on Ice: The Canadian Experience at the 1936 Olympic Hockey Tournament,' *Sport History Review* 34, 2 (2003): 190–212.

77 Kidd, *The Struggle for Canadian Sport*, 197.

78 Wong, *Lords of the Rinks*, 19.

79 Kidd, *The Struggle for Canadian Sport*, 197.

80 Metcalfe, *Canada Learns to Play*, 41.

81 *Sydney Post*, 15 January 1921, 8.

82 *Sydney Post*, 4 December 1924, 10.

83 *Sydney Post*, 29 January 1930, 10.

84 Ibid.

85 Ibid.

86 Ibid.

87 *Sydney Post*, 29 January 1930, 10.

88 Russell Field, 'Passive Participation: The Selling of Spectacle and the Construction of Maple Leaf Gardens, 1931,' *Sport History Review* 33 (2002): 35. Despite the criticisms levelled against the modernization thesis, Field implements it by suggesting that the transition of the 1920s from a culture of production to one of consumption was somehow suprahuman. Although the move to mass consumption involved 'willing participants,' the idea of disciplining an audience without resistance to such a move does not seem plausible. See also Howell, *Blood, Sweat, and Cheers*, 73–4.

89 Howell, *Blood, Sweat, and Cheers*, 82. For similar American developments that centred on mass consumer culture and sport see Mark Dyreson, 'The Emergence of Consumer Culture and the Transformation of Physical Culture: American Sport in the 1920s,' *Journal of Sport History* 15, 3 (Winter 1989): 261–81.

90 Donald J. Buckley was a druggist who operated Buckley's Busy Bend on the corner of Charlotte and Prince Street in Sydney. *The City Directories of Cape Breton including: Official City Catalogues of Sydney, North Sydney, Sydney Mines, Glace Bay, Dominion, New Waterford, Louisburg 1928*, 25. Though an avid local hockey fan, it is unclear if he was connected to the successful local pharmaceutical hockey team. It should also be noted that it was not unusual for prominent capitalists to trumpet support for the building of hockey arenas in Canada. See Metcalfe, *Canada Learns to Play*, 44.

91 *Sydney Post*, 31 January 1930, 10.

92 Metcalfe, *Canada Learns to Play*, 41.

93 *Sydney Post*, 10 March 1930, 12.

94 For some cancellations and ice problems due to the weather, see the *Sydney Post-Record*, 8 January 1935, 10, and 25 January 1935, 14.

95 *Sydney Post-Record*, 7 January 1936, 9.

96 *Sydney Post-Record*, 13 January 1936, 9.

97 *Sydney Post-Record*, 6 January 1937, 13.

98 Ibid.

99 *Sydney Post-Record*, 5 January 1937, 10.

100 Kidd, *The Struggle for Canadian Sport*, 29.

101 Cape Breton University, Beaton Institute of Cape Breton Studies, Insur-

ance Plan of Sydney, revised to July 1947, maps #618, 619, 620 – bin #5.

102 *Sydney Post-Record*, 5 January 1937, 10.

103 Ibid.

104 Ibid.

105 Alvin Finkel and Margaret Conrad, eds, *History of the Canadian Peoples: 1867 to the Present* (Toronto: Addison, Wesley, Longman, 2002), 369–74.

2 'Scientific Aggression': Irishness, Manliness, Class, and Commercialization in the Shamrock Hockey Club of Montreal, 1894–1901

JOHN MATTHEW BARLOW

The Shamrock Hockey Club (HC) of Montreal is usually referred to as the *Irish* hockey team of *fin de siècle* Montreal. The success of the Shamrocks, Stanley Cup winners in 1899 and 1900, is often pointed to as proof positive of the diffusion of the sport of hockey away from its elitist Anglo-Protestant roots at McGill College (now McGill University) in the last decade of the nineteenth century. The Shamrocks also represent an evolution away from the elite-level amateur Anglo-Protestant clubs of the city, the Montreal HC (affiliated with the legendary Montreal Amateur Athletic Association [Montreal AAA]) and the Victoria HC, which grew out of the elitist recreational site, the Victoria Rink.[1] Indeed, John Chi-Kit Wong points to the Shamrocks' success as evidence of the Irish breaking into the highest levels of the sport in the 1890s.[2] Michel Vigneault, for his part, points to the success of the Shamrocks at the turn of the twentieth century as key to the development of the sport in Montreal and the diffusion of elite-level hockey across ethno-religious lines to the bourgeois French Canadian classes, especially following the retirement of many of the Shamrocks' Irish-Catholic players after the 1901 season. They were eventually replaced with primarily French Canadian players.[3]

That the Shamrock HC was Irish (and Catholic) is indisputable and is evidenced by the club's Stanley Cup–winning roster, composed exclusively of Irish-Catholics: Jim McKenna, goal; Frank Tansey, point;[4] Frank Wall, cover-point; Harry Trihey (also the captain), Arthur Farrell, Jack Brennan,[5] and Fred Scanlan, forwards; and Barney Dunphy, coach. That the club was affiliated with the Shamrock Amateur Athletic Association (Shamrock AAA), Montreal's Irish-Catholic sport club, also speaks to the Irishness of the hockey club. Moreover, while the primary colour of the Shamrocks' jersey was grey, it was trimmed with Irish green.[6]

But if it is clear that the Shamrocks were an Irish-Catholic hockey club, what is less clear is what this means. What kind of Irishness did the Shamrock HC represent? Joy Parr has reminded us that the identities of the historical actors we as historians study were not lived sequentially, but simultaneously.[7] That is to say that identities are forged, reinforced, and policed out of contests and conflicts with one another. In *fin de siècle* Montreal, Irishness was contested terrain, a site of struggle between various stake holders in the community. Also contested, according to class and gender, was the right to call oneself Irish and exactly what it meant to call oneself Irish in the first place.

This chapter, then, is an examination of the Shamrock HC of Montreal through the concomitant lenses of ethno-religious, classed, and gendered identities at the *fin de siècle*. While the ethno-religious identities of the team and the players may have been of import to them and the Shamrock AAA, it was their classed and gendered identities that were of greater import when it came to the Shamrocks' presence in the Canadian Amateur Hockey League (CAHL).[8] And their acceptance not just by the other Anglo-Protestant clubs of the CAHL but also by hockey fans and Montreal's Anglo-Protestant press, most particularly the *Gazette* and the *Montreal Star,* was even more significant. The press was of central importance to the CAHL and the boosters of what was emerging as Canada's national winter sport, at least according to the sports editor of the *Gazette*.[9] It was through the press that upcoming matches in the championship-level senior league were not just advertised, but hyped, and that post-game coverage was provided, oftentimes in great detail.

The Shamrocks' Stanley Cup–winning seasons in 1899 and 1900 came at a critical juncture for élite-level amateur hockey in Canada. The *fin de siècle* saw the process of commercialisation at work in hockey, a necessary precondition to professionalism.[10] In other words, elite-level amateur hockey at the turn of the twentieth century in Montreal was undergoing a process of modernization. Richard Gruneau argues that sport is cultural text,[11] meaning that it is a manifestation of the society from which it emerges. In this regard, sport functions as a dialectic between culture and the actors in it; sport's meanings are both embedded in and act upon the culture from which it emerges. Thus, elite-level amateur hockey in *fin de siècle* Montreal was also embedded into larger cultural concerns about modernization and the so-called crisis of masculinity.

The sport editors and reporters of the *Gazette* and the *Montreal Star* became less concerned with the idea of fair play during this period. Rather, the press became more interested with winning and losing, though it did still make a point to praise the skill level of both clubs. However, this praising of both clubs had less to do with good sportsmanship than it did with the commercialization of the game and the need to sell tickets, the sport of hockey, and, ultimately, newspapers. Winning became of paramount importance. Meanwhile, the discourse surrounding the play of the game shifted, as now the newspapers became interested in describing the 'scientific' play of the hockeyists.[12] This rationalization of the sport can be clearly seen in the pages of the *Gazette* on the occasion of the release of a book on the playing of hockey by Arthur Farrell of the Shamrocks in 1899. The *Gazette* praised the book for offering 'particular reference to the game's incipient stages of development, and its present scientific aspect,' and praised Farrell himself for his 'technical' skill as a player.[13] In his book Farrell continually made reference to the scientific skills needed to excel at hockey, and even praised his own club, the Shamrocks, as the most scientifically skilled hockey club ever.[14]

This theorization of the sport and the development of a scientific style of play can be seen as keeping step with the modernization of society as a whole at the turn of the century in Montreal, and urban industrial Canada in general. This was the period of the rationalization of industrial capitalism and the rise of 'scientific' management principles in the business world.[15] Closely aligned to these new 'scientific' management principles was a new configuration of bourgeois masculinity, one that had to take into account the sedentary existence of the middle-class manager in his job. This development led to a variety of responses, including an increased focus on sport and the constructions of masculinity evident on, in this case, ice.

The Irish Experience in Montreal: Class, Nation, and the Postcolonial

The Irish-Catholic experience in Montreal has only recently been problematized by historians and it is only in the past decade or two that we have been able to move past the unfortunate cultural stereotyping of the Irish endemic in the works of the likes of Clare Pentland.[16] Most of this newfound attention, however, has focused on the city's Irish-Catholic industrial working classes in Montreal's *sud-ouest*, most particularly in

Griffintown.[17] The result of this focus is that very little attention has been devoted to the middle classes[18] of the Irish-Catholic population of nineteenth- and early-twentieth-century Montreal.[19]

Historical geographers Sherry Olson and Patricia Thornton have argued that the Irish-Catholics of nineteenth-century Montreal established themselves as a third cultural community in the city distinct from, and oftentimes between, Montreal's two 'majority' populations,[20] the French Canadians and Anglo-Protestants. The means by which Montreal's Irish-Catholics did this was their successful usage and manipulation of the Catholic Church, the St Patrick's Society, and Montreal's political institutions.[21]

In addition to these three institutions, sport was essential to the Irish-Catholic community of Montreal in assisting in the formation, reinforcing, and policing of identities. It also served as a means of easing the integration of the Irish-Catholic population, especially the middle classes, into the mainstream of Montreal's anglophone population. Historians have been especially fascinated with the Shamrock LC, a club whose players and fans were drawn from Griffintown in the Confederation era.[22] Alan Metcalfe has termed the Shamrocks the most successful lacrosse club in late-nineteenth-century Canada.[23] The Shamrock LC was firmly entrenched in the Irish-Catholic community of Montreal, mostly because its ownership and management was drawn from the elite of this community. It is necessary to focus on the Shamrock LC first, situating its place in Montreal's Irish-Catholic community as a manifestation of working-class culture. Thus, in one way, the lacrosse club serves as a counterpoint to the hockey club, which was both just as entrenched in the community and also represented the more bourgeois elements of the Irish-Catholic community of the city.

The lacrosse club also demonstrates an earlier attempt by the Irish-Catholic population of Montreal to force its way into the mainstream of anglophone culture, especially for the middle classes. Both the lacrosse and hockey clubs were affiliated with the Shamrock AAA. Central to this discussion, for both clubs, then, is an examination of colonialism, both in Ireland and in Canada, or, more specifically, Quebec, as well as the manner in which Irish national identity played out in this localized, Montreal Irish-Catholic community.

In the case of the lacrosse club, the Irish-Catholic working-class athletes used it as a means of challenging the economically and socially dominant Anglo-Protestant community of the city to gain a measure of respectability. The lacrosse club and its working-class supporters put a premium upon winning, long before it was fashionable to do so. It was precisely this emphasis on victory, along with the boisterous behaviour of the fans, that found the club in hot water with the middle- and elite-class sporting men on opposing clubs, most notably the Montreal LC, also affiliated with the Montreal AAA. As for the Shamrock LC's fans, Metcalfe has suggested that they were the first modern sports fans in Canada, 'living and dying with their team's fortunes.'[24] And their attitudes and behaviour apparently impinged upon the contemporary ideas of manhood.

Notions of masculinity and manliness were intimately tied up with the playing (and watching) of lacrosse. Gail Bederman makes a distinction between 'masculinity' and 'manliness' around the turn of the twentieth century. She argues that 'masculinity' was not a term in common usage before about 1890 in North America; instead, it was 'manliness' that men possessed. This is not to say that the two terms are interchangeable, however. Manliness, unlike masculinity, carried with it a moral dimension: to be manly was to follow a code that encompassed all that Victorians admired in men. By contrast R.W. Connell argues, 'masculinity' is a term that explains the 'male role,' and is variable according to time, place, and cultural setting.[25] In large part, this shift from manliness to masculinity was due to the rise of industrial capitalism and 'scientific' management principles at the *fin de siècle*. As capitalists and businessmen became increasingly focused on profit and growth and as bourgeois managers became increasingly sedentary in their jobs, concern with the male role in a capitalist culture became prevalent. Indeed, this is what led to the so-called crisis of masculinity at the *fin de siècle*, itself tied to the rise of modernity. Thus, the call to 'scientific' management in sport, both in the games themselves as well as in the management of organized sport, reflects this cultural shift.[26]

Notions of manliness and masculinity are given further complexity by Connell's notion of a hegemonic masculinity in any given society. Drawing upon the Gramscian notion of hegemony,[27] Connell argues that masculinity is a means of social control on the part of the dominant classes and, therefore, a site of contestation between the dominated and dominators.[28] In other words, the elite class creates its own code of masculinity, which it then seeks to impose upon the working classes, or any other group of subservient men.[29]

This middle-class masculinity promoted notions of respectability and, in the case of sport, fair play, with less of an emphasis on winning than on the joy of the sport itself, especially in the 1860s and 1870s as the Shamrock LC was rising to prominence. Unfortunately for the bourgeois opponents of the Shamrock LC, however, the Irish-Catholic lacrossists and their fans had differing ideas of masculinity and fair play. Nonetheless, Colin Howell surely exaggerates when he argues that 'middle-class commentators were inclined to exaggerate the rowdiness of working class Irish-Catholics. Fearful that the diffusion of sport across the social spectrum would lead to a breakdown of the social order, middle-class newspapers like the *Montreal Star* often commented on the crude language and raucous behaviour of the Shamrock supporters and their team's ungentlemanly play.'[30] First, Howell is wide of the mark in terms of newspaper commentary on the style of play of the Shamrocks. Rather than comment upon dirty play on the part of the Irish-Catholics, the Montreal Anglo-Protestant press was concerned with notions of scientific play. The Shamrocks were continually made to be mindful that their claim to respectability hinged upon their ability to play scientific lacrosse rather than a game based on sheer brute skill, size, and speed. In this manner, the Shamrocks always finished second to the bourgeois Montreal LC, but well ahead of the Iroquois Indian LC of the Kahnawà:ke Indian Reserve near Montreal. The Shamrocks' claim to scientific skill was dubious, according to the Montreal anglophone press, due to their class status. In the case of the Iroquois Indian LC, they were beyond the pale of science by the very fact of their aboriginalness.[31]

Second, it was not, as Howell claims, that middle-class commentators were fearful of a breakdown of the social order due to the diffusion of sport. Rather, there was more a fear that sport could not be used by the bourgeoisie to control working-class behaviours on the playing field. Instead, these skilled working-class athletes[32] saw the playing field as a space of freedom from the regulatory controls of job, church, and family.[33]

Similarly, the behaviour of the un- and semi-skilled working-class fans of the Shamrock LC also came under scrutiny by the Anglo-Protestant press of Montreal, for engaging in actions that were not regarded as manly in the eyes of the bourgeois commentators. These criticisms spoke to differing concepts of manliness across class divides, as the behaviour of these working-class Shamrock fans was, in fact, consistent with their own notions of manly comportment and conduct.[34] Thus, manliness became a site of struggle surrounding Shamrock LC matches, especially against the bourgeois Montreal LC or, for that matter, the Toronto LC, a club comprising mainly Irish-Protestants.[35] Moreover, there is probably something to be read into the fact that the Shamrock fans were Irish, Catholic, and working class. Concerns about this group were not repeated when it came to the fans of the other clubs.[36]

Thus, while those historians who have studied the Shamrock LC have tended to focus on the classed identities of the players and, especially, the fans,[37] a much deeper reading is worth exploring. If one examines the relationship between the dominated and the dominators in the last third of the nineteenth century in Montreal, it is not a stretch to argue that there was a symbolic equation, though not absolute equality, of a Shamrock victory over the Montreals as being akin to victories of colonized peoples over their colonizers in sport, as with Pakistan versus England in cricket, or the Maori versus England in rugby (or, for that matter, the Iroquois LC over the Montreals in lacrosse).[38] Hence, lacrosse is recognized as a postcolonial sporting form by John Bale and Mike Cronin in their pioneering work on the subject, in which they compile a list of seven types of postcolonial sporting forms. Of particular interest here are '2. Indigenous body-cultures [i.e., games] that were transformed into modern sports – e.g. lacrosse' and '3. Body-cultures that were "invented" by a former colony.'[39] Lacrosse, of course, was initially an aboriginal war game that was transformed into a modern sport, largely at the behest of Montreal dentist Dr George Beers[40] in the middle decades of the nineteenth century. While the Montreal Lacrosse Club was founded in 1856, Beers did not codify the rules of the game until July 1867,[41] two-and-a-half weeks after Confederation, when he had them published in the *Gazette*. The timing was not coincidental as Beers was attempting to propagandize lacrosse and to establish it as Canada's 'national sport.'[42]

Beers's attempt to establish lacrosse as the national sport of Canada in the wake of Confederation is significant.[43] As a brand new nation created out of four disparate British colonies in North America – one of which had a French Canadian (and Catholic) majority, Canada had a need to forge a new national culture. Moreover, this new Canadian culture needed to differentiate the young Dominion from the former colonial parent, Great Britain. That being said, however, Canada remained part of the British Empire and Canadians were not necessarily interested in breaking this bond. Thus, attempts to create a new Canadian culture were very much hybridized, to borrow from Homi K. Bhabha, and bore a fundamental ambivalence.[44] The British influence remained prevalent in Canada in the Confederation era, although that British culture became influenced by, and was influential upon, an indigenous Euro-Canadian culture that arose in Canada out of the mixture of its various ethno-religious groups. This is all the more pointed in the case of Quebec, a former European colony conquered and colonized by another European power before becoming a founder partner in Confederation. The British, though benign in some ways in their rule over Quebec during the colonial era, nonetheless exported their own legal, political, and cultural traditions to Quebec and attempted to enforce them there, to a greater or lesser degree.[45]

The postcolonial is an appealing framework within which to examine the experience of the Irish-Catholics of Montreal, as it situates them at the intersection of Ireland and Canada/Quebec. This approach highlights the subtleties of their ambiguity and ambivalence vis-à-vis both the old country and the new. An imagined Ireland remained part and parcel of the Irish-Catholic experience in Montreal, as this community found various means to represent the old country back to itself in Canada. At the same time, in many ways the colonial relations of Ireland to Britain, of colonized to colonizer, were replicated in Quebec for the Irish-Catholics, at least to some degree. The major difference, of course, was that, while in Ireland, the Irish-Catholics were the primary target of the imperial gaze from London. This gaze was modified in Quebec, where other 'Other' populations were the main target: French Canadians and aboriginals.

Both sport and the postcolonial can be viewed as sites of resistance. The emergence of organized sport in the Anglo-Atlantic world and its colonies in the mid-nineteenth century reflects Bhabha's concept of hybridity,[46] especially in the case of a sport such as lacrosse. The emergence of lacrosse can be equated with the emergence of Gaelic football in Ireland and Australian Rules football in that country, simultaneous processes all three. Roy Hay argues that Gaelic and Aussie Rules football are exactly what Bhabha makes reference to, given their hybridization of soccer forms with local contingencies and forms.[47] Similarly, lacrosse emerged out of a hybridized period and Beers, in particular, took his cue from cricket, setting up lacrosse as a Canadian sport in opposition to,[48] while at the same time taking part of, the British sport. Thus, it is appropriate to view the ongoing rivalry between the Shamrocks and the Montreals in lacrosse in this postcolonial light. Furthermore, this rivalry can be cast in a postcolonial masculinist light. A victory by the Shamrocks over the Montreals can also be seen as a victory, however small and symbolic, and however fleeting, over British imperialism and the dominant masculine ethos of the time, one that, in Canada, was based upon (though certainly not identical to) genteel British masculine ideals. This reading of the matches between the Shamrock and Montreal lacrosse clubs can be further highlighted and tied back to this postcolonial viewpoint when examined through the lens of Irish nationalism and nationality in Montreal in the late nineteenth and early twentieth centuries. Rosalyn Trigger argues that it was in the wake of the Fenian[49] threat to Canada in the 1860s that the Irish-Catholic church in Montreal attempted to divert Irish energies away from Irish nationalism towards an Irish national identity based upon the parish organization in the city.[50]

That being said, however, it is clear that an Irish nationalist community continued to agitate on Ireland's behalf in Montreal throughout the rest of the nineteenth century and in the early twentieth century. A minority group continued the Fenian tradition in Montreal and, by the end of the century, the Ancient Order of Hibernians (AOH) began to make its presence known there. The AOH was a republican, ultra-Catholic,[51] Irish nationalist organization with very clear and openly martial tones. Like the Fenians before it,[52] the AOH was a predominately working-class organization with its power base in the city's *sud-ouest*, Griffintown and Pointe-Saint-Charles.[53]

The majority of the Irish-Catholic community, of all classes, however, supported John Redmond and the parliamentary Home Rule movement,[54] which was meant to lead to Irish independence with a form of Dominion status and a national capital at Dublin. The communication of this Home Rule nationalist discourse can be seen in Montreal's St Patrick's Day parades in the late nineteenth century. As Susan Davis notes, nineteenth-century parades were a means of communication and were, among other things, 'modes of propaganda.'[55] The organizers of the St Patrick's Day parade in Montreal, a largely bourgeois outfit until the AOH became dominant in the 1910s,[56] made use of the parade exactly in this manner, as a medium to communicate their message concerning the plight of Ireland to the wider community of Montreal, especially, one would imagine, the Anglo-Protestants. Throughout the late nineteenth century, an Irish nationalist / Home Rule message was very carefully, and quite skilfully, conveyed through the parade. Its organizers, who before the formation of the Irish-Catholic Committee in 1893 were drawn exclusively from the St Patrick's Society and the Irish-Catholic clergy of Montreal, were always careful to ensure that their conservative Irish nationalist message was embedded in a larger message of Irish-Catholic loyalty to the Canadian state and the British Empire in general. The 1875 edition of the parade is perhaps the best example of this. Banners along the parade route declared that 'Ireland and France are True Friends' and demanded 'Home Rule for the Land of Our Forefathers.' However, a carefully constructed display of flags placed the British ensign as the centrepiece, surrounded by the Irish,[57] French, and American flags.[58] Finally, to ensure that the loyalist message got through, the British ensign was the only flag flying atop St Patrick's Hall.[59]

This fine balance was on display again in 1890, when a very strong Catholic identity was conveyed, together with a more respectable message concerning Home Rule for Ireland. The keynote speaker that year was J.J. Curran, Conservative Member of Parliament for Montreal Centre,[60] who, when asked about Home Rule, answered very carefully: 'Some people claimed that home rule meant separation. Did home rule in Canada mean separation? Were not the English, Scotch, and French in Canada loyal? And ... was there a more loyal body of men in this Dominion than the Irish-Catholics?'[61] Thus, if we look at the manifestation of Irish nationalism as viewed through the St Patrick's Day parade, it is clear that the majority of Irish-Catholic Montrealers identified themselves, at least in the late nineteenth century, very closely with Ireland and within an Irish diasporic identity, albeit within a framework of loyalty to the new country.

The Montreal Shamrock HC

It is through a lens of postcolonial bourgeois Irish-Catholicism that the Shamrock HC must be viewed. Indeed, hockey, like lacrosse, can be viewed as a postcolonial sporting form, given its genesis in Canada and that it arose out of a mixture of European and Canadian games in the 1870s.[62] Moreover, hockey, like lacrosse, was central to the forging of a unique Canadian identity in the Confederation era, and beyond.

Irishness was clearly important to the Shamrock players, as they chose to play for an Irish-Catholic club rather than jumping to any of the other Montreal-based clubs. It is not as if the Shamrock players would have had problems sticking with these other clubs, especially Shamrock captain Harry Trihey. The captain of the Shamrocks was widely regarded as the best player of his era and became legendary not only for his goal-scoring prowess,[63] but for the way he revolutionized the sport by speeding up the game.[64] Trihey and his fellow Shamrock forwards Fred Scanlan, Jack Brennan, and Arthur Farrell were all familiar with players from both the Montreals and Victorias from their time playing for McGill College in the mid-to-late 1890s.[65] Nonetheless, the Montreal HC and the Victorias were predominately Anglo-Protestant clubs; thus, it is not fair to point to the Shamrocks as the only club defined by the ethno-religious identities of its players. Moreover, the club continued its affiliation with the Shamrock AAA, and some of the players served on the board not just of the hockey club and the Shamrock AAA, but also of the lacrosse club.[66] Brennan, for example, also played for the Shamrock LC.[67] Goaltender Jim McKenna served on the Shamrock AAA board of directors in 1899.[68] As for Trihey, he was the Shamrock HC captain from 1898 to 1901, when he retired. In 1898 he was on the Shamrock AAA board of directors and was the lacrosse club's honorary secretary as well. Following his retirement from the game, he remained on the team's board as well as that of the Shamrock AAA, and served as the president of the CAHL in 1903–4.[69]

Trihey and several of his teammates, at least those who can be traced in the historical records, remained involved in the Irish-Catholic community of Montreal following their retirement from hockey. Brennan was a long-standing and prominent physician in the community. Farrell's father, William, was a merchant and had served as a city councillor, representing an Irish-Catholic middle-class neighbourhood. After he left the Shamrocks, Arthur Farrell entered his father's business and published at least two more books on the sport of hockey, including one in the prestigious and influential series of sporting books by the Spalding Company of New York City. As we saw earlier, Farrell's first book on hockey was published at the peak of his hockey career in 1899. Farrell, however, died young of tuberculosis at a sanatorium in the Laurentian town of Sainte-Agathe-des-Monts one day before his thirty-second birthday in 1909.[70]

With the outbreak of war in Europe in 1914, Trihey and several other prominent members of the Irish-Catholic community of Montreal took it upon themselves to organize the 55th Regiment, Irish Canadian Rangers, for the Canadian militia. Trihey was given the rank of lieutenant colonel.[71] Terence Fay notes that Trihey and the members of the 55th Regiment 'accepted the fact that Irish Home Rule was suspended for the duration of the war and that they should volunteer for service in a just war.'[72] Indeed, this appears to have been a common understanding among the bourgeoisies of the Irish-Catholic community of Montreal, at least at the outbreak of the war.[73] Fay, however, oversimplifies the rationale for enlisting in the Irish-Canadian Rangers. Irish-Catholics of

Montreal did not simply enlist for a just war. They enlisted to serve for Canada in that war. While they maintained an attachment to Ireland, for the majority Canada was their home. And serving for Canada in the war was in no way disloyal to Ireland, despite the fact that the Canadian Expeditionary Force (CEF) was subservient to the British Army.[74]

This ambivalence is made even clearer by the plight of Trihey, who was also the Commanding Officer of the 199th Overseas Battalion,[75] which began its recruitment campaign in Montreal at Easter 1916, rather unfortunate timing, given the events of that weekend in Dublin.[76] The Easter Rising in Dublin, combined with the brutal response of the British, seemed to have hurt recruitment campaigns on the part of the Rangers. It also certainly tried the patience of Montreal's Irish-Catholics vis-à-vis the postponement of the campaign for Home Rule in Ireland.[77] Nonetheless, the 199th departed for overseas at Christmas 1916, first for a tour of Ireland to try to drum up recruits for the British Army there, before they were to be deployed in France. However, the British High Command changed its policy, and despite promising the Canadian government that the Rangers would fight as a unit in France, the battalion was broken up to be fed into the line as individual reinforcements.[78] Enraged, Trihey resigned his commission and returned to Montreal.[79]

Upon his return, Trihey, still incensed at the British, wrote a letter to the *New York Daily Post* that perhaps encapsulated the ambiguity and ambivalence on the part of Montreal's Irish-Catholics vis-à-vis Ireland, Britain, and Canada. Trihey criticized the British decision to split up the 199th Battalion, noting that the Irish-Catholics of Montreal had willingly signed up to fight for Canada in the war and, more to the point, continued to do so in the wake of the Easter Rising in Dublin and the brutality of the British response. He then went on to question the need for conscription in Canada when there were 150,000 British troops imposing martial law in Ireland. His letter was reprinted in the *Gazette*, where it caught the attention of military authorities in Canada. Trihey only escaped trial for sedition because Charles Doherty, the minister of justice and Member of Parliament for Montreal West, interceded on his behalf.[80] Nevertheless, Trihey's opinions reflected the Irish-Catholic experience in Montreal vis-à-vis Ireland and Quebec/Canada, not just during the First World War, but for the entire generation leading up to the war and Irish independence. On the one hand, the Irish-Catholics of Montreal were proud Canadians willing to serve their country. On the other hand, they still maintained an interest in Irish affairs and in the plight of Ireland under the yoke of British imperialism.

However, if their Irishness (and Catholicism) was important to the players of the Shamrock HC, this was of lesser import to their opposition, their fans, and the newspaper reporters and editors who followed the CAHL in the anglophone press of Montreal. That the Shamrocks' ethno-religious status was not of any interest to their opponents and fans, of course, suggests that by the turn of the twentieth century the Irish-Catholics of Montreal were more or less integrated into the city's anglophone body politic. Instead of ethno-religious identity, what was important was the Shamrock players' class background as well as their willingness to share in, and adhere to, middle-class mores of manly behaviour at the hockey rink.

That the Shamrocks were a middle-class club is very clear, as a cross-listing of the Stanley Cup–winning roster with *Lovell's City Directory* for Montreal in 1899 and 1900 reveals that, at least for those who turned up in the directory, they were all of bourgeois backgrounds. That being said, however, it is important to note that they were not from the upper-middle class, let alone the elite of Montreal, as were the players on the other two Montreal-based clubs, the Montreal AAA and the Victorias. While both Frank Tansey and Arthur Farrell were from prominent local political families – both of their fathers had been city councillors – they were far from the elite of the city. The Tanseys' powerbase was in Griffintown, the district represented at city council by Frank's father, Bernard. Bernard had played for the Shamrock LC in the 1870s and he parlayed his fame as an athlete into the wildly successful Tansey House Tavern in Griffintown. By the *fin de siècle*, however, the family lived in the fashionable Little Dublin district,[81] in the shadow of St Patrick's Cathedral at the top of Beaver Hall Hill.[82] For their part, the Farrells lived at 706 Sherbrooke, on the fringe of the Golden Square Mile of Montreal,[83] the legendary district that then housed the majority of the wealth generated in Canada.[84]

Trihey, though he moved into Montreal's anglophone elite after his playing days with the Shamrocks, was a law student at McGill. The son of Thomas F. Trihey, a real-estate broker with offices on Great St James Street,[85] he owned a house on rue Sainte-Catherine in the exclusive west end suburb of Westmount.[86] Jack Brennan the son of a builder and contractor, was in medical school at McGill during his Shamrocks career. The Brennans lived on rue Saint-Hubert, near Parc Lafontaine in the eastern Plateau Mont-Royal. Then, as now, the area surrounding Parc Lafontaine was a fashionable part of town.[87] Finally, goaltender Jim McKenna was a bookkeeper who lived at 33 rue Saint-

Cuthbert, on the lower Plateau Mont-Royal, near the Hôpital Hôtel-Dieu and Fletcher's Fields[88] on the eastern slope of Mont-Royal. In 1900 McKenna's neighbourhood was a lower-middle-class one, populated by a mixture of Irish-Catholics and French Canadians. Within a decade or two, however, it became part of the famous Jewish ghetto of Montreal, immortalized in the fiction of Mordecai Richler.[89] Forward Fred Scanlan, cover-pointman Frank Wall, and coach Barney Dunphy do not appear in *Lovell's*.

Thus, while Trihey and Farrell were clearly the most affluent members of the team, hailing from Westmount and the fringes of the Golden Square Mile respectively, all the remaining players who can be traced in *Lovell's* were more solidly middle or lower middle class. But what is more striking about their socio-economic standing, aside from the residential patterns, is that more than half of the Shamrock players attended McGill College, the bastion of Montreal's elite, and elitist, Anglo-Protestant classes. This speaks to two things. First, by the dawn of the twentieth century, the sectarian divides of Montreal that were predominant in the middle third of the nineteenth century[90] had dissipated, at least within the anglophone community and within the middle and upper classes.[91] Second, the attendance of Trihey, Brennan, Scanlan, and Farrell at McGill speaks to the existence of a more elite bourgeois class among the Irish-Catholic community of Montreal by the last decade of the nineteenth century. This social mobility can be seen especially in the post-hockey careers of Brennan and Trihey, discussed above.

None of this is to suggest that the Irish-Catholics of Montreal had reached the highest level of the city's upper class. These socially ambitious men were still far away from the summit of Mont-Royal or, with a few exceptions such as Trihey, even the exclusivity of lower Westmount. This is apparent in a comparison between the Montreal AAA and the Shamrock AAA; the former charged a $10 annual fee on its members, in addition to the $10 initiation fee upon joining, as a means to ensuring that the Montreal AAA's membership remained exclusive and elitist. Membership fees in the Shamrock AAA, for its part, were much cheaper, reflecting its less exclusive membership.[92]

The Hockeyist's Body: Gender, Violence, and Fair Play

As previously noted, hockey was in a state of flux at the time of the Shamrocks' Stanley Cup victories in 1899 and 1900. Not only were the

Shamrocks changing the way in which the game was played on the ice, through Trihey's innovations, but the sport was caught in a cultural paradigm shift. Notions of manliness were in flux in the face of modernity and all that entailed. Within the context of the sport itself, notions of fair play and sportsmanship were under fire amidst the growing commodification of the sport at the elite senior amateur level and the concomitant importance placed upon winning.[93] This new focus on winning led to more physical and aggressive play and an accompanying shift in attitude on the part of the players, fans, and press towards violence and rough play. (See also chapter 5.) Michael Robidoux notes that hockey was a violent game by nature and this is part of what made it central to the forging of a Canadian myth and nation; the violence of the sport was part of its appeal.[94] Meanwhile, John Chi-Kit Wong reports that there was more importance placed on winning by the early 1890s at the expense of the doctrine of fair play.[95]

This erosion of the importance of gentlemanly play can be seen in an examination of two events involving the Crystal HC of Montreal in the late 1880s and early 1890s. The Crystals were the predecessor club of the Shamrocks, the Shamrock AAA obtaining their franchise in 1894 and forming its own hockey club.[96] In 1886, at the Montreal Carnival, the Crystals were playing the Quebec HC when one of the visiting players was injured and had to leave the game. The Quebecs, winning the game at the time, asked the Crystals to take off a player as well, to make the match fair. The Crystals refused and went on to win. Seven years later, the Crystals were playing the Montreal AAA, when one of their players was kicked out of the match, though he was eligible to return for the overtime period. The Montreals refused to let the punished player back onto the ice. Subsequently, the Crystals appealed to the league, which ruled against them. Indeed, the decision of the AHAC was particularly galling for the *Gazette*, as it showed the erosion of gentlemanly behaviour on the ice in favour of a win-at-all-costs mentality. However, while the *Gazette* was appalled in 1886 by the behaviour of the Crystals, arguing that they had no right to call themselves champions, the newspaper was more resigned to the rise of this new mentality by 1893, despite its criticism.[97]

Further evidence of the erosion of gentlemanly play can be seen around the Shamrocks' defence of the Stanley Cup against the champions of the Ontario Hockey Association, Queen's College (now Queen's University), in 1899. In the aftermath of the Shamrocks' easy and successful defence of the Cup, there was some incipient trash-talking on the part of the Queen's team. Despite 'being satisfied with the game they put up' in a 6–2 shellacking at the hands of the Shamrocks, the Kingston newspaper reported that Queen's was 'confident [that] they can whip the Shamrocks either on Kingston ice or in Montreal when [Queen's] are in condition. In conversation, Capt. Curtis said: – "The Shamrocks are altogether over-estimated, and I am sure that if we had been playing in the Quebec league with them this year we could have won out without much trouble."'[98] Queen's also complained about its share of the gate receipts from the match, about having to pay for the referee, and about the fact that the Shamrocks used sticks that were six inches longer than those of the Queen's club.[99] With the exception of the complaints about the sticks (which Queen's could have easily remedied by obtaining new sticks in Montreal), the Queen's players, or at least Curtis, showed an almost total disregard for bourgeois concepts of sportsmanship and more of a concern with, if not winning, at least finding a good excuse for losing, as well as with the commercialized, commodified aspect of elite-level amateur hockey.[100]

This shift to a focus on winning can also be seen in the pages of the *Gazette* in its coverage of a 4–3 victory by the Shamrocks over the Montreals in league play in 1899. The newspaper reported some rather questionable behaviour on the part of the victorious Shamrocks:

> Time and again Montreal, according to all probabilities of the game, should have scored. They did not primarily on account of inaccuracy in direction, secondarily, because the Shamrocks got into a habit of moving round the goal posts and dropping them into some place where they were not supposed to be.
>
>   This habit of removing goal posts is an excellent one, if nobody is looking and the referee is charitable enough to think incidents of this description are accidental.[101]

In other words, the Shamrocks were outright cheating against the Montreals by moving the goal around to disrupt their opponents' shots at McKenna in the Shamrock net. What is interesting, however, is the *Gazette*'s tone in reporting this behaviour. Rather than outright condemning the Shamrocks for cheating, the newspaper instead took on a bitingly sarcastic tone. This approach rather blunts the newspaper's criticism of poor sportsmanship on the part of the Shamrocks. At any rate, both the actions of the Shamrocks and the muted response from the *Gazette* (as well as a complete lack of response from the Montreals) show this shift in attitude. The question of fair play seemed moot and irrelevant; what mattered now was victory.

Attitudes towards the violence inherent in hockey also underwent a shift in the 1890s.[102] Violence became less an issue to be problematized. Instead, newspaper reporters and their editors chose to contextualize it and to embed it in the discourse of scientific play that came to dominate accounts of hockey during this decade.[103]

At first, it appears rather odd that Canada, which has created for itself a reputation of tranquillity and peaceful-mindedness, would have as its national winter sport hockey, one of the more violent sports known to humankind. Hockey is also not exactly the sport one would expect 'gentlemen' of the late nineteenth century to be playing due to its violence and occasional brutality.[104] However, Robidoux argues that the violent play inherent in hockey allowed the sport to be separated from other important bourgeois pastimes, including and perhaps especially, baseball.[105] He also suggests that 'the distinction ... hockey received as being a rough sport served as a means for Canadians to display their proficiency in the clearly demarcated context of a sporting event'; this is precisely what made hockey ideal for Canadian identity.[106] In this way we can see hockey, and its attendant violent and occasionally brutal play, as a response to the crisis of middle-class masculinity at the turn of the twentieth century. Hockey became a means for these bourgeois players to reclaim some of the physical vitality that they, as a class, perceived themselves to have lost through the process of urbanization, industrialization, modernization, and bureaucatization.

This is exactly what made the sport useful not just for Canadian national identity, but for bourgeois masculine identities as well; and this is also what drew upwards of 10,000 fans to the Montreal Arena on Wednesday and Saturday nights to see senior-level amateur hockey.[107] Finally, the threat of violence is what drew the sports reporters and editors of Montreal's anglophone press to the sport. It was largely *due* to its violent nature, then, that hockey became a uniquely, and distinctively, Canadian sport.[108] This is not to say, however, that hockey at the turn of the twentieth century was all about violence and resembled the movie *Slapshot!* Far from it, as hockeyists were expected not only to follow the rules of the sport, but to conform their behaviour to acceptable norms and standards of behaviour on the ice, and not to engage in gratuitous violence.[109] In other words, this violence was ritualized for the most part.[110] This was, argues Robidoux, in keeping with Canadian stereotypes of the frontiersman and his stoic nature.[111]

With the violence of hockey contextualized into the discussion of scientific play, what did become a subject of discussion in the sports pages of the *Gazette* and the *Montreal Star* by the turn of the twentieth century was the body of the hockeyist and his physical condition. In reporting on the team's practices prior to its matches, the *Gazette* made several comments on the physical fitness of the Shamrocks over the course of the 1898 and 1899 seasons, suggesting that the players were 'all in the pink of condition.'[112]

The press went further than this, however, in discussing the physical condition and body of the hockeyist and the sport's attendant violence. Indeed, the hockey player's physical fitness was intimately tied up with the question of violence in the sport. The hockeyist's body *had* to be in the pink of condition, as, according to the *Gazette*, 'men who are not in absolute perfect physical condition should not be permitted to play. Modern developments have made the conditions as hard on a man who is to play championship[-level hockey] for a [*sic*] hour's actual time as on the prize-fighter, who boxes for a limited or unlimited number of rounds. The prize-fighter does get various rests during the course of his little séance. According to the rules[,] the amateur hockey player only gets it at half time.'[113] This physical health was necessary to engage in the 'aggressive science' of a hockey game: 'A man did not need to show a homicidal eye, when he was coming at you like an express train's headlight flashing around the curve, with an intoxicated mechanic controlling the throttle. But the forwards met each other with the same impetus, and the speed of some of the skaters, doubled up like jack knives, with nothing in view but a bit of rubber and an idea of direction, could apparently give an express train points.'[114]

The choices of metaphor here are interesting. Despite the sophomoric writing of the *Gazette* reporter, the train analogy is entirely in keeping with the rise of modernity in late-nineteenth-century Montreal. Moreover, we can see that this discourse surrounding a match between the Shamrocks and Montreal HC creates a very nuanced image of the masculine identities of the hockeyists. The *Gazette*, while praising the 'aggressive science' of the players in the match, downplays the actual violence in what was, if we read between the lines, a violent game.[115] Rather than needing to act 'homicidal,' a hockeyist was better served to engage in a controlled 'scientific aggression' against his opponent, to couch his violent impulses within a scientific approach that privileges reason over emotion and skill over passion in a match that was 'clean, hard, and very fast.'[116] In short, we have the expression of a bourgeois manliness in this focus on reason and skill, initially developed as a counterpoint to working-class manliness and its focus on physical strength as middle-class men began to become sedentary in their jobs.[117]

That the report felt it proper to comment on the need for physical fitness on the part of the players is also significant, as it speaks to another facet of the construction of a masculinist identity for the players, this time focusing on their bodies rather than their emotions. The place and function of the body in sport is, indeed, central. This commentary also echoes the sort of body-typing engaged in with sports such as boxing, where the body is much more on display than is the case with hockey. That the *Gazette* chose the prizefighter as a point of comparison to the hockeyist reflects this focus.

None of this is all that surprising. Howell argues that 'at its most basic level ... sport is about the body: how it is used, how it is imagined, how it is watched, and how it is disciplined to meet the requirements of living or to conform to social expectations.'[118] Indeed, this focus on the body can be seen in a Foucauldian sense, as sport is a form of modernity and technology that is then used to train and discipline the body. The athlete's body is displayed on the ice under the gaze of the audience and the press. In other words, the physical fitness of athletes was a form of discipline and power and was therefore closely tied to themes of modernity in industrial, modern Montreal at the *fin de siècle*.[119]

The boxing comparison is significant for other reasons as well. Boxing was seen as the ultimate individualistic sport, a triumph of the body over the soul, of power over pain. In the ring, the prizefighter was reliant upon his body, skill, training, and discipline in order to defeat his opponent. For this reason, boxing was known as 'the sweet science,' a notion the *Gazette* writer was referring to in calling hockey an 'aggressive science.' But the linking of the boxer to a Foucauldian discourse on the body of the prizefighter is much easier to demonstrate, given the relative lack of clothing the boxer wears in the ring: boxing trunks and no shirt, with his body and musculature on open display. The focus on the boxer's body as a carefully constructed and disciplined modern weapon is obvious.[120] In comparing the hockeyist, who was fully clothed and wore at least some rudimentary padding on his hands and shins, to the nearly naked boxer, the *Gazette* was attempting to focus attention on the masculine, sculpted, disciplined, and 'scientifically' controlled body of the player.

Indeed, photographs of hockeyists and their teams from this era were very carefully constructed and reflect, first, this focus on the body and the masculine identity of the players and, second, their controlled emotions. Following their Stanley Cup victory in 1899, the Shamrock HC paid a visit to the studios of William Notman & Sons, Montreal's premier photography studio, to be photographed with the trophy (see figure 1). The players in the photograph either glower off into the middle distance, looking away from the camera, or glare directly into it. Some of the players are carefully posed in a vaguely threatening manner, others appear solitary and aloof, all in the guise of contemporary middle-class manliness.

During this so-called crisis of masculinity at the *fin de siècle*, contemporaries feared the declining virility of the white, middle-class male and the apparent strength of 'Other' men, those from the working classes or of different ethnic or racial background, among others.[121] Part of the response to this was to hyper-masculinize white, middle-class men in order to counter the alleged over-civilization and feminization of these men around the turn of the twentieth century. This response entailed the fetishization of the (white) middle-class male body and its reconstruction in the image of 'the perfect man,' as John F. Kasson argues.[122]

It is in this light that we must view the photograph of the Stanley Cup–winning Shamrocks. All the players, including one of the spares, Charles Horner, were wearing their Shamrocks sweaters, which were remarkably tight and conformed to the musculature of the players' arms. In the case of Trihey, seated in the middle of the picture, his lips are pursed, his arms cocked and resting on his thighs, as he stares off slightly menacingly into the middle distance, gazing to the left of the camera. Scanlan is sitting to the left of Trihey, looking much more relaxed, leaning back in his chair with his legs spread in front of him and his arms casually resting on his thighs. On his face, his lips pursed as he stares directly into the camera, is what can only be described as an arrogant expression. Farrell is standing at the end of the back row to the right of Trihey, his back leaning against a chair that he holds onto with his hands. His face shows determination and his arms and muscles are taut as he stares off into the same middle distance as Trihey, to the left of the camera. Jim McKenna looks the most threatening of all. His arms are folded to emphasize his biceps and he glares directly into the camera. None of the players or club officials are smiling, though the officials, as well as spare player John Dolby, look much more relaxed than the players. In other words, the very structure of the hockeyists in the

Figure 1. Montreal Shamrocks, Stanley Cup Champions, 1899. Back row, from left to right: Jim McKenna (goaltender), John Dolby (spare), Frank Tansey (point), C. Foley (treasurer), Barney Dunphy (coach), Frank Wall (coverpoint), Arthur Farrell (forward). Front row, from left to right: Charles Horner (spare), Fred Scanlan (forward), Harry Trihey (forward, captain), Jack Brennan (forward). (Notman Photographic Archives, Musée McCord, Montreal)

photograph reflects middle-class concerns about masculinity at the *fin de siècle*, with their hyper-masculinized poses, as they seek to reclaim the masculine nature of middle-class men and engage in a clear display of their manliness *vis-à-vis* the violent sport in which they excelled.

The sitting for this photograph was carefully controlled by the photographer, the Shamrock HC, and the Shamrock AAA. The players were carefully posed to display the heroic qualities of the stoic, manly hockeyist. In doing so, the Shamrocks were following the ritual established with the first Stanley Cup winners, the Montreal AAA of 1893, shown in figure 2. Figure 3 shows the Montreal Victorias, the champions in 1888, in the pre–Stanley Cup era. What we see is that the posing of the players changed rather dramatically over the decade preceding the Shamrocks' cup victory in 1899. The Shamrocks were much more aloof and vaguely threatening in their poses before Notman & Sons' photographic eye than were the 1893 Montreals or 1888 Victorias, both also photographed by Notman & Sons. It is not quite the case that the Montreal HC players are smiling for the camera, but they appear much more relaxed than the Shamrocks. In the case of the Victorias, other than the player sitting second from the right in the front row, all the players are relaxed. The players standing in the back row, as well as the club officials, gaze directly into the camera. The players lying at the front and those seated in the front row, however, avoid the camera, gazing off into the middle distance to the camera's left.

Despite the *Gazette*'s emphasis on the discourse of 'scientific aggression,' it remains that hockey *was* violent and that violence could threaten to overshadow the game. For example, during a game between the Shamrocks and the Montreals early in the 1900 season, there was a conflagration with less than two minutes to play in a lopsided 8–3 Shamrock victory. With the game well out of hand, Brown of the Montreals slashed Trihey, the Shamrocks' best player, hard over the ankles. Trihey did not take kindly to this infraction and responded with a 'stiff right hook' to Brown's neck, sending him to the ice, 'and a general melee followed.'[123] According to the *Gazette*, referee Graham Drinkwater's quick response prevented a total breakdown and tranquillity was quickly restored.[124] There was no further commentary on the fight between Brown and Trihey, though the recounting of the violence, in all of two sentences, was under a subheading 'The Fight.' However, while the *Gazette* and the *Montreal Star* were usually content to editorialize on the state of the game, to comment on the skill of the players, and so on, neither newspaper felt much need to make any substantive editorial

Figure 2. Montreal AAA, the first Stanley Cup champions, 1893. The Cup is in the front foreground. (Notman Photographic Archives, Musée McCord, Montreal)

Figure 3. Montreal Victorias, 1888 champions. (Notman Photographic Archives, Musée McCord, Montreal)

comment on the violent slash by Brown on Trihey nor Trihey's assault on Brown in response.[125]

This episode echoed the general lack of commentary from the *Gazette* following another melee that erupted during the second game of the 1899 Stanley Cup challenge series between the Victoria HC of Winnipeg and the Montreal Victorias.[126] McDougall, of the Montreal club, was sent off for slashing after a rather vicious attack on Winnipeg's Gingras, who was hurt and had to leave the game. The Winnipegs demanded that McDougall receive a match penalty, which the referee refused. The Winnipeg club then insulted the referee, who simply skated off the ice and left the building. This effectively postponed the match, as the Montreal club refused to play with another referee in charge. A search party was sent out into the cold Montreal night to cajole the referee into coming back to the Arena to continue the match, but by the time he returned, the Winnipegs had left the ice as well, retreating to their dressing room. They refused to return to the ice to continue the match, and so the Cup was awarded to the Montreal Victorias, who had won the first game of the series and were leading in the second when the incident between McDougall and Gingras occurred. The *Gazette* had plenty to say about the actions of the referee and the attendant controversy, and also reported on the Winnipeggers' complaints; but the newspaper had little to say about McDougall's slash on Gingras. While some of this selective reporting can no doubt be chalked up to home-town boosterism on the part of the *Gazette*, it should also be noted that the paper reprinted excerpts from the Winnipeg papers from over the wire. The Winnipeg papers gave less attention to the original slash by McDougall than to the conflagration that emerged around the referee's actions.[127]

Hype, Modernization, and Commercialization in the Press Narratives of the Shamrock HC

As Paul Braganza notes in his history of baseball in Montreal, the press had a major impact on the spread of that sport: 'If covering games and creating rivals could increase interest, the newspaper would profit – and if this meant lying about attendance or creating an imagined excitement, so be it.'[128] This observation can also be applied to hockey. In the case of hockey in *fin de siècle* Montreal, it was not so much that attendance figures had to be fudged as it was a case of creating and hyping rivalries, especially among the Montreal-based clubs, all in the name of the commodification and commercialization of the sport; and the anglophone press of Montreal was a key partner in this process. We can particularly see this around matches between the Shamrocks and the Montreal HC, a team whose fortunes were in decline around the turn of the century.[129] A rivalry was quickly invented for the two clubs, who had not played each other before the Shamrocks joined the AHAC in 1894.[130] This imagined rivalry between the Shamrocks and Montreal HC was based upon the long and storied rivalry between the Shamrock and Montreal lacrosse clubs. Matches between the Shamrocks and Montreals were hyped in advertisements in both the *Gazette* and the *Montreal Star* as featuring 'The Old Rivals,'[131] and mention was made of this rivalry in nearly every account of games between the two clubs, despite the fact that by 1899 they were hardly 'old rivals.' Indeed, so celebrated was this 'rivalry' that the very first match played in the new Montreal Arena when it opened to start the 1898 season was 'between those old-time rivals, Shamrocks and Montreal.'[132]

This commercialization and commodification of championship-level senior hockey can also be seen in the pre- and post-game coverage of matches in the press, especially in the *Gazette*. For example, before a Shamrock-Quebec match in February 1898, the *Gazette*, rather breathlessly, stated that 'the topic in athletic circles is narrowed down to the skating championship and tomorrow night's hockey game.'[133] Oftentimes, however, the paper was forced to admit that the game had not been all that entertaining. Following a 10–2 drubbing of the Shamrocks by the Montreals in January 1898, the *Gazette* noted that the game was 'not the acme of perfection by any means,' complaining that play was too individualistic and not team-oriented. Nonetheless, the *Gazette* concluded, it was pretty to look at.[134] Following a 6–5 loss to Quebec by the Shamrocks in February 1898, the *Gazette* reported that 'the game was a clean and hard one, but was not characterized by brilliant hockey.' Still, the paper went on to praise the skill of both clubs.[135] Following another Shamrock loss, this time to the Montreal HC, 4–0, the *Gazette* gushed over the skill of both clubs, and noted that the Shamrocks had just as much licence to win the match, as they had played just as well, despite the lopsided score. However, noted the *Gazette*, 'it is not to be understood, by ay means, that the style of play should be characterized as "good." It was not, in fact, it was decidedly rotten.'[136] Finally after a 5–0 victory over Quebec in a February 1898 match that was marred by poor ice, the *Gazette*, along with praising the play of the Shamrocks, reported that 'the play was certainly not brilliant, the visitors [i.e., Quebec] particularly playing a bad game.'[137]

In all these instances, however, despite complaints about poor or weak play, or shoddy ice, the negative comments were made quickly and coverage moved on to the finer points of play during the match and a recounting of all the scoring, including the plays that led to the goals. Accounts the scoring plays, moreover, rarely made mention of defensive breakdowns or mistakes that led to the goals. Instead, the *Gazette* (and the *Montreal Star*) focused on the skill of the attacking players. Such positive accounts of the games effectively served as a form of (free) advertising for the CAHL and its member clubs. This, in turn, drove sales of the newspapers up as fans sought to read coverage of the CAHL season in the sport pages of the *Gazette* and *Montreal Star*.

The *Gazette* also hyped games by the Montreal-based clubs especially, it seems, when the teams were not all that evenly matched. In these instances, the newspaper made a point of speaking to the skill level of the weaker team. For example, in an article before the first meeting between the Shamrocks and Victorias in January 1898, the *Gazette* reported that, 'according to supporters of both teams, the match ought to prove a very good one.' And while the paper noted that not much was known about the Shamrock team, due to a number of new players joining the club,[138] 'they are credited with doing good work in practice, but it is thought that they will have to take second place with the Vics.'[139] The Shamrocks did indeed take second place that night, by a 7–3 count,[140] which is perhaps not all that surprising given that the Victorias were the defending Stanley Cup champions and the Shamrocks a newly configured club. The *Gazette*, however, found much to praise in the Shamrocks' play that night and used it to hype the next game, against Ottawa. The paper noted that 'the work of the Shamrocks in the first game with the Victorias was a great surprise, and it is now quite certain in consequence that when they face the Ottawas on Saturday evening there will be a very large audience present.'[141] The next day, in another article previewing the Shamrock/Ottawa tilt, the *Gazette* praised the local side: 'The Shamrocks gave an excellent account of themselves when they met the Victorias [despite being pummelled 7–3], and judging from that day's play, they should defeat the Ottawas or at least succeed in making a draw with them, as the Winnipegs did. But better things hould [*sic*] be expected, for if the Winnipeggers depended on forward speed and the Ottawas were only able to hold them down, then a little combination work up front and a bit of steadiness behind the line should bring the Shamrocks out victors.'[142] Just in case the *Gazette*'s readership had not yet got the point, in yet another preview on the day of the game, the paper suggested that the Shamrocks, 'since their struggle with the Vics, have picked up wonderfully, and in consequence may be relied upon to make the pace hot from the start. They are in the pink of condition, and can keep up the pace during the hour.'[143] The Shamrocks made good on the *Gazette*'s prediction, and came away with a 2–1 victory.[144]

The *Gazette* continued to lavish praise on the Shamrocks in the 1898 season, arguing that while they were still an unknown quantity, 'they can play good hockey as already been demonstrated, and they are capable of still better things.'[145] These approbations continued even as the losses mounted, and the Shamrocks finished in third place in the five-team CAHL with a 3-5 record. Perhaps the praise lavished by the *Gazette* was earned as the 1898 season was an improvement on the 1-7 records the Shamrocks had posted in 1896 and 1897 and their attendant dead-last finishes.

The following season, 1899, partly on the basis of their improved play in 1898, the *Gazette* counted upon the Shamrocks to contend for the championship. However, in the first game of the season, they stumbled out of the gate and lost 4–3 to Ottawa in the capital. Despite this defeat, the paper still pegged the Shamrocks 'to be a factor in the championship race.'[146] The following week, in advance of the Shamrocks' match with their 'old rivals,' the Montreals, the *Gazette* attempted to create a buzz: 'The Shamrock team is the strongest that has ever represented that club, the players are all in the pink of condition, and will do their best to defeat the boys in blue. Harry Trihey has recovered from his recent indisposition and will be on the forward line to help Farrell, Scanlan, and Brannan to get the puck past Montreal's stalwart defence. McKenna, Tansey, and Wall is a defence of no mean ability, as was shown in their match in Ottawa on Saturday night.'[147] The Shamrocks began to live up to their hype in 1899, and they beat the Montreal HC 4–3 in this match.[148] Indeed, the loss to Ottawa in the first game was their only setback that season, as they went on to win the Stanley Cup by dint of their first-place finish in the CAHL.

The *Gazette*'s conversion to the Shamrocks' cause can especially be seen in two of the three challenges they turned aside in defending the Cup over the next two seasons. In its coverage the *Gazette* gave up any pretence of fair play or any real demonstration of respect for the Shamrocks' opponents, with the exception of the Winnipeg Victorias, where the paper fell back on hometown boosterism. These incidences clearly show the shift in middle-class mores of manliness away from notions of fair play towards a focus on winning. In its coverage of the Shamrocks'

Stanley Cup matches, the *Gazette* was more interested in taunting not just the Shamrocks' opponents, but the newspapers in the other cities as well. Of course, the hype the paper placed on the challenge matches played in Montreal only helped to fill the stands of the Arena and to sell newspapers in the lead-up to and after the matches.

We have already seen the complaints and boasts made by the rather unsportsmanlike captain of the Queen's College side, which lost 6–2 to the Shamrocks in a Cup challenge in 1899. In its coverage of the actual match, the *Gazette* rather arrogantly stated that 'the Stanley Cup is still in the custody of the Shamrock Hockey Club. Everybody who has watched hockey this season knew it would stay there.'[149] Of course, in advance of the match the *Gazette* ran a story from the wire from Kingston, which reported that while the supporters of Queen's were generally of the opinion that their team would lose, the team itself had boasted how it had 'easily demonstrated that they were without a doubt the fastest hockey aggregation in Ontario, having defeated all comers in the OHA series without any trouble. In their southern trip, Queen's were triumphant, closing out four teams without allowing them to score.'[150] So, goaded like this by the Kingston paper and the Queen's team itself, it is perhaps not surprising to read the *Gazette*'s tone following the Shamrocks' easy victory.

In 1900 the Shamrocks received a Cup challenge from the Victoria HC of Winnipeg, who had won the Cup in 1896. The Winnipeg Victorias were a much more serious opponent than was Queen's. Thus, the tone of the *Gazette*'s coverage of this series was much more respectful of the challengers although the Shamrocks were still expected to win.[151] When Winnipeg won the first game of the best-of-three series, 4–3, the *Gazette* easily conceded that the visitors deserved the victory.[152] Following the Shamrocks' victory two nights later to tie up the series, the coverage in the *Gazette* was practically breathless: 'The same exciting features characterizing the first contest were re-enacted. The hockey was sensation in its perfection. Intense excitement prevailed throughout. The final ten minutes, with Shamrock leading by one point and their western opponents straining every resource of nerve and sinew in desperation of pulling down the vital margin, developed the wildest demonstration. The cheering of ten thousand throats was deafening.'[153] When the Shamrocks won the deciding game 5–4, the headline on the *Gazette*'s sports page declared: 'IT STAYS HERE – The Stanley Cup Likes Not The Western Weather.' If the paper had been about breathless after game two of the series, now it was gasping and grasping for words: 'Narrative in the superlative can only convey an imperfect sense the paragon of perfection and sensational detail of this, the last and premier exhibition of a week's great hockey.'[154]

Following that display of hockey between the Shamrocks and the Victorias, however, the next challenge for the Cup, from the Maritime champions, the Halifax Crescents, could not be anything but a letdown. There was some history between the two clubs. In 1899 the Shamrocks had travelled to New York City and then back through Halifax, where they played the Crescents in an exhibition game the Shamrocks won 4–2. The game was characterized by Trihey's brilliant play.[155] So the teams were not complete unknowns to each other when they met in the spring of 1900 in Montreal for the Stanley Cup. Nevertheless, the two-game challenge series was not even close, as the *Gazette* had predicted, and the Shamrocks won easily, by a combined score of 23–2. What is perhaps more interesting, though, is the almost total lack of interest on the part of the *Gazette* in this Cup challenge. Whereas for the series against Queen's and the Winnipeg Victorias, the paper provided comprehensive coverage, as we have seen, when it came to the Crescents, the *Gazette* could barely stifle a yawn and provided minimal coverage of the games, other than noting the Shamrocks' easy victories.[156] This lack of interest and excitement in the Shamrock/Halifax series, though, is not all that surprising. The Winnipeg Victorias were former Stanley Cup champions when they challenged the Shamrocks. Indeed, while the Shamrocks defeated the Victorias in 1900, they were not able to hold them off in 1901. The Shamrocks lost the Cup to the Winnipeggers after being swept in two straight games at the Montreal Arena. The second game was the first time in Stanley Cup history that a match had gone to overtime. Queen's, while not regarded as a top-flight club like the Winnipeg Victorias, were nonetheless the champions of an increasingly competitive Ontario Hockey Association. The Crescents, by contrast, were from the Maritime league which was not regarded as being of particularly high quality. And the Shamrocks' easy handling of the Halifax side reflected this.

Conclusion

The Shamrock Hockey Club at *fin de siècle* Montreal provides us with a unique opportunity to study a hockey club at a confluence of cultural events. Both the sport of hockey and the club itself provide an interesting window into the culture of Canada's largest and most important city of that time, due to the classed, gendered, and ethno-religious identities of the Shamrock players. The turn of the twentieth century was a period that saw a general crisis of masculinity among the middle classes across the Anglo-Atlantic world. Faced with the growth of industrial capitalism and the rise of the managerial class, middle-class men were left to find a new way to reconfigure their manliness in the face of a sedentary existence at work. These men no longer worked with their hands or their bodies, and thus, in this realm of their life, there was less of a focus on their physicality and their bodies. By playing elite-level amateur sport, especially within the commercialized world of hockey in Montreal at the *fin de siècle*, these men were putting their bodies on display, under the discerning gaze of 10,000 spectators at the Montreal Arena on Wednesday and Saturday nights. In so doing, they were also putting their manliness on display for each match. The mores of middle-class men were under flux throughout this period, and there was an ambivalence between the cool, detached, reasonable rational behaviour a man was supposed to show and what happened on the ice. Part of what drew middle-class men (to say nothing of the spectators and commentators) to the sport of hockey *was* its violence. These men were able to engage in an ultraviolent sport, and do so within the recognized strictures of their middle-class cultural norms. Thus, the violence of hockey became, for the most part, ritualized. There was an acceptable norm for the level of violence on the ice, beyond which there were penalties, not the least of which were the penalties under hockey's rules. Expulsions from the game, suspensions from the league, as well as the censure of 10,000 passionate fans and the withering glare of the newspaper writers, oculd all come down on the man who overstepped the boundaries of acceptable violence on the hockey rink. Indeed, as Stacy Lorenz and Geraint Osborne show us in chapter 5 of this book, this is exactly what happened to Charles Masson of the Ottawa Victorias when he clubbed Cornwall's Bud McCourt over the head with his stick in a 1907 match. Thus, it behoved the hockeyist to stay within the rules of the sport. And while the sport was occasionally brutally violent, for the most part the rules were followed.

In addition to being under the gaze of the spectators at the Montreal Arena, the hockeyist fell under that of the sportwriters and editors of the Montreal anglophone newspapers. These writers and editors were more than happy to conspire with these athletes, constructing narratives around the hockeyist's body that compared him to a prize-fighting boxer. This is significant for the very fact of the comparison: the boxer was a man in peak physical condition, with well-toned muscles and power. Yet boxing was also the 'sweet science,' and in comparing the hockeyist with the boxer the press was also drawing upon this trope. The key to good hockey at the turn of the twentieth century was to engage in a scientific game and to make use of 'aggressive science.'

The elite-level amateur hockey clubs of the CAHL, including the Shamrocks, were owned by businessmen, some of whom were from the upper ranks of Canada's industrial capitalist class. At the turn of the twentieth century, they were employing scientific management models and were rationalizing their business empires along these lines. It occurred to them that they could also operate their sporting clubs in the same manner and make a profit in so doing. Thus, the massive (for its time) Montreal Arena was built in 1898 at the corner of rue Sainte-Catherine and Wood Street in Westmount, a few blocks west of the future location of the iconic Montreal Forum, itself constructed in 1924. The Arena was constructed explicitly for hockey and, more important, for the spectators, who were becoming consumers of hockey. In order to sell those 10,000 tickets twice a week, the hockey club operators, as well as the Arena's owners, needed help. Thus, artificial rivalries were created, such as that between the Shamrocks and the Montreals, who were chosen to play the first game in the Arena on the basis of their 'old rivalry.' By the time the Arena opened in 1898, the Shamrocks and the Montreals had been 'old-time rivals' for all of four years. But the Shamrock Lacrosse Club, the most successful of all time up to that point, did have a long-standing rivalry with the Montreal LC. These clubs were operated by the Shamrock AAA and the Montreal AAA, respectively, as were the hockey clubs. Thus was born the hockey rivalry.

And the newspapers were complicit in the commercialization. As we have seen, the newspaper writers for the *Gazette*, especially, made it their business to create a hype around the games at the Arena. The paper sought not only to interest the casual reader, but to get him passionately interested. To this end, the *Gazette* published a series of over-hyped articles in the lead-up to big games, especially Montreal derbies. There were long recaps of all the games involving the Montreal clubs, especially detailing the play. Though the sportwriters made it a point to praise the skilful play of both clubs, it was not done in the interests of fair play. Rather, they sought to create a market, not just for the hockey games at the Arena, but for the newspapers as well. In short, a passionate hockey following led to increased circulation, which helped the newspapers' bottom lines. The relationship, then, between the CAHL, its member clubs, the Montreal Arena, and the Anglo newspapers of Montreal was deeply symbiotic.

For the hockey commentators in the media, and presumably for the

20,000 men, women, and children who packed the Arena each week, it was these middle-class gender norms that were important. For the Shamrock players, however, hockey held another attraction. That hockey was a middle-class, if not upper-middle- or elite-class, sport is clear. That Montreal's Irish-Catholic population did not, as a rule, occupy spots in this upper rung of the middle or elite classes is also clear. Hockey, then, became important as a vehicle to carry some of the Shamrocks, Harry Trihey in particular, into this elite class. But it was more than a matter of social mobility for the Irish-Catholic men who laced up their skates for the Shamrock HC. The fact that they continued to play for an Irish club is significant. It was not that they could not make the cut on the other Montreal clubs, nor that the Montreal HC and the Montreal Victorias were not their own kind of ethno-religious club (the players on both those clubs tended to be Anglo and Protestant). Thus, the Irish Catholicism of the Shamrock players made them unique in that sense, but it did not make their club unique in that it was one of players of similar background.

The late nineteenth and early twentieth centuries were turbulent times for the Irish-Catholics of Montreal, caught between a loyalty to Canada and an enduring, abiding interest in the old country. This imagined Ireland continued to play a major role within the Irish-Catholic community of the city during this period, especially insofar as the Irish Question played out between Ireland and Great Britain, the period of the most concentrated and clearest agitation in Britain and Ireland for Home Rule. This agitation extended beyond the British Isles and across the Atlantic to the Irish diaspora in North America; and the Irish of Montreal were no different. Montreal's Irish-Catholics, especially those among the bourgeoisy, were drawn into the struggle for Home Rule. Yet although they demonstrated simple support for the struggle for Irish independence, Montreal's Irish-Catholics were bifurcated in their identity, caught between their two countries. But their identity in Canada was bifurcated as well. In short, their ambivalence and ambiguity *vis-à-vis* Canada/Quebec and Ireland left them as a truly hyphenized ethno-religious group. They were Irish-Canadians.

NOTES

1 The Victoria Rink was constructed in 1862 by a group of upper-class Anglo-Protestants as a location for socially exclusive winter recreation. In the 1870s, however, the rink management became increasingly dismayed

at the costs of maintaining a building that was idle for upwards of nine months of the year, and was even then only used on a handful of evenings during the winter. Thus, it decided to open the rink to a more middle-class crowd, which used the rink for its own recreational purposes. See John-Chi-Kit Wong, *Lords of the Rinks: The Emergence of the National Hockey League, 1875–1936* (Toronto: University of Toronto Press, 2005), 11. Victoria Rink was the site of the first hockey match ever played, in March 1875. Today's sport of hockey still carries vestiges of that game, most notably the size of the ice, at least in North America – 200 by 85 feet – and the use of a flat disc, instead of a ball, initially to prevent spectator injuries. See Richard Gruneau and David Whitson, *Hockey Night in Canada: Sport, Identities and Cultural Politics* (Toronto: Garamond, 1993), 37–8.

2 Wong, *Lords of the Rinks*, photograph caption between pp. 112 and 113.

3 Michel Vigneault, 'La naissance d'un sport organisé: Le hockey à Montréal, 1875–1917, unpublished PhD dissertation (Université Laval, Sainte-Foy, QC, 2001), 138–40. In the 1902–3 season, the Shamrocks had two French Canadian players on the roster: Théophile Viau and Louis Hurtubuise. Preceding the advent of French Canadian players on a very bad Shamrock team (0–8 in 1902–3 and outscored by their opponents 56–21), however, and probably more important to the diffusion of hockey in Montreal across ethno-religious lines were the teams at the two classical Jesuit colleges shared by the Irish-Catholics and their French Canadian co-religionists, Collège Sainte-Marie and Collège Mont-Saint-Louis. Three of the players who went on to star for the Shamrocks' cup-winning teams played at Collège Sainte-Marie in the mid-1890s – Jack Brennan, Arthur Farrell, and the captain, Harry Trihey. After 1896 the Irish moved to their own college, Loyola, a founding institution of Concordia University in 1974. See Michel Vigneault, 'Farrell, Arthur,' Dictionary of Canadian Biography, on-line edition, at http://www.biographi.ca/EN/showbio .asp?BioID=40827&Query=Farrell (accessed 26 January 2006). See also Vigneault, 'La naissance d'un sport,' 137–8, 158–60, 221–3.

4 Tansey was the son of Bernard Tansey, a long-time city councillor for St Ann's Ward in Montreal's south-west. Bernard was himself a former athlete, playing for the Shamrocks Lacrosse Club (LC) in the 1870s, as well as a member of the board of the Shamrock Amateur Athletic Association (Shamrock AAA), to which both the Shamrock LC and the Shamrock HC belonged. *Lovell's City Directory of Montreal, 1899*; Don Morrow and Kevin Wamsley, *Sport in Canada: A History* (Toronto: Oxford University Press, 2005), 96–7; John Matthew Barlow, '"The House of the Irish": Irishness, History, and Memory in Griffintown, Montréal, 1868–2009,' unpublished PhD dissertation (Concordia University, Montreal, 2009), ch. 2.

5 Brennan's name is also spelled 'Brannon' in the records.

6 The club's logo, however, was not a shamrock, but a winged foot. The winged foot of the Shamrock HC was green on their grey jerseys.

7 Joy Parr, *The Gender of Breadwinners: Women, Men, and Change in Two Industrial Towns, 1880–1950* (Toronto: University of Toronto Press, 1990), 245–6.

8 The CAHL was formed out of the ashes of the Amateur Hockey Association of Canada (AHAC) in 1898, when the Ottawa Capitals, a club of dubious skill, was granted permission to join the league. The Capitals had applied to the AHAC on the basis of their Stanley Cup challenge the previous season, although they were pasted 15–2 in a single-game challenge for the Cup by the holders, the Montreal Victorias. When the AHAC admitted the Capitals, the other five teams in the league resigned in protest and formed the CAHL. These five were the Montreal HC. Victoria HC (Montreal), Shamrock HC, Ottawa HC, and Quebec HC The CAHL lasted until the 1905–6 season, when it was folded by its member clubs and the Eastern Canada Hockey Association (ECHA) was formed. *Gazette*, 12, 13, 14, and 15 December 1898; Wong, *The Lords of the Rinks*, 27, 38–9.

9 Numerous references were made to hockey as Canada's national winter sport in the pages of the *Gazette*. Lacrosse, of course, was the national summer sport. See, for example, *Gazette*, 15 December 1898, 21 February 1899, and 30 December 1899.

10 Wong, *The Lords of the Rinks*, chs. 2–4. Professionalism of elite-level hockey came to Montréal later in the decade, when the Wanderers declared themselves professionals following their Stanley Cup victory in 1906.

11 Richard Gruneau, *Class, Sport, and Social Development* (Windsor, ON: Human Kinetics, 1999 ([1983])), 44–7.

12 Hockey players were more commonly referred to as 'hockeyists,' as part of the attempt to rationalize and apply scientific principles to the sport. The same is true of lacrosse players, who were known as 'lacrossists.'

13 *Gazette*, 30 December 1899.

14 Arthur Farrell, *Hockey: Canada's Royal Winter Game* (Montreal: Corneil, 1909), 36–7.

15 Parr, *The Gender of Breadwinners*, 140–64; Robert Lewis, *Manufacturing Montreal: The Making of an Industrial Landscape, 1850–1930* (Baltimore: Johns Hopkins University Press, 2000), 78–99.

16 See, in particular, H. Clare Pentland, 'The Lachine Canal Strike of 1843,' *Canadian Historical Review* 29, 3 (1948): 255–77; Pentland, *Labour and Capital in Canada, 1650–1860* (Toronto: James Lorimer, 1981), esp. 191–9, for an examination as to how Pentland characterized and stereotyped Irish-Catholic workers in British North America as little more than drunken, primitive tribesmen. Michael Cross, in his work on social violence in the mid-

nineteenth century in British North America does little better, concluding that the Irish were, by nature, violent. See, in particular, his 'The Shiners' War: Social Violence in the Ottawa Valley in the 1830s,' *Canadian Historical Review* 54, 1 (1973): 1–26.

17 Griffintown has captured the attention of historical geographers such as Sherry Olson, Patricia Thornton, Robert Lewis, and Rosalyn Trigger, of feminist historians such as Bettina Bradbury, of sports historians such as Alan Metcalfe, Don Morrow, and Barbara Pinto, as well as of cultural historians such as Daniel Horner and myself. See, for example, Alan Metcalfe, *Canada Learns to Play: The Emergence of Organized Sport in Canada, 1807–1914* (Toronto: McClelland & Stewart, 1986), esp. 196–203, where Metcalfe discusses the Shamrock LC; Barbara S. Pinto, 'Ain't Misbehavin': The Montreal Shamrock Lacrosse Club Fans, 1868–1884,' unpublished MA thesis (University of Western Ontario, London, 1990); Robert D. Lewis, 'The Development of an Early Suburban Industrial District: The Montreal Ward of St. Ann, 1851–71,' *Urban History Review / Revue d'histoire urbain* 19, 3 (1991): 166–80; Don Morrow, 'The Institutionalization of Sport: A Case Study of Canadian Lacrosse, 1844–1914,' *International Journal of the History of Sport* 9, 2 (1992): 236–51; Bettina Bradbury, *Working Families: Age, Gender, and Daily Survival in Industrializing Montreal* (Toronto: Oxford University Press, 1993); Rosalyn Trigger, 'Protestant Restructuring in the Canadian City: Church and Mission in the Industrial Working-Class District of Griffintown,' *Urban History Review / Revue d'histoire urbain* 31, 2 (2002): 5–18; Daniel Horner, '"A Barbarism of the Worst Kind": Negotiating Space and Gender in the Aftermath of Montreal's Gavazzi Riot,' unpublished paper presented to the Annual Conference of the Canadian Historical Association (2005); John Matthew Barlow, '"Forgive My Nostalgia": Looking Back at Griffintown, Montreal, 1960–2004,' unpublished paper presented to the Annual Conference of the Canadian Historical Association (2005); and Barlow, '"The House of the Irish."'

18 In referring to class and the class background of the various historical actors of this study, I am not relying solely upon a socio-economic definition of class. Instead, I view class within a constellation of cultural factors, which include things such as socio-economic and societal questions. To that end, while a person's occupation is partly determinative of her class standing, so too are other factors, such as education, living arrangements, and household location. Similarly, in determining class as a cultural grouping, other factors, such as attitudes, mores, and cultural manifestations must also be taken into account.

19 An exception to this is Kevin James, 'Dynamics of Ethnic Associational

Culture in a Nineteenth-Century City: Saint Patrick's Society of Montreal, 1834–56,' *Canadian Journal of Irish Studies / Revue canadienne d'études irlandaises* 26, 1 (2000): 47–68. The work of Rosalyn Trigger and of Sherry Olson and Patricia Thornton deals with the Irish-Catholic middle classes of Montreal within the context of larger examinations of the Irish-Catholic community of the city. See Rosalyn Trigger, 'The Geopolitics of the Irish-Catholic Parish in Nineteenth-Century Montreal,' *Journal of Historical Geography* 27, 4 (2001): 553–72; and Sherry Olson and Patricia Thornton, 'The Challenge of the Irish-Catholic Community in Nineteenth-Century Montreal,' *Histoire Sociale / Social History* 35, 70 (2002): 35–70.

20 'Majority' is in quotation marks because the Anglo-Protestant population of Montreal was, in fact, a minority, and a declining one at that, from about the 1860s onwards. However, due to the inordinate amount of economic, social, and political power wielded by this community, it is often referred to as a 'majority' population, despite its demographic deficiencies. See Jean-Claude Marsan, *Montreal in Evolution: Historical Analysis of the Development of Montreal's Architecture and Urban Environment* (Montreal: McGill-Queen's University Press, 1981 [1974]), 176; Paul-André Linteau, *Brève histoire de Montréal* (Montreal: Boréal, 1992), 65; and Marc V. Levine, *La reconquête de Montréal*, trans. Marie Poirier (Montreal: VLB Éditeur, 1997 [1990]).

21 Olson and Thornton, 'The Challenge of the Irish-Catholic Community.' See also Rosalyn Trigger, 'The Role of the Parish in Fostering Irish-Catholic Identity in Nineteenth-Century Montreal,' unpublished MA thesis (McGill University, Montreal, 1997).

22 The Shamrock players and most of their fans hailed from Griffintown, though the Shamrock LC itself was owned by members of Montreal's Irish-Catholic elite class and was affiliated with the Shamrock AAA. See Pinto, 'Ain't Misbehavin''; and Barlow, '"The House of the Irish,"' ch. 2.

23 Metcalfe, *Canada Learns to Play*, 196.

24 See ibid., 192–203; Morrow, 'Lacrosse as the National Game,' in *A Concise History of Sport in Canada*, ed. Don Morrow et al. (Toronto: Oxford University Press, 1989), 54–6; Pinto, 'Ain't Misbehavin''; Colin D. Howell, *Blood, Sweat, and Cheers: Sport and the Making of Modern Canada* (Toronto: University of Toronto Press, 2000), 37–9; and Barlow, '"The House of the Irish,"' ch. 2. Quote taken from Howell, *Blood, Sweat, and Cheers*, 38.

25 Gail Bederman, *Manliness and Civilization: A Cultural History of Gender and Race in the United States, 1880–1917* (Chicago: University of Chicago Press, 1995), 17–19; R.W. Connell, *Masculinities* (Cambridge, UK: Polity Press, 1995), 28–30.

26 Bederman, *Manliness and Civilization*, 17–19; Connell, *Masculinities*, 28–30.

See also E. Anthony Rotundo, *American Manhood: Transformations in Masculinity from the Revolution to the Modern Era* (New York: Basic Books, 1993), 10–30. It is also worth noting that because this chapter is concerned with the time period of this paradigm shift in North American culture, there is necessarily some overlap between the concepts, both in contemporary culture and in my analysis of the Shamrock HC.

27 Antonio Gramsci, *Selections from the Prison Notebooks*, trans. and ed. Quintin Hoare and Geoffrey Nowell Smith (New York: International Publishers, 1971), 12; T.J. Jackson Lears, 'The Concept of Cultural Hegemony: Problems and Possibilities,' *American History* 90, 3 (1985): 568.

28 Connell, *Masculinities*, 77–8.

29 I refer to the working *classes*, and not *class* for specific reasons. First, while I do not deny that there was, at times, something akin to working-class consciousness, this was still an elusive state, and the fragmentation of the working classes was far more common than their unity. Moreover, this fragmentation was not always the fault of the capitalists, but rather arose spontaneously from the workers themselves, who identified themselves with their trade, their ethnicity, their religion, their location, and so on before they identified themselves as part of any imagined community (to borrow from Benedict Anderson) of the working class. Second, often left out of the equation in the search for working-class solidarity by historians are the majority of the workers, the un- and semi-skilled. It is also clear that in many instances, working-class organizations and unions had little interest in these workers, which further reinforces the notion of castes within this 'working class.' Thus, for these reasons, I prefer to speak of the working *classes*. See, for example, Bryan D. Palmer, *A Culture in Conflict: Skilled Workers and Industrial Capitalism in Hamilton, Ontario, 1860–1914* (Montreal: McGill-Queen's University Press, 1979); Gregory S. Kealey and Bryan D. Palmer, *Dreaming of What Might Be: The Knights of Labor in Ontario, 1880–1900* (New York: Cambridge University Press, 1982); Roy Rosenzweig, *Eight Hours for What We Will: Workers and Leisure in an Industrial City, 1870–1920* (New York: Oxford University Press, 1983); Parr, *The Gender of Breadwinners*; Victor A. Walsh, '"Drowning the Shamrock": Drink, Teetotalism, and the Irish-Catholics of Gilded-Age Pittsburgh,' *Journal of American Ethnic History* 101–2 (1990–1): 60–79; Gregory S. Kealey, *Toronto Workers Respond to Industrial Capitalism, 1867–1892* (Toronto: University of Toronto Press, 1991 [1980]); Noel Ignatiev, *How the Irish Became White* (New York: Routledge, 1995); and Lynne Marks, *Revivals and Roller-Rinks: Religion, Leisure, and Identity in Late-Nineteenth-Century Small-Town Ontario* (Toronto: University of Toronto Press, 1996). Similarly, and as I argue below with

respect to the Irish-Catholic middle class of Montreal, the middle classes were just as fragmented and diverse as the working classes.

30 Howell, *Blood, Sweat, and Cheers*, 38.

31 Barlow, '"The House of the Irish,"' ch. 2.

32 The players for the Shamrocks in the Confederation era were all either mechanics or machinists. Ibid.

33 Ibid.

34 Ibid.

35 Morrow, 'Lacrosse,' 55. Of course, the fact that the Toronto LC was a primarily Irish-Protestant club, hailing from the 'Belfast of Canada,' added yet another dimension to clashes between the Torontos and Shamrocks. Other than in the late 1870s, when sectarianism was rife in Canada, clashes between the Shamrocks and Torontos did not really lead to issues on the playing field or in the stands. See Barlow, '"The House of the Irish,"' ch. 2.

36 Pinto, 'Ain't Misbehavin',' ch. 4; Barlow, '"The House of the Irish,"' ch. 2.

37 See Alan Metcalfe, 'Working-Class Physical Recreation in Montreal, 1860–1895,' *Working Papers on the Sociological Study of Sports and Leisure* 1, 2 (1978): 12–15; Metcalfe, *Canada Learns to Play*, pp. 192–203; Morrow, 'Lacrosse,' 54–6; Pinto, 'Ain't Misbehavin''; Howell, *Blood, Sweat, and Cheers*, 37–9; and Morrow and Wamsley, *Sport in Canada*, 96–101.

38 See, Laura Fair, 'Kickin' It: Leisure, Politics, and Football in Colonial Zanzibar, 1900–1950s,' *Africa* 67, 2 (1997): 224–51.

39 John Bale and Mike Cronin, 'Introduction: Sport and Postcolonialism,' in *Sport and Postcolonialism*, ed. John Bale and Mike Cronin (New York: Berg, 2003), 4. Italics mine.

40 Beers was member of the Montreal AAA and its various member clubs, including the Montreal LC, for whom he played goal. He was also the goaltender in a lacrosse match played between a team of 'gentlemen' from Montreal and a team from Kahnawà:ke and Akwasasne before the Prince of Wales in Montreal in July 1860. Away from the lacrosse pitch, Beers was also a path-breaking dentist in Montreal who played a key role in the professionalization and standardization of that profession. Finally, he was among the founders in the early 1860s of the Victoria Rifles Volunteers militia unit, formed as a response to the Fenian raids. He retired from the military with the rank of captain in 1881. Morrow and Wamsley, *Sport in Canada*, 91–9; J. Thomas West, 'Beers, George,' *Dictionary of Canadian Biography*, on-line edition, at http://www.biographi.ca/EN/ShowBio .asp?BioId=40079&query=beers (accessed 10 October 2005).

41 The Montreal LC was followed by the Hochelaga and Beaver Lacrosse Clubs in 1858 and 1859, respectively. There were also aboriginal teams from

Akwasasne and Kahnawà:ke. However, these earlier matches were much more informal and recreational. As Morrow and Wamsley point out: 'In the early years of the M.LC, members met up in the field behind St. James the Apostle Church, piled their surplus clothes in a heap, and played a lacrosse match among themselves before breakfast.' The codification of the rules in 1867 is recognized as the 'invention' of the sport, as codification of rules and regulations (as well as a standardization of the playing field and the disciplining of the game to the notion of time) is recognized by sport scholars as one of the key moments in the transfer from games to sports. See Morrow and Wamsley, *Sport in Canada*, 91–3, quote on 91.

42 *Gazette*, 17 July 1867; Morrow and Wamsley, *Sport in Canada*, 91–3.

43 Morrow and Wamsley, *Sport in Canada*, 91–5. Interestingly, Anglo-Protestant bourgeois norms of behaviour at lacrosse matches were also borrowed from cricket. It is also worth pointing out that cricket remained a popular sport in Montreal during lacrosse's heyday, judging by the coverage of the sport in the Anglo-Protestant newspapers of the city, most notably the *Montreal Herald*. This, however, did not stop *The Herald* from poking fun at the staid nature of cricketers: 'Cricketers do not, as a rule, crow over victory; nor do they, on the other hand, brood over defeat. Their game is, perhaps above all others, a good-humored one and affords few opportunities for unpleasantness. The hard hitter and heavy scorer who is dismissed for a "duck" harbours no thought of revenge against the lucky bowler who has taken his wicket or the lightning fielder whose snap-catch has sent him back to the pavilion minus the usual round of applause. It is the "fortune of war"; he resigns himself philosophically to his fate and is almost ready to cry, "Well played, sir!" to the man who causes his downfall' (10 August 1885). Of course, it is interesting to note that *The Herald* lampoons cricket for its *politesse* in 1885, nearly two decades after the advent of the Shamrock LC and its fans and the massive sea change they portended for the playing of sport and for spectatorship in Montreal and, ultimately, in Canada.

44 Homi K. Bhabha, *The Location of Culture* (New York: Routledge, 1994).

45 Quebec presents something of an anomaly, however, in that the primary legal tradition there, at least insofar as the civil law goes, is French civil law (criminal law follows the English common-law tradition). However, despite this, following the creation of the Supreme Court of Canada (SCC) in 1874, justices on the bench who came from the rest of Canada were ignorant of civil law and showed a reluctance to accommodate Quebec's distinct legal tradition, much to the chagrin of French Canadian Quebeckers. In this sense, then, Quebec's civil-law tradition was nullified at the national level until the SCC became more sensitized in the twentieth

century, following the advent of Canada's first French Canadian prime minister, Sir Wilfrid Laurier, in 1896. The issue of the law, Quebec's distinct legal tradition, and the colonial relation of Canada to Britain was further demonstrated in the fact that, before 1948, the Judicial Committee of the Privy Council in London was the highest court of appeal in Canada. The Law Lords of the Judicial Committee rarely, if ever, had an understanding of the French civil-law tradition. John Dickinson and Brian Young, *A Short History of Quebec*, 3rd ed. (Montreal: McGill-Queen's University Press, 2003), 253; H.V. Nelles, *A Little History of Canada* (Toronto: Oxford University Press, 2005), 160, 210; *The Canadian Judicial System*, website of the Supreme Court of Canada, at http://www.scc-csc.gc.ca/aboutcourt/system/index_e.asp (accessed 2 January 2007).

46 Bale and Cronin, 'Introduction,' 7–8. See also Bhabha, *The Location of Culture*.

47 Roy Hay, 'The Last Night of the Poms: Australia as a Postcolonial Sporting Society?' in *Sport and Postcolonialism*, ed. Bale and Cronin, 18–22, 25–6. Of course, local contingencies differ greatly across Canada and Australia, on the one hand, and Ireland, on the other. Whereas Aussie Rules football and lacrosse emerged out of white European settler societies, Gaelic football emerged out of a colonized (albeit white European) society. As such, the cultural meanings attached to Gaelic football differed greatly from those attached to Aussie Rules and lacrosse (with the exception of the aboriginal players). Whereas the latter were tied to nascent nationhood, the former was tied to colonial oppression and resistance. See Patrick McDevitt, 'Muscular Catholicism: Nationalism, Masculinity, and Gaelic Team Sports,' *Gender & History* 9, 2 (1997): 262–84.

48 Indeed, Beers wrote a good number of screeds against cricket during this time, praising lacrosse instead. See, in particular, George W. Beers, 'A Rival to Cricket,' *Chambers Journal* 18 (6 December 1862): 366–8.

49 The Fenians were an Irish revolutionary group, based in New York City and Dublin, agitating for independence. Their strength in the Irish diaspora separated them from earlier Irish revolutionary groups. One of the Fenians' plans for obtaining Irish independence was to invade Canada and effectively hold it ransom for Ireland. To this end, several raids were launched across the American border from Vermont and New York into Ontario and Quebec, with no success. Montreal was their major power base in Canada, and the Montreal Fenians were among the most radical throughout the diaspora. See David A. Wilson, 'The Fenians in Montreal: Invasion, Intrigue, and Assassination,' *Eire/Ireland* 38, 3–4 (2003): 109–33.

50 Trigger, 'The Geopolitics of the Irish-Catholic Parish.'

51 The AOH's ultra-Catholicism was somewhat ironic, given that it was regarded as a secret society by the Catholic Church and therefore was not looked upon with any great favour by the clergy. Indeed, the AOH was excommunicated by the archbishop of New York, who urged his colleague in Montreal to do so the same. See Peggy Regan, 'Montreal's St. Patrick's Day Parade as a Political Statement: The rise of the Ancient Order of Hibernians, 1900–1929,' unpublished BA (Hons.) thesis (Concordia University, Montreal, 2000).

52 Montreal's Fenian past included support for the cross-border raids of the American Fenians in Vermont and upstate New York (though it does not appear as though any Montreal Fenians actually travelled out to the countryside to fight with their American Fenian brothers) and appears to have extended to the assassination of the Irish-Catholic Father of Canadian Confederation and Member of Parliament for Montreal West, which included Griffintown, Thomas D'Arcy McGee. McGee had been an Irish revolutionary himself in his youth, a member of the Young Irelanders, who rebelled in 1848. McGee was assassinated on Sparks Street in Ottawa on 7 April 1868, allegedly by the Montreal Fenian Patrick James Whelan. McGee became a target of the Fenians not simply due to his opposition to the group, but because he published an exposé of the Fenian movement in Montreal in the pages of the *Gazette* in the midst of the 1867 general election, as McGee, a Conservative, was embroiled in a bitter campaign with the Liberal Bernard Devlin. Though not a Fenian himself (indeed, Devlin fought against the Fenians in 1866), Devlin had the support of the Fenians of Griffintown and Montreal as a whole. See Thomas D'Arcy McGee, 'Account of the Attempts to Establish Fenianism in Montreal,' *Gazette*, 17, 20, and 22 August 1867; Robin B. Burns, 'McGee, Thomas D'Arcy,' *Dictionary of Canadian Biography*, on-line edition, at http://www .biographi.ca/EN/ShowBio.asp?BioId=38705&query=mcgee (accessed 7 August 2007); J-C Bonenfant, 'Devlin, Bernard,' *Dictionary of Canadian Biography*, on-line edition, at http://www.biographi.ca/EN/ShowBio .asp?BioId=39064&Query=devlin (accessed 7 August 2007); Wilson, 'The Fenians in Montreal.'

53 Regan, 'Montreal's St. Patrick's Day'; Wilson, 'The Fenians in Montreal.'

54 Home Rule Members of Parliament from Ireland sat in the imperial parliament in London.

55 Susan G. Davis, *Parades and Power: Street Theater in Nineteenth-Century Philadelphia* (Philadelphia: Temple University Press, 1986), 2–4.

56 The AOH began to assume a more prominent role in the parade's organization following the creation of a special committee for the parade in

1893, the Irish-Catholic Committee (it had been organized earlier by the St Patrick's Society). As the twentieth century dawned, the AOH was among the leadership of the committee; in 1919, the year before the outbreak of war between Ireland and Britain, the AOH officially gained control over the organization of the parade and the Irish-Catholic Committee was disbanded. In 1929 the AOH ceded control to the newly created United Irish Societies of Montreal, of which it was a member. Regan argues that this was possible due to the stabilization of the political situation in the newly independent Irish Free State by the end of the 1920s. Given the rise of the AOH, especially following the Easter Rising in 1916 in Dublin, and its prominence vis-à-vis the St Patrick's Day parade in Montreal, it is quite possible that the more republican and extremist Irish nationalist messages conveyed by the AOH in the parade were tacitly acceptable to the more 'respectable' elements of the Irish-Catholic community of Montreal. This, however, must be countered with the fact that the Irish-Catholics of Montreal raised two battalions for the Canadian militia in the First World War, the 55th Irish Canadian Rangers, raised for home defence purposes, and the 199th Overseas Battalion, Irish Canadian Rangers, to be sent into battle in France. *Gazette*, 3 July 1917; Robin B. Burns, 'The Montreal Irish and the Great War,' *Historical Studies* 52 (1985): 67–82; Regan, 'Montreal's St. Patrick's Day Parade'; Barlow, 'The House of the Irish,' ch. 3.

57 This Irish flag was not the now-familiar Irish tricolour republican flag of green, white, and orange, but the more traditional cross of St Patrick, which itself is a constituent element of the Union Jack flag of the United Kingdom.

58 Canada, of course, did not yet have a flag of its own, and flew the British ensign instead.

59 *Gazette*, 18 March 1875.

60 Curran was solicitor general in the Conservative governments of Sir John Thomson and Sir Mackenzie Bowell from 1892 until his retirement from federal politics in 1895. 'Justin M'Carthy in Montreal,' *New York Times*, 10 November 1886; Parliament of Canada website, at http://www2.parl .gc.ca/Parlinfo/Files/Parliamentarian.aspx?Item=68df3a04-5588-41f6-80b7-e4cb81571c76&Language=E&MenuID=Lists.Members.aspx& MenuQuery=http%3A%2F%2Fwww2.parl.gc.ca%2FParlinfo%2FLists% 2FMembers.aspx%3FParliament%3D%26Riding%3D%26Name%3Dc% 26Party%3D%26Province%3D%26Gender%3D%26New%3DFalse% 26Current%3DFalse%26Picture%3DFalse (accessed 24 October 2005).

61 *St. Patrick's Day, Montreal 1890* (Montreal: Herald Press, 1890), 32.

62 Bale and Cronin, 'Introduction,' 4–8.

63 Hockey in this era was a defensive sport, largely because the forward pass was illegal. Nonetheless, in the 1898–9 season, Trihey netted 19 goals in 7 games. The following season, he scored 17 goals in 7 games. In five Stanley Cup matches in 1900, he potted 12 goals. See Trihey's page on the 'Legends of Hockey' website, part of the Hockey Hall of Fame's website, at http://www.legendsofhockey.net:8080/LegendsOfHockey/jsp/LegendsMember.jsp?mem=p195008&type=Player&page=statsaward&list=ByTeam&team=Montréal%20Shamrocks (accessed 30 October 2005).

64 Since the forward pass was illegal in this era, most teams simply had their pointmen (or defencemen) lob the puck out of the defensive zone with the intention of having their forwards forecheck to recover the puck. Trihey, however, developed a new technique with the Shamrocks, wherein he and the other three forwards (hockey was played seven-aside at this point) rushed the puck out of their end together, in close quarters, using quick backward and sideways passes, together with manoeuvring around the opposing forwards and pointmen, to carry the puck into the attacking zone.

65 *Gazette*, 23 February 1900; Earl Zuckerman, 'McGill's Contribution to the Origins of Ice Hockey,' McGill University Athletics website, at http://www.athletics.mcgill.ca/varsity_sports_article.ch2?article_id=81 (accessed 21 October 2005).

66 The Shamrock HC lost money throughout its existence, even during its Stanley Cup–winning years, and the shortfall was made up by the Shamrock AAA. This arrangement was generally how such amateur athletic associations in the late nineteenth century tended to operate, including the Montreal AAA, which was the Canadian model amateur athletic association of this era. *Gazette*, 19 April 1898; Wong, *The Lords of the Rinks*, 21.

67 Donald M. Fisher, *Lacrosse: A History of the Game* (Baltimore: Johns Hopkins University Press, 2002), 316.

68 *Gazette*, 19 April 1898.

69 The presidency of the CAHL rotated among member clubs on an annual basis. *Gazette*, 19 April 1898; Wong, *The Lords of the Rinks*, 34.

70 *Gazette*, 30 December 1899; *Gazette*, 7 January 1901; Vigneault, 'Farrell.' Further biographical information on Farrell was taken from his webpage on the 'Legends of Hockey' website, part of the Hockey Hall of Fame website, at http://www.legendsofhockey.net:8080/LegendsOfHockey/jsp/LegendsMember.jsp?mem=p196503&type=Player&page=bio&list=ByTeam&team=Montréal%20Shamrocks (accessed 15 October 2005).

71 *The Irish-Canadian Rangers* (Montreal: Gazette Printing Co., 1916), 12–17.

72 Terence J. Fay, *A History of Canadian Catholics: Gallicanism, Romanism, and Canadianism* (Montreal: McGill-Queen's University Press, 2002), 172.

73 Concordia University Archives, PO26, Saint Patrick's Society of Montreal fonds, box HA 1540: Meeting minutes, 4 April 1916 to 27 January 1919, Meetings of 14 March 1917, 7 May 1917, and 6 May 1918.

74 Burns, 'The Montreal Irish'; Barlow, '"The House of the Irish,"' ch. 3.

75 The 55th Regiment, Irish Canadian Rangers was raised for home-defence purposes only, though it released some members to serve in other overseas battalions before the formation of the 199th Overseas Battalion in 1915. *The Irish-Canadian Rangers*, 15–25.

76 At Easter 1916 the Irish Republican Brotherhood (IRB, a precursor to the Irish Republican Army, or IRA), with a force of 1000 volunteers and 200 members of James Connolly's Irish Citizen Army, seized the General Post Office (GPO) and a few other sites in Dublin. Connolly was an Irish socialist revolutionary who had joined the conspiracy with other prominent Irish republicans, such as Joseph Plunkett and Patrick Pearse, earlier in 1916. Following the seizure of the GPO, Pearse and his colleagues proclaimed a Provisional Irish Republic. The insurrectionists were shelled by the British Army and were forced into surrendering five days later, on 29 April. Other, smaller, risings had occurred around Ireland, all of which were easily put down. Approximately 64 insurgents were killed during fighting at the GPO, along with 132 British soldiers (some of whom were Irishmen serving in the British Army) and 230 civilians. Much of central Dublin was devastated by the artillery fire. The British government responded with brutality, declaring martial law and instituting mass arrests that, historians argue, converted initial hostility towards the IRB into widespread sympathy and support. Fifteen of the leaders of the GPO Rising were shot, including Pearse, Plunkett, and Connolly. Connolly was gravely wounded in the fighting at the GPO and he had to be strapped upright into a chair in order to be shot in the yard of the Kilmainham Jail in Dublin. The GPO Rising is generally regarded as the opening salvo in the war for independence from Britain that culminated in the 1920–2 Anglo-Irish War and the creation of the Irish Free State in 1922, which led to the Irish Civil War in 1922–3. See R.F. Foster, *Modern Ireland, 1600–1972* (Toronto: Penguin, 1989), 461–94.

77 Concordia University Archives, PO26, Saint Patrick's Society of Montreal fonds, box HA 1540: Meeting minutes, 4 April 1916 to 27 January 1919, Meetings of 14 March 1917, 7 May 1917, and 6 May 1918.

78 This was not, however, a policy decision against the Rangers, but a reflection of British policy, as all newly recruited units were to be broken up in this manner due to pressing needs for both seasoned soldiers and reinforcements on the front.

79 *The Irish Canadian Rangers*, 23–40; Burns, 'Montreal's Irish,' 74–7; Barlow, '"The House of the Irish,"' ch. 3.

80 *Gazette*, 3 July 1917; Burns, 'Montreal's Irish,' 77; Barlow, '"The House of the Irish,"' ch. 3.

81 Little Dublin was initially a working-class district, but was gentrified over the course of the nineteenth century, especially after the construction of St Patrick's in 1847. The neighbourhood has long since been dismantled through the construction of warehouses, the Southam Paper Company's head offices and plant, and, in the late twentieth century, the massive Palais de Congrès, as well as various government complexes along boulevard René Lévesque (formerly Dorchester Blvd). In the early years of the twenty-first century, Little Dublin has begun to see something of a revival, as some of the warehouses and some of the remaining stands of townhouses were converted into condominiums.

82 *Lovell's City Directory of Montreal*, 1899 and 1900. The listings in *Lovell's* also demonstrate the great spatial distribution of the Irish-Catholic middle classes in Montreal around the turn of the twentieth century. Whereas in other 'Irish' cities of the diaspora, such as Liverpool, Boston, or New York City, the Irish controlled the political system in various neighbourhoods, this was not possible in Montreal due to the varied settlement patterns. Thus, they operated as a swing vote in various neighbourhoods where there was a concentration of Irish-Catholics in order to have their interests represented at the municipal, provincial, and federal levels. Olson and Thornton, 'The Challenge of the Irish-Catholic Community.'

83 The Golden Square Mile, much of which has long since been demolished, comprised roughly the territory between rue Sherbrooke on the south, Mont-Royal and avenue des Pins on the north, McGill's campus to the east, and rue Côte-des-Neiges on the west. At the turn of the twentieth century, approximately 70 per cent of Canada's wealth was concentrated in the 25,000 or so residents of the Golden Square Mile. Marsan, *Montreal in Evolution*, 257.

84 *Lovell's City Directory of Montreal*, 1899 and 1900.

85 Great St James Street is now part of rue Saint-Jacques. It was that portion of rue Saint-Jacques in Vieux-Montréal where the city's business district was located in the nineteenth and early twentieth centuries.

86 Largely developed and settled in the late nineteenth century, Westmount was intended to be (and is) an exclusive, elitist residential neighbourhood. Montreal's Anglo-Protestant capitalists were lured to build their estates atop Mont-Royal in Westmount, while anglophone professionals and the manager class were enticed to lower Westmount, where the Triheys lived. See John

A. Dickinson and Brian Young, *A Short History of Quebec,* 3rd ed. (Montreal: McGill-Queen's University Press, 2003), photograph caption, 201.

87 Marsan, *Montreal in Evolution,* 304–6.

88 Fletcher's Fields, which lie across avenue du Parc from the eastern entrance to Parc Mont-Royal and directly north of the walls of Hôpital Hôtel-Dieu, is now part of Parc Jeanne-Mance.

89 At the turn of the twentieth century, the burgeoning Jewish population of Montreal was mostly located on the Lower Main, that part of boulevard Saint-Laurent below Sherbrooke. Like Little Dublin, this lower part of the Plateau Mont-Royal has seen a considerable amount of gentrification in the 1990s and the first decade of the twenty-first century.

90 James, 'Dynamics of Ethnic Associational Culture'; Horner, '"A Barbarism of the Worst Kind."'

91 Montreal's experiences during the small-pox epidemic of 1885, however, suggest that the sectarian divide between the city's Anglo-Protestant and French Canadian Catholic populations, especially across class divides, remained very much alive. See Michael Bliss, *Plague: How Smallpox Devastated Montreal* (Toronto: Harper Perennial, 1991).

92 The actual amount of the fees for the Shamrock AAA is not known, just that they were lower than the Montreal AAA's. *Gazette,* 19 April 1898; Don Morrow, *A Sporting Evolution: The Montreal Amateur Athletic Association, 1881–1981* (Montreal: Montreal AAAA and Don Morrow, 1981), 58–9; Wong, *Lords of the Rinks,* 23.

93 See the following section.

94 Michael A. Robidoux, 'Imagining a Canadian Identity through Sport: A Historical Interpretation of Lacrosse and Hockey,' *Journal of American Folklore* 115, 456 (2002): 219–21.

95 Wong, *Lords of the Rinks,* 24–6.

96 Farrell, *Hockey,* 29.

97 *Gazette,* 20 and 26 March 1886, 13 and 14 March 1893; Wong, *Lords of the Rinks,* 24–6.

98 *Gazette,* 17 March 1899. There was no actual Quebec league, even though the CAHL was predominately Quebec-based, with three clubs, in Montreal and Quebec. Ottawa was also in the league. Indeed, it was not necessarily geography that determined membership in the CAHL, but quality of play. As we saw in note 8, above, the CAHL was formed when the AHAC was folded after it had admitted the Ottawa Capitals, whose bona fides as a top-flight club was not certain. *Gazette,* 12, 13, 14, and 15 December 1898; Wong, *The Lords of the Rinks,* 27, 38–9.

99 *Gazette,* 17 March 1899.

100 See Wong, *Lords of the Rinks*, for a discussion of the commercialization and commodification of elite-level amateur hockey in the 1890s and early twentieth century.

101 *Gazette*, 16 January 1899. Goal nets were not yet in usage in 1899.

102 In earlier years Montreal's anglophone newspapers were concerned about the violence inherent in the sport. See, for example, *Gazette*, 20 January and 26 March 1886; *Montreal Star*, 20 January 1886.

103 Indeed, in chapter 5, Stacy Lorenz and Geraint Osborne, in examining the case of the death of Cornwall HC's Bud McCourt in a match against Ottawa, show how attitudes towards hockey violence had changed even more by the middle of the first decade of the twentieth century.

104 There are, of course, precedents for this. For example, rugby in England was popularized in the mid-nineteenth century by the headmaster of Rugby School, Thomas Arnold. Rugby, according to one popular saying in Ireland and the United Kingdom, is a thug's game played by gentlemen, whereas football (i.e., soccer) is a gentleman's game played by thugs. This reflects the working-class roots of Association football in England in the late nineteenth century, as opposed to the more bourgeois roots of the Rugby Union.

105 Robidoux's comparison of hockey's emergence is a rather odd, and largely artificial one, given that hockey is a winter sport and baseball a summer one. Paul Braganza is correct to compare baseball with lacrosse in the late nineteenth century. In general, Robidoux places too much emphasis on Canadian identity being formed in comparison to the United States in explaining the emergence of lacrosse and, especially, hockey, as national sports. Robidoux, 'Imagining a Canadian Identity,' 219–21; Paul Braganza, 'Montreal's First Nine: A Study of Nineteenth Century Baseball in Montréal,' unpublished MA thesis (Concordia University, Montreal, 2005), ch. 4.

106 Robidoux, 'Imagining a Canadian Identity,' 219–20. Of course, the same could be, and has been, said for lacrosse.

107 Shamrock forward Arthur Farrell, in his book *Hockey: Canada's Royal Winter Game* (63), published at the height of his hockey career in 1899, reports that the Arena had a capacity of 10,000.

108 This does not mean that the sport was not played in other nations, most notably the United States, by the 1890s.

109 Of course, other Canadian sporting forms, most notably lacrosse and Canadian rules football, are also violent and occasionally brutal. There is, however, a connection between Canadian conceptualizations of the nation as a northern one with an unforgiving winter climate, especially

as seen a decade or two later in the paintings and popular images of Tom Thomson and the Group of Seven, and the growth and popularization of hockey during the late nineteenth / early twentieth centuries. While it is true that central Canada experiences summer weather that can be uncomfortably hot and humid, and that its Pacific Coast does not experience a cold, snowy winter at all, it remains that Canadians see themselves as inhabitants of a cold, northern climate. This might go some distance to explain how and why hockey has captured the national imagination, across ethno-linguistic lines, in a way that lacrosse, baseball, and Canadian rules football never have.

110 See chapter 5 below.

111 Robidoux, 'Imagining a Canadian Identity,' 217–18.

112 *Gazette*, 8 January 1898 and 13 January 1899.

113 During this era, hockeyists played the entire 60-minute match, consisting of two thirty-minute halves; there were no line changes. *Gazette*, 16 January 1899.

114 Ibid.

115 *Montreal Star*, 16 January 1899; *Gazette*, 16 January 1899.

116 *Gazette*, 16 January 1899. However, as Lorenz and Osborne show in chapter 5, phrases such as 'clean, hard, and very fast' could also be employed by the press as a means of downplaying the ultra-violence in a game, so as to focus instead on the skill of the players.

117 For more detail on how this played out in the development of sport, see Barlow, '"The House of the Irish,"' ch. 2.

118 Howell, *Blood, Sweat, and Cheers*, 106.

119 See Michel Foucault, *The Birth of the Clinic: An Archaeology of Medical Perspectives*, trans. A.M. Sheridan Smith (New York: Pantheon, 1973) and 'Body/Power,' in *Power/Knowledge: Selected Interviews and Other Writings, 1972–1977*, ed. Colin Gordon (New York: Pantheon Books, 1980), 55–63. See also Howell, *Blood, Sweat, and Cheers*, 106–8.

120 Gail Bederman explores the relationship between the boxer's body, masculine identity, and race in the case of the first African-American heavyweight champion, Jack Johnson, in her *Manliness and Civilization*, 1–5, 8–10.

121 See, for example, M. Marsh, 'Suburban Men and Masculine Domesticity, 1870–1915,' in *Meanings for Manhood: Constructions of Masculinity in Victorian America*, ed. Mark C. Carnes (Chicago: University of Chicago Press, 1990), 111–27; Parr, *The Gender of Breadwinners*; David Roediger, *The Wages of Whiteness: Race and the Making of the American Working Class* (New York: Verso, 1991); Bederman, *Manliness and Civilization*; Marks, *Revivals*

and Roller Rinks; Dana D. Nelson, *National Manhood: Capitalist Citizenship and the Imagined Fraternity of White Men* (Durham, NC: Duke University Press, 1998); and John F. Kasson, *Houdini, Tarzan, and the Perfect Man: The White Male Body and the Challenge of Modernity in America* (New York: Hill & Wang, 2001).

122 Kasson, *Houdini, Tarzan, and the Perfect Man.*

123 *Gazette*, 15 January 1900.

124 Drinkwater was a former player for the Montreal Victorias, retiring following the 1899 season. He was inducted into the Hockey Hall of Fame in 1950, the same year as Harry Trihey. See his biography on the 'Legends of Hockey' website, part of the Hockey Hall of Fame's website, at http://www.legendsofhockey.net:8080/LegendsOfHockey/jsp/LegendsMember.jsp?mem=p195002&type=Player&page=bio&list=#photo (accessed 30 October 2005).

125 *Gazette*, 15 January 1900; *Montreal Star*, 15 January 1900.

126 The two Victoria clubs faced off for the Cup in February 1899, several weeks before the end of the CAHL season, when the Shamrocks were awarded the Cup by virtue of finishing atop the CAHL regular-season standings. The Montreal Victorias had won the Cup in 1898 and the Winnipeggers challenged them for it during the 1899 season; thus, Montreal was allowed to defend its Cup before losing it to the Shamrocks in March.

127 *Gazette*, 20 and 22 February 1899.

128 Braganza, 'Montreal's First Nine,' 4.

129 The Montreals had three consecutive mediocre seasons around the turn of the century, despite finishing second in 1898 and 1900. Their win-loss records in the 1898, 1899, and 1900 seasons were, respectively, 4–4, 3–5, and 5–3. The Montreals, initial winners of the Stanley Cup in 1893, a feat they repeated in 1894, did not win the Cup again until 1903.

130 See Vigneault, 'La naissance d'un sport,' 120, for details concerning the merger with the Crystals and the formation of the Shamrock HC in 1895.

131 *Gazette*, 15 January 1899; *Montreal Star*, 15 January 1899.

132 *Gazette*, 2 January 1898.

133 *Gazette*, 3 February 1898.

134 *Gazette*, 17 January 1898.

135 *Gazette*, 7 February 1898.

136 *Gazette*, 10 February 1898.

137 *Gazette*, 14 February 1898.

138 These new players, including pointman Frank Wall and goaltender Jim McKenna, completed the lineup that would go on to win the Stanley Cup in 1899. Trihey, Farrell, and Brennan had all joined the club for brief ap-

pearances during the 1897 season. Trihey only appeared in one game that season before establishing himself as a regular in 1898.

139 *Gazette,* 4 January 1898.

140 *Gazette,* 5 January 1898; *Montreal Star,* 5 January 1898.

141 *Gazette,* 6 January 1898.

142 *Gazette,* 7 January 1898.

143 *Gazette,* 8 January 1898.

144 *Gazette,* 10 January 1898.

145 Ibid.

146 *Gazette,* 9 January 1899.

147 *Gazette,* 13 January 1899.

148 *Gazette,* 16 January 1899.

149 *Gazette,* 15 March 1899.

150 *Gazette,* 14 March 1899.

151 *Gazette,* 10 February 1900.

152 *Gazette,* 13 February 1900.

153 *Gazette,* 15 February 1900.

154 *Gazette,* 17 February 1900.

155 *Gazette,* 9 March 1899.

156 Ibid.

3 Arenas of Debate: The Continuance of Professional Hockey in the Second World War

J. ANDREW ROSS

It is hard to conceive of a more important crucible for national identity formation than military conflict. Nation-state formation is often connected to violent revolution or military conflict with other nations. Even when national survival is not at stake, war may figure prominently in national mythologies. Canadian national identity formation is often seen as having suffered the absence of such a formative conflict, a clear break point provided by an American-, French- or Russian-style revolution that dated independence and began the national myth.[1] This void has been filled with a national narrative based on the gradual acquisition of 'peace, order and good government,' and an emphasis on constitution-making and consensus-building.[2] Nevertheless, Canadians have still been tempted to assign nation-building weight to wars: the War of 1812 prevented assimilation into the United States; the Boer War gave the new nation its first opportunity to assert itself on the world stage independent of the British;[3] the First World War came to function as Canada's 'war of independence';[4] and the Second World War saw the emergence of a 'genuine nationhood.'[5] In many of these conflicts Canada's involvement was controversial and resulted not in increased national identity fusion, but in fission – most often between English Canadians, who usually supported British imperial interests, and French Canadians, who generally did not. The volatile debates over policies such as conscription in the First and Second World Wars highlight the English-French divide, but there were many other issues that illustrated social rents that have not been acknowledged. Indeed, popular social memory of the war experience is often revised to conform to post-war sensibilities and rationalizations that simplify or subordinate home-front conflict to a master narrative of justified victory.[6]

The prevailing social memory of the Second World War is one that has often understated the many ambivalences, dissensions, and conflicts of the period. Jeffrey Keshen confronts its conception as 'the good war,' arguing that 'in many ways the popular memory has sanitized and simplified a "complex and problematic event" whose legacies for Canada were not just profound, but also contradictory.'[7] Other authors have discussed the failures of the manpower mobilization system and the compromises forced on political leadership, but Keshen points out that a 'not-so-good-war' was also manifest in war profiteering, black markets, moral decay, soldiers' conduct, and veteran reintegration.[8] These issues reveal fundamental social fissures that have been left unstudied. For example, there is little analysis of social resistance to the impingement of war policies on the home-front standard of living, or analysis of the political imperative to maintain civilian morale.[9]

The debates over the place of professional hockey during the war provide an opportunity for such an analysis. The hockey industry produced a seemingly frivolous and intangible entertainment product, leaving it open to a kind of criticism to which the essential 'guns or butter' industries were not subject. Hockey and other entertainment industries also directly influenced wartime Canadian civilian and military morale in a way that traditional war industries did not. Addressing the question of how hockey's wartime role was negotiated and fulfilled, and how and why the decisions to allow the sport to continue were made, provides insight into the many wartime ambiguities, contradictions, and conflicts among business, the state, and the individual. Through discussions over military exemptions, passports for players, the motives of capitalist club owners, and American criticism, hockey's importance to the war effort – and implicitly to the national identity – was negotiated and ultimately confirmed in the arenas where debate took place.[10]

War Declared

On 7 September 1939, the same day that the Canadian parliament met to discuss the war in Europe, the National Hockey League (NHL) owners gathered in their own emergency session to discuss how war might affect business in the fall.[11] Like the politicians, the hockey men already had a British model to follow; after legislation had rendered all men aged eighteen to forty-one liable for service, both the Football Association (soccer) and National Ice Hockey League had suspended operations to put their facilities at the disposal of the War Office.[12] In Canada, the situation was not yet so dire, and with no imminent fear of attack and no active engagement, the fear that the league would lose its players or its Canadian arena facilities was soon allayed. The indications were that even as Canadian prime minister William Lyon Mackenzie King spoke of full economic support – mainly agricultural and financial aid to Britain – as yet he was making no commitment on military participation.[13]

From the outbreak of hostilities, sportswriters discussed the war's possible effect on the large amounts invested in assets and player contracts. They pointed out that many US arenas depended on hockey for survival, and the likelihood of conscription did not augur well. The owner of the Chicago Black Hawks, Major Frederic McLaughlin, did not expect the war to affect attendance or the player supply, as he assumed Canada would send its regulars to the front first. However, '[i]f the United States should be forced into the struggle, then it would be another story.'[14] Charles Mayer, sports editor of Montreal's *Le Petit Journal*, saw not Canadian but US government policy as the deciding factor, surmising that the Canadian government might not want to defend sports in wartime and, even if it did, the American government might change *its* policy and no longer allow Canadians to cross the border to work anyway. This possibility had Frank Calder making enquiries in Washington as well as Ottawa.[15]

Hockey Declares

Amid these speculations the NHL decided at its 7 September meeting to carry on as usual, and Calder confirmed the league's patriotic commitment while citing the game's importance to morale: 'We will just as in the last Great War, patriotically assist the government in every possible way. Any of our players who wish to volunteer will be assisted in doing so. We feel that a well-conducted sport will be of great benefit to the national morale in these days of worry and mental stress.'[16] As a pre-emptive move against anticipated labour shortage, the seven NHL clubs reduced their playing rosters from sixteen to fifteen men.[17] But by mid-October enlistments had dropped off and, of all the NHL's players, only Bill Cowley of the Bruins had signed up. At age thirty-seven, there was little chance of even him being called up to serve.[18]

Fear of hockey's suspension waned along with public interest in the war as the lack of military action through late 1939 and early 1940 allowed Canada to settle into what became known as the 'phoney' war. Mackenzie King even called a snap federal election for 26 March 1940, winning a solid majority in a campaign marked by an ambivalent attitude towards war preparedness.[19] But a few months later everything changed. Due to the collapse of the Anglo-French front in May 1940 and the evacuation at Dunkirk, 'the complacent attitude that had characterized Canadian response to the war ... was dramatically altered.'[20] The government quickly passed the National Resources Mobilization Act (NRMA) in June 1940, providing for national registration of all Canadians, and giving great powers to the government, now 'almost unlimited in [its] ability to determine the role of every individual.'[21] The NRMA allowed conscription for domestic defence, but overseas service remained strictly voluntary, recognition that a good proportion of the populace – and most Quebeckers – still resisted any notion of overseas obligation. The immediate intent of the Act was to provide for national registration and a training period (initially thirty days) for men who were eligible for call-up, to be administered by a newly formed Department of National War Services (DNWS).[22] Since it was also announced that voluntary militia enlistment would end on 15 August 1940, thousands volunteered in August to avoid the stigma of being conscripted and labelled as unwilling to fight for their country.[23]

In response to the NRMA, NHL managers actively encouraged their players to sign up with Non-Permanent Active Militia (NPAM) units. Conn Smythe, managing director of the Toronto Maple Leafs, outlined the reasons clearly in a 17 July letter to his players, advising players to 'sign up immediately with some Non-Permanent Militia Unit and get your military training in as soon as possible.'[24] If the player were called, he would then be ready, but in the meantime he 'will have complied with the regulations and be free to play hockey until called on.'[25] Meanwhile, the Maple Leafs club was working on a plan to have its players join the Toronto Scottish Regiment and club executive officers were joining government agencies in management capacities. Smythe also recommended that players obtain passports for travel to the United States. Lester Patrick, the manager of the New York Rangers, wrote a similar missive to his players: applications for passports should be made early in the summer as it was 'easy then'; but he prophesied that 'it might become difficult later' due to increasing governmental restrictions on cross-border travel.[26]

Getting the Green Light

Planning players' pre-season military training to avoid mid-season labour interruption was prudent, but government fiat might still bring
the season to an instant halt. To forestall this, Frank Calder spent 'considerable time at Ottawa getting the green light from government agencies for hockey.' He lobbied government officials, telling the press, 'We
desired assurances ... that we would not be molested by war agencies
during our playing season. Failing that we would hardly have con-
templated operating.' By 5 September his efforts had paid off and he
declared that 'everything is in order.'[27] At the NHL semi-annual meeting held the next week in New York, it was reported that 'practically
all' NHL players had done military training and joined NPAM.[28] As a
result, the feeling of the meeting was that there was 'little possibility
of hockey players being taken into the military in such numbers as to
make the operation of professional hockey impossible.'[29] NHL hockey
would continue in its second wartime season.

The press also chimed in with discourses on the cultural importance
of hockey – especially its contribution to civilian morale. The author of
an article in *National Home Monthly* offered that hockey was 'a welcome
diversion' at which spectators might 'rid their minds of the strain of
war news and the constant knowledge that the future of democracy
and freedom hangs in the balance.'[30] He applauded the 'very wise' decision to let hockey continue and responded to those who might criticize
hockey players as engaged only 'in mimic warfare' that the problem of
the Canadian Active Service Forces was a shortage not of manpower,
but of equipment. This message of hockey's value as a 'wartime diversion' was a common theme among sportswriters, and contributed to
public perception of the league as an essential morale booster.[31]

Economic Help

The commitment to allow hockey to continue may be at least partly
attributed to tangible economic help from the NHL. The onset of war
brought rapid Canadian industrial expansion fuelled by large purchases
of capital equipment and materiel from the United States. In combination with several loans to Great Britain – and with more being con-
templated – this buying spree tilted Canada's balance of payments and
strained its US dollar supply to the limit, and the government was looking for any means of acquiring currency.[32] In July 1940 Conn Smythe sug-

gested a plan whereby Canadian players employed by American teams would receive a small stipend for living expenses, with the bulk of their earnings being converted from US dollars and deposited in Canadian-dollar bank accounts, thereby providing foreign exchange to the Foreign Exchange Control Board (FECB).[33] The plan was expected to make available $500,000 in foreign exchange and was eagerly taken up and publicized by the FECB.[34] Thereafter, it was often cited when professional hockey's contribution to the war effort was discussed. And aside from administrative tasks, it cost the league nothing at all. At least one writer noted that the balance-of-payments problem was actually a boon to American club owners, insofar as it encouraged the Canadian government to allow Canadian hockey players to continue to travel south of the border as an alternative to insisting on their enlistment.[35]

The financial requirements of the war also intruded into the arena in the form of an amusement tax proposed in May 1941. The Special War Revenue Act initially created a 20 per cent Moving Picture Amusement Tax, but after intense lobbying, the minister of finance, James Ilsley, broadened it to include 'all entertainments,' including hockey, baseball, and other sports. Conn Smythe was advised by his local member of parliament (MP), Rodney Adamson, to 'get hold of a lawyer accustomed to dealing with the Government' and fight it. Adamson told him to point out to Ilsley the difficulty of collecting tax in small rinks; the damage the tax would do to amateur hockey and 'Canada's National Sport'; the value of sports to the nation's youth ('getting out and playing games rather than sitting in stuffy movie houses watching frustrated sex dramas'); 'the value of the Toronto Maple Leafs as an advertising medium for Canada'; and any other points that he could think of.[36] Sure enough, when the tax came up for debate in the House of Commons, Adamson and other Toronto Conservative MPs lined up to denounce its effects on amateur, youth, and public participation in sport. One cited the FECB deal and the importance of hockey as 'a source of revenue, of United States dollars, which are brought back by Canadians playing in big-league hockey in the United States.'[37] Another, Thomas Church, lauded Maple Leaf Gardens as 'a patriotic enterprise' built by men who did 'great work for Toronto, and never got a nickel out of it.'[38] He used the tax issue to argue for conscription, suggesting the government study the question more closely and make a survey of the enlistments for each sport with a view to adopting a national policy, and 'so that everyone will do his part, and that we would cease to have everything as usual in Canada.'[39] Despite these arguments, the government was not inclined to exempt the sport, and the Act was passed on Dominion Day (1 July 1941). For the rest of the war, Maple Leaf Gardens and the Montreal Forum, as well as smaller arenas, movie houses, and theatres, all served as collection points for the coffers of war. Even though the tax was paid directly by customers, the Gardens and others would disingenuously imply that they were paying the tax as another example of their patriotic contributions to the war effort.[40]

Passport Crisis

Despite a modicum of publicity, the FECB plan, the amusement tax debate, and even the occasional hockey player enlistment, generated little public comment. It was only as the NHL was gearing up for its third wartime season in the fall of 1941 that controversy was stirred. It concerned permission for professional hockey players to travel to the United States for the winter season.

According to NRMA regulations, men who were eligible for call-up (twenty-one to twenty-four years of age) required a letter from the chairman of their local National War Services (NWS) Board in order to obtain a passport.[41] On 12 September 1941 the Manitoba NWS Board chairman, Justice J.E. Adamson, refused to give such permission to six U.S.-bound professional hockey players, telling 'the athletes Canada needs men and that they are the type who would make good soldiers.' Perhaps warning off other would-be applicants, he also promised that 'the ruling would affect all hockey players of military age in Manitoba who seek to enter the United States.'[42] Reached for comment, the minister of NWS, J.T. Thorson, seemed to concur with the decision, saying that 'since the needs of our army services come first, any board rulings must override any of the conveniences of sport in time of war.'[43] He predicted that the precedent would no doubt 'have a tendency to influence decisions in other regions' and also confirmed that there could be no appeal of this type of decision.[44]

The day the Manitoba decision was reported, the NHL was holding its semi-annual meeting in Toronto. Frank Calder seemed resigned to the news and responded by reformulating Tennyson: 'Ours is not to reason why, but to follow any and all decisions of the national war services.'[45] But the sportswriters and editorial-page writers were less acquiescent and a regional divide was evident: the *Winnipeg Free Press* and other western papers lined up behind the Manitoba decision, but the eastern papers did not. Ralph Allen, the *Globe and Mail* columnist, saw hypocrisy and discrimination against the players, and attacked the government for allowing its agents to victimize hockey players while refusing to ask the question 'Why aren't you in the army?' of the rest of the population.[46] The *Evening Citizen* in Ottawa agreed, arguing that there was a fine line between moral suasion and coercion, and that if 'voluntary participation' was the government's policy, then it should let every man decide for himself, or else apply selective service (i.e., conscription) for overseas service to all.[47]

Reporters asked the chairmen of the other regional boards if they concurred with the Manitoba decision. Justice J.F.L. Embury sided with his colleague in Manitoba and said the Saskatchewan board would allow no man eligible for call to leave the country. Justice J.G. Gillanders of Toronto said his board was permitting players to go under certain circumstances.[48] Justice John Doull of Nova Scotia said his board had not considered it yet. The New Brunswick board had allowed one player to go for a short time, and might consider others. The Quebec, British Columbia, and Prince Edward Island boards had not yet had any applications, but the chairman of the latter said his personal opinion was that 'men with the necessary physical qualifications for hockey would get scant consideration if they sought to leave the country.'[49] The chairman of the London, Ontario, board weighed in on 17 September, saying that he would also refuse permission to hockey players aged twenty-one to twenty-five to cross the border to play in the United States. Five NHL players would be affected by this, including two members of the NHL Boston Bruins' famous 'Kraut Line,' Milt Schmidt, twenty-three, and Woody Dumart, twenty-four.[50] Sure enough, the next day the *London Free Press* reported that those members of the Western Ontario Reserve Army aged between twenty-one and twenty-four who had enlisted before 13 August 1940 would hereafter be required to undergo four months' compulsory military training. Schmidt and Dumart were included.[51]

Meanwhile, the Manitoba board had sent copies of its decision to the other boards, summarizing its reasoning:

1. Young men of athletic ability should be serving in Canada's army at this time, instead of playing hockey.
2. If Canadian hockey players were allowed to play in the United States it would cause criticism of Canada and would be used as a pretext by men, such as Colonel Lindbergh and Senator Wheeler, who allege that Canada is not making an all-out war effort.[52]

The first reason reflected a common opinion, but the second indicated sensitivity to American opinion, and a fear that Canadian actions might help dissuade America from entering the war as a belligerent.

After only a week, the issue started to die down, but not before a few parting shots were taken by each side. Justice Embury of Saskatchewan got his chance to refuse passport permission to several hockey players.[53] Ralph Allen of the *Globe and Mail* pursued his persecution thesis and noted the lack of attention paid to Canadian baseball players playing in the United States as well as the many American baseball players who were still allowed to play in Canada.[54] The *Winnipeg Free Press* editorial page claimed the board decisions had been met with 'universal approval across Canada,' and suggested that 'young men who are physically fit and not in uniform are shirking the major duty that citizenship imposes on them.'[55] But, sharing common ground with Ralph Allen, it pointed out that while the youth who asked for a passport to play hockey was, of course, 'a glaring example... what of the case of many thousands of young men who will never be in the limelight but are deliberately choosing the safety and earnings of civilian life in preference to the non-lucrative hazards of wartime responsibilities?'[56]

Frank Calder was trying to keep a low profile in the public debate, but his movements behind the scenes were tracked by the press. Calder and D.C. Coleman of the Canadiens met with the associate deputy minister of NWS in Ottawa and reportedly assured him that the NHL did not want to interfere, but merely wanted to be kept informed of the situation.[57] Amid rumours that the NHL was developing a contingency plan whereby its American clubs would be moved to Canada, Calder flew west to lobby the Manitoba board in person.[58] Calder, Col. J.R. Kilpatrick, the president of the Rangers, and Mervyn Dutton, the manager of the New York Americans, arranged a meeting with Justice Adamson and Calder also planned to visit Regina to see Embury and the members of the Saskatchewan board.[59] Caught by a *Free Press* reporter at the Fort Garry Hotel in Winnipeg, Calder insisted the NHL would comply with the laws of the land, but also emphasized how even war-plagued Britain was continuing to play football (soccer), watched and supported by none other than Churchill himself.[60] The *Free Press* editors disparaged the Calder message that 'business as usual' helped the war effort or, as they put it, that 'in order to smash Hitlerism ... the front line of the Boston Bruins must be kept intact.'[61] Showing sensitivity to American opinion, they cited sports columnist Dave Egan of the *Boston Sunday Advertiser*, who had complained that 'something is phony' when Hank

Greenberg of the Detroit Tigers and others had to settle for $21 a month, while 'our Canadian cousins continue to ring the cash register.'[62] The editors of the *Free Press* agreed, and contended there was absolutely no 'business-like argument' for hockey in wartime.

The meeting with Adamson bore no fruit, so Calder and Kilpatrick flew back east.[63] That same day, the *Winnipeg Tribune* reported that the papers of two local Toronto Maple Leafs players, Wally Stanowski and Pete Langelle, had been transferred to an Ontario NWS board, noting that 'the board here [Manitoba] was of the opinion the request for the transfer was made only because Ontario restrictions were more lenient.'[64] In response to the news, Toronto coach 'Happy' Day glibly commented that the Leafs had assured authorities that its players would be on hand for military call if and when the occasion demanded it. At least six western players crossed the border through Ontario.[65]

This 'passport crisis' was directly relevant to the increasing public disenchantment over the slow pace of Canadian recruitment policy in 1941, and the result was increased scrutiny and criticism of the DNWS, most notably in the House of Commons. Among other issues, there was concern over the department's lack of consistency regarding medical rejections and exemptions for military call-ups, due to the lack of central oversight over the discretionary power of the local NWS boards. The Manitoba passport ruling was cited by MP Tommy Douglas of Weyburn, Saskatchewan, as a case in point, a 'glaring example' of the lack of consistency in the policy, made worse by the lack of a right of appeal to the minister.[66] Thorson responded that 'this subject has received in the sports columns of the newspapers a great deal more attention than it deserves,' but did admit that the various board chairmen had dealt with the subject 'in a manner that is not altogether uniform.'[67] He noted that sixty hockey players had been given permission to travel: twenty-two from Toronto; thirteen from Edmonton; seven from London; six from Kingston; five from Montreal; four from Port Arthur; one each from Quebec, Regina, and Saint John (New Brunswick); and none from Halifax, Charlottetown, Winnipeg, and Vancouver. When Douglas took this as evidence of a 'total lack of uniformity,' Thorson argued that 'the facts' and 'the human factor' made each case unique. Douglas countered with stories of players transferring to more favourable districts, insisting that an appeal process was needed to 'obviate much of the feeling of uneasiness which has arisen in consequence of these different decisions that are handed down by the boards in identical cases.'[68]

Not Necessarily Conscription, but Conscription if Necessary

The discussion over standards featured hockey players, but it represented a growing disenchantment with the Canadian recruiting system in general. Over the course of 1941 more voices had been raised in support of conscription, and the Mackenzie King government reacted in two ways. First, in December 1941 the Cabinet formed a Cabinet Manpower Committee to study the civilian and military manpower situation more closely.[69] The sudden attack on Pearl Harbor and the prospect of a two-front war gave added focus to the committee's work. By March 1942 the committee reported and Mackenzie King announced the creation of the National Selective Service (NSS) under the Department of Labour. The NSS would take over coordination of both NRMA *and* civilian manpower allocation. Liability for service under the NRMA was extended, with all single men and widowers born between 1912 and 1921 now liable for call-up.[70] In addition, farmers and farm labourers were forbidden to seek employment elsewhere except with NSS permission, and no physically fit man seventeen to forty-five could be employed in various non-essential occupations.[71] In June 1942 an order-in-council was passed providing that no man or woman could take employment anywhere without a permit from an NSS officer. This meant that 'for the first time the war was felt at home.'[72] The second stratagem Mackenzie King used to appease the conscriptionist camp was the calling of a plebiscite for 27 April 1942 to release him from his election promise not to impose conscription for overseas service. When it was held, every province but Quebec voted to release him from his obligation, but there are indications that rural Canadians were less supportive than urban voters.[73] Mackenzie King was still personally uncommitted, and on 10 June 1942 uttered his famous phrase 'not necessarily conscription but conscription if necessary.'

The new NSS structure, though still regional in emphasis (the NWS boards became NSS boards and retained the same membership), may have given professional hockey magnates more hope of establishing a consistent national policy. However, early omens were not promising. On 20 April the *Ottawa Journal* reported that 'no player of military age will be permitted to report next season to any of the American teams in professional hockey leagues.'[74] 'The lack of a general all-over policy' the year before had resulted in 'unfair discrimination' that would be eliminated this year 'with all draft boards refusing any permit applications.'[75] The report was widely reprinted, but as the next season was months away, it provoked little public comment. At the May 1942 NHL annual meeting in Toronto, Jack Adams, manager of the Detroit Red Wings, said he would 'buck' any move to cancel hockey for the duration of the war, citing its necessity as an alternative to movies as war-worker recreation.[76] The official press statement released at the conclusion of the meetings was less confrontational, reflecting Calder's calm and seemingly compliant stance. The league expected to operate and, 'like any other business, will do whatever the governments of Canada and the United States request it to do.'[77]

Back to the Lobby

Yet even as several major NHL stars began to enlist, behind the scenes Calder started lobbying the new NSS director, Elliott Little, for the league's continuation.[78] Calder met Little on 6 August 1942 to make the case for the NHL.[79] The meeting went well, and afterward Little issued a statement: 'It may be necessary to give some consideration to maintaining the N.H.L. in some form, or on some basis, or else we would face the problem of replacing what it at present means to hundreds of thousands of Canadians in entertainment and maintenance of morale.'[80] Significantly, this was the first official recognition of the league's importance to morale. Little said he would assess the league's manpower situation before arriving at a firm decision, but spokesmen at the NSS 'intimated strongly that their chief is inclined to believe the N.H.L. should be continued, at least for the 1942–43 season.'[81] It was suggested that the issue would be reduced to 'a straight decision between morale and manpower requirements,' that is, if many men were needed, then the needs of the forces would take precedence; if few, then the 'morale factor of the N.H.L. is likely to swing the case.'[82] The morale factor was taking on a concrete value. The assurance of Little's statement reflected the growing influence of the NSS; while the NWS board chairmen still officially decided the exemptions, Little must have believed that a uniform national policy was his to formulate and impose.[83]

Calder hoped it was, and pressed on in a follow-up memorandum the day after their meeting, noting that 'to one so conversant with the conduct of the winter sport, I need hardly emphasize the place which the National League holds in the public mind in the Dominion.'[84] His theme was not just morale, but also the economic importance of the sport. Calder pointed out that not only had over 500,000 fans personally attended games in Montreal and Toronto, but several million listened to the weekly Imperial Oil Hockey Broadcast, the Saturday radio show sponsored by Imperial Oil, which had replaced its own advertisements with spots featuring War Savings and Victory Bond Drives, among other government appeals. These shows were then distilled by Maple Leafs broadcaster Foster Hewitt into thirty-minute recordings for transmission and rebroadcast by the BBC to Canadian troops overseas on Sunday afternoons. Calder enclosed a public statement by Imperial Oil claiming it had received thousands of letters testifying to the hockey broadcast's popularity both for the servicemen and also at home in 'the maintenance of public morale by diversion.'[85] The economic value was also evident. Maple Leaf Gardens estimated it would pay over $95,000 in income and excess profits taxes, in addition to $134,506.00 in amusement tax. Furthermore, the FECB regulations alone had brought in approximately a quarter of a million dollars in 1941–2.[86] Calder ended his letter with a request for NSS permission to enter into contracts with the players (an NSS regulation), reiterating that the league was 'firmly of the opinion that it is to the interest of national morale that our activities should be carried on for this coming winter.'[87] He did not mention passports or border crossing.

While the American clubs of the NHL could argue the importance of their being allowed to obtain players, based on the importance of the NHL's contributions to the Canadian war effort, the exclusively U.S.-based American Hockey League (AHL) had a more difficult case to make.[88] Though it seems to have escaped mention by the newspapers, Little was also visited by Charles Sawyer, a lawyer from Cincinnati, Ohio, who was acting on behalf of the AHL club owners. Sawyer was no ordinary lawyer, but a former lieutenant governor of Ohio and a current member of the Democratic National Committee.[89] His visit had been arranged through Hugh Keenleyside, assistant undersecretary of state for external affairs, at the request of Pierrepont Moffat, the U.S. ambassador to Canada.[90] After making his 'urgent appeal' in a meeting with Little on 14 August 1942, in Ottawa, Sawyer followed up with a fourteen-point memorandum outlining the issues to consider.[91] While Calder had avoided direct mention of the issue of passport permissions, Sawyer could not, so he confronted it head-on.[92] He adduced the fact that American baseball players were playing on Canadian teams without negative public comment, implying that Canadian hockey players in the United States would attract none. Furthermore, hockey was a very popular and 'clean' entertainment that did not require spectators to use their automobiles, and the number of hockey players required

was small, less than four hundred in all leagues. Economic considerations were also manifold: hockey was the major source of income for
American arenas; Chicago Stadium and others provided both funds to
charities and space for their fundraising benefits; and players' salaries
and American clubs' training camps provided foreign exchange to Canada. Finally, Sawyer promised that at its next meeting the AHL would
initiate a program of war charity donations to be divided equally between Canadian and American organizations, on the pattern of the All-
Star Game played the year before.[93]

After these meetings, Little forwarded the Calder and Sawyer memoranda to Keenleyside, confirming that the NSS was willing to allow
Canadians *not* subject to military service to cross the border if American authorities 'agreed that it was desirable to maintain professional
hockey.' He asked Keenleyside to ascertain the views of the US officials.[94] Keenleyside duly wrote to Ambassador Moffat, explaining that
'the policy of the Canadian Government at the present time is to refuse
exemption from military service to hockey players unless they would
be eligible for such exemption on other grounds. In other words hockey
playing is to be treated like any other business – if the player is eligible
for military service he will be called up; if he is not, he will not be called
up.'[95] Keenleyside asked Moffat to determine the views of the responsible US officials to the matter, which he called 'largely a question of
public relations.'[96] In due course, Paul V. McNutt, the chairman of the
recently established US War Manpower Commission (WMC), agreed
to the policy, and Keenleyside provided a draft of a joint press release
that was issued in both Ottawa and Washington at eleven o'clock on 15
September 1942: 'While neither country has any intention of granting
exemption from military service to hockey players or other athletes,
there is no objection to allowing any men who are not subject to military service to continue their professional athletic activities unless and
until they are requested to engage in some non-military war duty.'[97]
Although this did not give any special treatment to players per se, a
subsequent NSS press release on 22 October did specify that, in Canada
at least, 'If a person is engaged in work of low priority and there is no
vacancy in work of high labour priority for which he is particularly
skilled, he may be given a permit to play professional sport.'[98]

Although this policy suggested the NHL would have to rely increasingly on married players and younger players, Calder and the
other governors were pleased.[99] Unlike the AHL, which often relied
on younger and single players, the NHL featured older, often married

players, who were less likely to be subject to call, and the NHL could obtain players from the AHL and other leagues when the need arose.[100] At the September 1942 NHL semi-annual meeting in Toronto the league issued a statement that 'the authorities have recognized the place which the operations of the league hold in the public interest and have, after lengthy deliberation, agreed that in the interest of public morale the league should carry on.'[101] It was also reported that it had been 'approved as a matter of general policy, that the N.H.L was opposed to employment by any club of any person who should properly be in the active service of his country, whether of Canada or the U.S.A.'[102] The definition of 'properly be' would, of course, be left to the authorities.

McNamara's Rules

As the 1942–3 season began play, Little was replaced, having lost a power struggle over wartime labour management policy. He had proposed a plan that was attacked as likely to result in a spartan Canada with widespread rationing and a huge bureaucracy. Mackenzie King and the Cabinet rejected Little's seemingly draconian proposals and Little was forced to resign in November 1942.[103] His successor was the chief commissioner of the Unemployment Insurance Commission and associate deputy minister of the Department of Labour, Arthur Mac-Namara.[104] Like King, MacNamara was also highly sensitive to public opinion. When he first addressed the hockey player issues, MacNamara's first priority was to avoid a repeat of the 'unfortunate publicity' arising out of variations in treatment to professional hockey players on applications for passport permits.[105]

MacNamara intended to formulate a policy well in advance of the 1943–4 season, in order to give early guidance to the local and regional NSS offices and mobilization boards. He sought comments from the NSS staff, and provided his own to start the discussion:

> The number of men involved is, of course, very small and the number of those men having some particular skill is very limited. If the players are given the impression that the possibilities of their continuing with their clubs next winter are dependent upon the type of employment in which they engage during the off-season, there will, no doubt, be a strong tendency to get into the least essential work. This obviously, is not desirable and I think the players should be encouraged to work in war industry as much as possible. But, if we do encourage them to take employment in

war industry and agree that professional hockey may be permitted to continue next season, then, I think perhaps they could be permitted to leave that employment at the commencement of the next season.[106]

MacNamara's suggestion here that compromises be made to encourage hockey players to get into essential civilian war work is pragmatic, but not to be misinterpreted as relieving military obligations: staff members were to bear in mind that 'any policy agreed upon from the civilian angle would not affect in any way the man's status under the Mobilization Regulations.'[107]

MacNamara also thought it prudent to confirm with the Americans that the policy of 15 September 1942 would still apply for the 1943–4 season, and directed a member of his staff to make inquiries through External Affairs.[108] Keenleyside solicited the opinion of the Canadian embassy staff and received a response from Lester Pearson, the number-two man at the embassy in Washington, through Norman Robertson, the undersecretary of state for external affairs. Pearson was not in favour of hockey's continuance. He enclosed a typed copy of a 1 April 1943 column by Dave Egan of the *Boston Daily Record* excoriating Canada for allowing hockey players to play while Americans were dying in foxholes in Guadalcanal: in the 'FOURTH season of hockey, everything is just dandy in never-never land with the heroes of the hockey rinks ... and I do know that our national sport will do well to finish its second wartime season, and I do know that their national sport is finishing its fourth wartime season without the slightest show of distress.'[109] Commenting to Robertson, Pearson wrote that he recognized Egan's statement was

a very one-sided statement of the case and that we might as well complain of the [American League baseball] Washington [S]enators opening the base-ball season next week while Canadians are losing their lives bombing Berlin. There is, however, a difference in the two cases, and one which I feel personally would justify us preventing Canadian hockey players coming to this country next winter; namely, that while American base-ball teams consist of Americans playing in their own country, American professional hockey teams consist of foreigners brought in from Canada to play here. There is a difference.[110]

Keenleyside forwarded Pearson's letter to the NSS, noting that although he himself still supported the continuance of the hockey policy 'in principle,' he believed the issue would have to be decided 'not on the basis of principle but on expediency.'[111] His inclination was to agree with Pearson in advocating that Canadian hockey players should be prevented from playing in the United States next winter, but he was 'not, however, sufficiently convinced that it is the right decision to present it to you officially as the view for the Department of External Affairs.'[112] He suggested a meeting of the interested parties to work out a policy, but 'it may be ... that the National Hockey League will not in any event be able to continue next winter. If that should be the case, the problems would be pretty largely solved.'[113]

In August 1943 the NHL made its annual pilgrimage to Ottawa, this time without its canny diplomat, Frank Calder, who had died the previous February.[114] After meeting with MacNamara, the NHL governors and the president of the AHL, Maurice Podoloff, reported that the federal government still 'realizes that hockey is a great morale-builder' and that MacNamara had told them they might expect 'certain' concessions to keep the league functioning the next season.[115] Recognizing the analogy to US baseball, the NHL had suggested the Canadian government consult with the US government, hoping that the green light given to baseball might incline them to do the same for hockey.[116]

What Do the Americans Think?

The hockey men seemed to recognize that American policy was an important factor. Luckily for them, Paul McNutt seemed to support the sport. He sent a letter to MacNamara on 25 August agreeing that 'the continuance of hockey along with other recognized sports is desirable and we would be glad to see granted whatever clearances are needed ... to maintain hockey in the United States and Canada during the coming winter.'[117] Interpreting this as a signal to go ahead, MacNamara sent out NSS Circular Memorandum no. 283 in September, directing the mobilization boards and divisional registrars to grant permits to play hockey to any person not in the military call-up age group, or who had been rejected, unless they were employed in an establishment with an A or B labour rating (essential).[118]

All seemed well and good until October, when the Canadian legation in Washington asked for information on the agreement, complaining that it had not been kept up to date. When they were apprised, MacNamara's ignorance of the American recruitment policy environment became clear. The diplomats pointed out that 'if McNutt's policy is the only policy, we will have trouble getting players back who have stayed over three months,' because while the McNutt's WMC might have a positive stance towards the maintenance of hockey, the law stipulated that after the three-month period all males between the ages of eighteen and thirty-eight residing in the United States were subject to the draft. Not only this, but the embassy also noted that the US age range for draftees was much wider than Canada's, so exemption from the Canadian draft did not necessarily exempt them from the US draft. The wider publicity aspects also had to be considered. The US policy of drafting fathers was provoking 'hard feelings' in the public, and the American press generally was prone to make 'invidious and inaccurate statements with regards to the war efforts of other nations.'[119] Robertson relayed these warnings to MacNamara and added, 'Our past experience has shown that the Local [US Draft] Boards exercise their rather considerable powers with more energy than discretion.'[120] He also reiterated his concern over 'the publicity aspect,' noting in particular the negative American press reaction to Canada's recent reorganization of Home Defence Forces. To avoid these repercussions, 'it would therefore be appreciated if the instructions concerning professional hockey players would be administered in such a way as to give the least possible cause for criticism of Canadian manpower policy in the United States.'[121] Robertson asked to be advised 'before any major decisions on policy with respect to Canadians going to the United States are taken, so that the Canadian Minister in Washington may be forewarned and given an opportunity to express an opinion.'[122]

By the time of Robertson's letter, Labour Exit Permits (LEPs) had already been issued to most of the players required by the various teams, issued on the authority of MacNamara's Memorandum no. 283, which had been based on McNutt's 25 August letter. MacNamara now became aware that Canadian permits might not prevent players from being called up by American authorities, and to head this off, he wrote to McNutt, hoping to get him to agree that since the players had complied with the Canadian regulations, they should not become subject to the US regulations during their temporary residence in the United States.[123] McNutt did not respond before MacNamara got his answer: in November Canadian players were called up by local US draft boards. MacNamara sent McNutt a telegram immediately: 'Situation now urgent. Stop. Would appreciate by return advice as to motion you contemplate to bring situation under control.'[124] McNutt replied by wire, reiterating the WMC position that hockey players were not exempt and clarifying that the three-month rule would continue to apply. He promised help only to correct any situations of players in the United States *less* than three months who had been called up in error.[125] MacNamara was forced to admit to McNutt that the Canadian LEPs had been given without considering US mobilization regulations, and asked McNutt to make an exception and defer the players involved for five months (that is, the rest of the hockey season). He promised that the situation would not be repeated in future.[126] McNutt would not budge: deferment of the hockey players over three months was not possible. The solution was simple: the players' return to Canada within three months 'should alleviate any existing difficulty.'[127]

In December MacNamara wrote back to Robertson to give him an update. He was pessimistic and resigned to the fact that the local draft boards in the United States would be proceeding to draft without reference to a player's non-resident status.[128] He expected that it was 'entirely likely that all professional hockey will stop sometime in January as the players would no doubt return to Canada before the expiration of the three-month period. We would consider this a rather unsatisfactory development as the entire question would no doubt, then, become a public issue.'[129] The prospect of returning players was worrisome to both MacNamara and Robertson, but for opposite reasons. While MacNamara was concerned about negative publicity that showed the government sacrificing hockey to the war effort, Robertson was worried about just the reverse – while he recognized hockey's usefulness to morale, he did not think its 'cessation for the duration of the war is a development greatly to be deplored.' On the contrary: 'Judging from press comment on the hockey question both in Canada and in the United States, and in view of the expected increase in the tempo of the war in coming months, I believe that we would evoke much more unfavourable publicity by making any special effort to assure continuation of the sort than by permitting it to become a war casualty. In any event, I doubt whether anything useful could be achieved even if we were to attempt to bring about a modification in the attitude of the United States authorities.'[130] Echoing Keenleyside, he wrote that the matter would have to be decided 'not on the basis of principle but of expediency.'[131] If the WMC policy resulted in 'the disappearance of professional hockey for the duration, my inclination would be to let matters take their course.'[132] Robertson was content to let the Americans decide, and he would make no special efforts to push them either way.

In any event, professional hockey did continue for the rest of the

1943–4 season. It had little to do with MacNamara, the one man who seemed intent on pushing for continuation, as he was powerless to change US mobilization regulations or the mind of the man who executed them: Paul McNutt. The status quo persisted because there was no real willingness to stop the sport. McNutt supported continuation in principle, but not at the expense of effective mobilization, and even if he had gone to bat for the sport, it would likely have made little difference. For by coincidence, in December 1943, just before the three-month permits were to expire in the first months of 1944, the US Congress made the Selective Service independent of McNutt's control. This was a direct result of McNutt's attempts to eliminate certain exemptions, which had met with resistance from individual draft boards.[133] A partial explanation of why hockey players were allowed to continue to work in the United States lies within the discretionary power of these local US draft boards.[134] As in Canada, it was up to the individual boards to call up players and decide their status, but the decision of December 1943 confirmed the US Selective Service's ability to resist McNutt's application of a uniform policy of fewer exceptions. But this should not be overemphasized. By this point in the war, most eligible recruits had already enlisted. Although there were examples of Canadian players being called up by US draft boards, and of some even being sent back to Canada mid-season, the NHL rosters were by now dominated by men who, by virtue of age and dependency status, were less threatened by the American draft. Even after Rangers players Ott Heller and Bryan Hextall were called up by a New York draft board, they were still allowed to play out the season in New York.[135]

The Broda Affair

While professional hockey continued, another scandal in the fall of 1943 showed the limits of the overt intrusion of commerce into the central institution of war society, the military. Toronto Maple Leafs goalie Walter 'Turk' Broda had been called up in October 1943 and, like most Maple Leafs, intended to enlist locally, likely with the Royal Canadian Artillery. But his mind was soon changed when he was offered $2400 on top of his military pay to join a unit in Montreal and play for the Montreal Army senior hockey team in the amateur Quebec Hockey Association. Someone got wind of this transfer of allegiance and arranged to have the RCMP arrest him while he was on the train to Montreal.[136] That Broda was arrested before the midnight deadline for his reporting, and that he was being accompanied by a sergeant major from Montreal at the time, were subjects of some discussion in the ensuing press coverage, but it was the commercialization of hockey in the military that became the topic of the day. A *Calgary Herald* editorial was typical: why should 'the cream of young Canadian manhood ... be allowed to continue to play [hockey] to the detriment of war service'?[137]

At the outset of the war, military hockey had been seen as a valuable component of the military training regimen, but teams soon discovered that some of their enlisted men had the talent to allow them to compete beyond military house leagues. They joined senior amateur competition, both provincial and national, and soon dominated. Ottawa military teams won the Allan Cup in both 1942 and 1943 using players such as Milt Schmidt, Woody Dumart, and Bobby Bauer – aka the Boston Bruins 'Kraut Line.' Soon the combination of regimental pride and commercial opportunity seemed to overtake physical training purposes, and the Broda incident brought to light how hockey was being run 'by the same entrepreneurial ethos as peacetime, professional hockey.'[138] Military teams even traded players, taking advantage of the Canadian Amateur Hockey Association (CAHA) Wartime Regulations that had exempted military players from the residence rule to allow for inter-unit transfers.[139] And Broda's salary, though undoubtedly large, was not unusual; Dink Carroll reported in the *Montreal Gazette* that it was well known that former professionals were being paid to play for service teams.[140] While press criticism could show ambivalence on the issue of non-military players crossing borders, it was united in its criticism of military hockey's violation of the amateur-professional barrier. As a result, in December 1943 the Royal Canadian Air Force withdrew its teams from Allan Cup competition, and in January the Army did the same, having already instructed its commanding officers to send their athletes overseas.[141]

In a secret memorandum of January 1944, Col. E.A. Deacon, Director of Auxiliary Services, explained the change in the hockey policy:

The idea behind the playing of Hockey and all other games by Army teams has been the maintenance of morale and the creation of an 'esprit de corps' in the units, and as long as the interest created by such contests were of Service significance mainly, games and competition in which teams composed of civilians were involved, were not discouraged.

As matters proceeded however, such competitions and the service teams playing in them, were found to be in danger of coming under the domination of civilian organizations who were for commercial reasons using the teams for their own purposes with the result that instead of the teams being organized in the interests of the service there was a possibility of their becoming revenue earning units of commercial corporations.[142]

'When this trend was realized,' Deacon continued, the decision was taken after consultation 'to withdraw all service teams from competitions in organized leagues.'[143]

Although Deacon seemed to blame external commercial interests rather than the unit commanders themselves, it seemed that even the military command had difficulty maintaining uniformity of regulations. Even while there was an active campaign to press NPAM men into agreeing to serve overseas, domestic military commanders were holding on to skilled hockey players on the home front. And Deacon's statement that service teams had been withdrawn from 'competitions in organized leagues' was not accurate: Army teams had withdrawn to garrison leagues, but Navy teams still continued to play in senior amateur hockey, albeit not in Allan Cup competitions. However, the Broda affair did spell the end of high-profile competitive military hockey. While it was more visible as a new phenomenon that only appeared during the war, in its perceived perversion from war-making to profit-making it became unacceptable.[144]

Internal Dissension

As an institution, the NHL also constantly negotiated its aims and activities to conform with its own clubs' perception of the league's wartime role. While the NHL lobbied hard for the right of all hockey players to travel to the United States to play, the clubs were in less agreement about which players should be eligible for play. The legitimacy of exemption from military service for hockey players on either occupational or medical grounds came to a head in 1944. Generally speaking, NHL owners and managers spoke positively of their fellow member clubs' contributions to the war effort, but there was criticism, and while the war suppressed much of it, a long tradition of internecine conflict made it inevitable some would emerge in the press. With two sons in the military, Art Ross, manager of the Bruins, was very critical of the Canadian teams' lack of charitable contributions in general, and his comments about the Canadiens cancelling a charity exhibition game with the Bruins had been reported in the newspapers.[145] He also sarcastically referred to the Montreal Canadiens, whose players were mostly employed in Montreal war industries, as 'The Essential War Workers.'[146] To a great extent, Ross was correct. Despite Canada's early belligerent status, it was American clubs – Boston and Chicago – that led the way in charity events, raising money with war-bond drives and charity games. Chicago owner Frederic McLaughlin had even offered the Black Hawks' entire 1942–3 season profits to charity.[147]

Ross was not content to take shots only through the press, and brought the issue to the table of the NHL board of governors in the form of a resolution at the May 1944 annual meeting. He wanted it stipulated that 'for the duration of the war, no person will be eligible to play in the National Hockey League whose induction into the Armed Forces of the Dominion of Canada or of the United States of America has been deferred or may hereafter be deferred for other than physical reasons. This rule, however, shall not apply to a student who is attending school, or college and whose induction has been deferred as a student, nor shall it apply to any person whose induction has been deferred as a farmer and who, as of the date of January 21st, 1944, is recognized as a farmer by occupation.'[148] Senator Donat Raymond, the Canadiens' governor, clearly saw the motion as an attack on his team, and he countered by proposing an amendment to the motion: 'That in view of the object of Mr. Ross' motion, the National Hockey League go further and request the Dominion government that no permit to leave Canada be granted to any professional hockey player who could be used for any purpose in connection with our war effort.'[149] By suggesting the league voluntarily end the very foundation of its continuance – player border crossing – Raymond certainly made his point, but with four American teams at the table there was no hope the amendment would pass.[150]

The NHL governors passed the Ross resolution unaltered, but held off publicizing its contents until the fall, presumably to preserve the chance to amend or change it if necessary, or perhaps to adjust rosters. By 9 September 1944 Frank Selke reported that none of the Maple Leafs would be affected by the ruling.[151] On 24 December 1944 Bill Tobin said his Black Hawks 'all either have been rejected, discharged, or are over or under the military age limit.' To his knowledge all men eligible for call-up were over thirty, and the Canadians on the club had been rejected for military service in their country.[152] The ruling did, however, affect at least one prominent player. Phil Watson had been on loan to the Canadiens from the New York Rangers owing to passport permission difficulties, and the new regulation meant he would not be able to play even for the Canadiens in the upcoming season. When in November he obtained his medical deferment, he was able to join the Rangers for the season.[153] Other than Watson, the policy seems to have had little real effect, other than for public relations.

Harmonization

By the fall of 1944 the US and Canadian central administrative bodies now seemed to be on the same page, but an NSS board's lack of adherence to the national uniform policy could still create problems.[154] The Hon. Mr Justice A.M. Manson, chairman of the Vancouver mobilization board, wrote to MacNamara about 'ten or a dozen' hockey players who 'have popped up in the last two weeks, all asking to go down to the United States to play professional hockey.'[155] Manson said he just could not see his way clear to giving them permits, and so the only fair thing to do was to refuse them all, offering to MacNamara, 'You believe in uniformity. This is a case for uniformity.'[156] Manson also thought it funny that 'most of these applicants are medically unfit and yet they can play one of the fastest and roughest games known to man.'[157] In response, MacNamara politely admitted that there was 'a variety of opinion' on the issue, but then outlined the history of the policy for Manson, enclosing the related circulars and memoranda that had been issued by the NSS.[158] For MacNamara, the policy was now fixed, and the 'great lack of uniformity in the manner of treatment of individual applications' at the various regional boards in 1942–3 was a thing of the past: Manson would have to toe the line. On the issue of medically unfit men playing hockey, MacNamara agreed that it was 'anomalous,' but blamed this on 'the physical standards of the Armed Forces' and concluded by assuring Manson that 'the great majority of players engaged in the professional leagues last winter were men who had been rejected for service or discharged from active service.'[159] While Manson continued to be a thorn in MacNamara's side, the NSS director did succeed in bringing the boards into line with a relatively uniform national policy, which itself was becoming more consistent with the American approach.[160]

The influence of the United States on Canadian policy became most evident in a 18 January 1945 NSS circular issued to all NSS officers and mobilization boards: 'Effective immediately and for the balance of the current hockey season a Labour Exit Permit may not be granted to any man to leave Canada to play professional, semi-professional, or amateur hockey, unless the applicant is a veteran entitled to the preference, that is, a veteran who has had overseas service or is in receipt of a pension.'[161] This policy effectively restricted professional hockey to using only veterans. Lester Patrick of the Rangers saw this as a serious blow, predicting that 'hockey may be stopped next season,' but NHL President Red Dutton was more optimistic and noted that only three or four players would be affected.[162] The question still remained: what had prompted this hardening of policy?

In late November 1944, with the Allies fully engaged in the war in several theatres, and with rationing tightened up, the US War Department announced that, owing to charges of favouritism towards athletes, especially baseball players, the decision to approve release of 'prominent' personalities would be taken out of the scope of individual unit commanders.[163] On 9 December 1944 James F. Byrnes, head of the US Office of War Mobilization and Reconversion, suggested to the Selective Service director, General Lewis B. Hershey, that athletes with medical discharges be recalled and 4-F ballplayers be re-examined. Six days later, Hershey directed local draft boards to review athlete cases.[164] Byrnes also ordered horse racetracks closed to address war plant absenteeism. Finally, in the 6 January 1945 State of the Union Address, President Roosevelt spoke of the need for an act making use of the 4-Fs, essentially calling for so-called 'work or fight' legislation that might threaten all professional sports.[165] On 20 January the War Department announced it would review any professional ballplayer rejected by draft boards, and major league baseball began making plans to play the 1945 season with draft rejects.[166]

It was against this American background that the circumstances of MacNamara's 18 January circular must be drawn. T.R. Walsh, the NSS chief enforcement officer, characterized the new Canadian policy response as 'rather drastic' but 'probably justified by existing circumstances.'[167] However, he was ambivalent about whether MacNamara should issue a press statement on the issue. Publicity was once again at the forefront: 'I am of two minds whether the circular would constitute a good basis for a press statement by you. It might have some good effects and indicate that we are taking a strong stand in regard to any further movement of this kind to the United States during the present season, but, on the other hand, it might only have the effect of stirring up a lot of questions about those who are already engaged in athletics and might bring about a demand for recall of all of those presently engaged in hockey. I hardly think this would be a desirable debate to stir up.'[168] Walsh recognized that the new policy would only affect those applying for a new permit, and not those already in possession of one. In the interests of consistency – and perhaps in a bid to pre-empt criticism that US clubs were being discriminated against – on 24 January Walsh informed the Montreal and Toronto NSS boards that the same principle would apply equally to the Canadian clubs, namely, that 'no permit (Form NSS 122) [would be issued to a man] to enter the employment of the Toronto or Montreal professional clubs, unless he is a veteran entitled to the preference.'[169]

Arguably, the 18 January letter and Walsh's 24 January addendum are the closest Canada came to a policy that firmly prioritized hockey-playing *behind* essential war employment and military service. The latitude exercised in the early war years, when the war was not as close to home, had dissipated. But it still did not stop professional hockey from continuing. Had the war (and the policy) persisted into the next season, there surely would have been further strains on the NHL and AHL. As it was, the NHL relied on many teenagers and veterans who would not last into the post-war era.[170] Aside from a small skirmish in February 1945, where Conn Smythe demanded hockey players be demobilized to play, the end of the war in the summer of 1945 ended the issue.[171]

Conclusion

While the controversy over hockey players only gained nation-wide attention on a few occasions over the course of the war, behind the scenes there was extensive discussion of the place of professional hockey and its players. There was no one decision that confirmed hockey's place, but rather several decisions that addressed the issue from different perspectives and areas of control; taken together, they allowed hockey to continue, but with increasing restriction as war demands became more insistent.

The NHL and AHL succeeded in having hockey acknowledged as an industry that both boosted morale *and* contributed to the war's economic needs through the FECB and tax contributions. On the one hand, the professional clubs behaved in a predictable capitalistic manner that was arguably little different than that of the pre-war period, and that behaviour was often ascribed by themselves and others to patriotic rather than profit-making goals. On one level, the NHL was able to take advantage of a state that was unwilling to compromise a popular home-front activity overtly until the demands of war labour forced it to. However, men such as Art Ross were keenly aware of the necessity of contributing to the war beyond excess profits, taxes, and complimentary tickets, and pushed the NHL to refuse exempted players. Others, such as Conn Smythe, were even willing to put their own lives on the line by enlisting, even while defending business and the home front status quo. The NHL's fight to maintain itself is consistent with Canadian and American wartime policy and social sentiment, which recognized that the requirements of morale (read as normalcy or maintaining the standard of living at home) were just as imperative as military requirements overseas.

Bureaucrats reflected the ambivalence of the public and political masters. The men most central to the administration of recruitment – MacNamara and McNutt – evinced less concern over foreign relations and more over the bureaucratic goal of centralization and uniformity. Of the two, MacNamara was the more adept at reconciling bureaucratic rules with political reality. Those who decided the fates of individual players – NSS board chairmen such as Manson – struggled to apply an approach consistent with their own perceptions of the resources needed, but they were trying to apply consistently the principles of a mobilization system that was arguably not designed to be consistent. Thus, the chairmen's decisions were often at odds with a central administration that was treading the line between the need for effective mobilization and labour control and the political desire to maintain a measure of normalcy while keeping social conflict to a minimum. Elliott Little was an early casualty of this tightrope, and MacNamara, like the Mackenzie King government itself, continued the balancing act throughout the war.

The diplomats of External Affairs were caught between Canadian and American interests, and emphasized the principle of 'expediency,' which meant adapting to American policy if it avoided negative publicity. But they were not alone. While the effect of American lobbying – such as that by AHL club owners for continuation of border-crossing – is difficult to assess, it is clear that even the mere opinions of American media were important factors for many Canadian observers and stakeholders.

Thus, the Second World War provided an opportunity for the redefinition of hockey's cultural and industrial roles, and the importance of the national sport was made manifest through an acknowledgment of its contribution to civilian and military morale. Until the war, the state had had little influence over, or interest in, hockey. When the war began, many assumed that the sport would be put on hold, but as the war intensified, diplomats, bureaucrats, politicians, and businessmen were required to acknowledge the value of hockey as entertainment on the home front and to accommodate public opinion by constantly negotiating and defining this role against mobilization requirements. Far from being frivolous fodder for the sports pages, the debate over hockey reproduced the social tensions and conflicts over the extent and character of individual, business, and national participation in the war that stretched into the highest reaches of Canadian and American government policy-making and administration. In the end, the debate in these arenas was forced to accommodate a society that, while not rejecting the war outright, was not willing to submit either its economy or its national social identity entirely to the war's demands.

NOTES

The author wishes to thank Michael D. Stevenson and Richard Holt for comments and source suggestions, as well as John Wong, and commentators at the University of Western Ontario McCaffrey Seminar, the 2005 Canadian Historical Association Meeting, and the 'Canada's Game?' conference held at Bridgewater State College, Plymouth, MA, in April 2005. The Foreign Exchange Control Board documents are used with permission from the Bank of Canada. My thanks go to Heather Ryckman and Jane Boyko for their help with these documents.

1 This notion has a long genealogy and is most often seen in comparisons between Canadian and American national ideologies. For an example, see Seymour Martin Lipset, *Continental Divide: The Values and Institutions of the United States and Canada* (New York: Routledge, 1990).
2 The quotation is from section 91 of the Constitution Act, 1867 (formerly the British North America Act, 1867).
3 Carman Miller, *Painting the Map Red: Canada and the South African War, 1899–1902* (Montreal: Canadian War Museum and McGill-Queen's University Press, 1993), xi, 440. The Nile expedition of 1884 and the rebellions of 1837, 1869–70, and 1885 have also figured in national lore.
4 Jonathan F. Vance, *Death So Noble: Memory, Meaning, and the First World War* (Vancouver: UBC Press, 1997), 10.
5 J.L. Granatstein, *Canada's War: The Politics of the Mackenzie King Government, 1939–1945* (Toronto: Oxford University Press, 1975), vi–viii, 424.

6 Vance addresses the importance of studying the gap between the objective reality of the First World War and how contemporaries themselves perceived it. Vance, *Death So Noble*, 4. Granatstein emphasizes that, in the Second World War, Canada went to war only because Britain did: 'It was not a war for Poland; it was not a war against anti-Semitism; it was not even a war against Nazism ... Canada did not enter it to fight the good fight.' Granatstein, *Canada's War*, 420. Later, the 'good fight' or other contemporary justifications became important. As a popular example, at the 2001 Remembrance Day ceremony in Ottawa, the author recalls a speaker justifying the war partially on the grounds that it was 'fought against racism.'

7 Jeffrey Keshen, *Saints, Sinners and Soldiers: Canada's Second World War* (Vancouver: UBC Press, 2004), 5, 9. Michael Bliss asks: 'But what if we misunderstood our war experience and drew the wrong lessons from it?' He believes the prevailing 'pretty good war' interpretation has had far-reaching – and negative – effects insofar as it has provided the justification for the post-war growth of big government and 'intrusion of government in our lives.' Bliss notes the lack of public appetite for historical revision of 'the notion of the war as Canada's heroic age,' as shown by the controversy over 'The Valour and the Horror,' an early-1990s documentary that re-examined the 'dark side' of the Canadian war effort. Michael Bliss, 'Canada's Swell War,' *Saturday Night* 110, 4 (May 1995): 38–40. By contrast, Vance contends that Canada's social memory of the war is 'dominated by overtones of negativity' and 'has come to emphasize mismanagement, injustice, failure and cupidity.' As such, he sees 'The Valour and the Horror' as a simple articulation of conventional social memory. Vance, *Death So Noble*, 10–11. These differences of opinion highlight the importance of a critical examination of the relationship between the war experience, its historical interpretations, and popular social remembrance.

8 Keshen, *Saints, Sinners, and Soldiers*, 9. Stevenson has concluded that one of the most crucial institutions of the Canadian wartime state – its manpower allocation system – was more aptly described as a 'muddle.' Michael D. Stevenson, *Canada's Greatest Wartime Muddle: National Selective Service and the Mobilization of Human Resources during World War II* (Montreal and Kingston: McGill-Queen's University Press, 2001).

9 Literature on the role of civilian morale in the Second World War is sparse. The contribution, real or imagined, of business and commerce to this aspect of war is certainly in need of more attention.

10 There has been some discussion of the place of hockey in the Second World War, but the central issue that drives much of the existing litera-

ture is the degree to which Canadian hockey players may have avoided military service by virtue of their athletic or cultural status, and the degree to which this avoidance was abetted not only by the National Hockey League (NHL) and its member clubs, but also by Canadian military and civilian authorities. Several authors contextualize the treatment of players within prevailing Canadian conscription and manpower policies, but do not ask the more basic question of why the sport was allowed to continue in wartime society at all, at any level – professional, amateur, recreational, or military. Academic analysis of the role of hockey during the war has been sporadic. Using mainly newspaper sources, an article by Bruce McIntyre frames the 1941 passport debate as emblematic of a more general Canadian social ambivalence to the conscription issue, and argues that hockey players were singled out unfairly to compensate for failures in the selective service system. Bruce McIntyre, 'Which Uniform to Serve?' *Canadian Journal of History of Sport* 24 (December 1993): 68–89. Another short article generally supports the view that players were eager to join up but were thwarted by military commanders eager to use them for military hockey teams in Canada. Bill Twatio, 'Wartime Wonders,' *Queen's Quarterly* 100 (Winter 1993): 833–40. The most detailed analysis of professional and military hockey during the war is provided by G.S. Panunto, who tracks the careers of war-era players through their amateur, military, and professional careers. Despite missing much of the internal government correspondence, he argues convincingly that hockey had a special status and 'was afforded much leniency by the government, military and public.' Gabriel Stephen Panunto, 'For Club or Country? Hockey in Wartime Canada, 1939–1945,' MA thesis (Carleton University, 2000), 13.

Popular writers usually highlight the military contributions of the few unrepresentative players who actually saw combat, and tend to uncritically accept that hockey was allowed to continue on the basis of its contribution to morale. For representative examples, see Brian McFarlane, *50 Years of Hockey: An Intimate History of the National Hockey League* (Toronto: Pagurian Press, 1967), 84; and Neil Isaacs, *Checking Back: A History of the National Hockey League* (New York: W.W. Norton & Co., 1977), 131. Douglas Hunter contextualizes Toronto Maple Leafs managing director Conn Smythe's role with reference to the conscription policies of the Mackenzie King government and uses several case studies of the few players who did see combat. Douglas Hunter, *War Games: Conn Smythe and Hockey's Fighting Men* (Toronto: Viking, 1996).

11 Jim Hurley, 'Meeting to Decide Hockey Fate Today,' *New York Daily Mirror*, 7 September 1939, 37. The group comprised President Frank Calder, Conn

Smythe of Toronto Maple Leafs, Jack Adams of Detroit Red Wings, Lester Patrick of New York Rangers, and W.A. Hewitt of the Canadian Amateur Hockey Association (CAHA). The NHL was composed of seven clubs: Montreal Canadiens, Toronto Maple Leafs, Detroit Red Wings, Chicago Black Hawks, New York Americans, and New York Rangers. For the 1941–2 season the Americans became the Brooklyn Americans, but suspended operations after that season.

The Second World War began in Europe after the German invasion of Poland on 1 September 1939 and the subsequent French and British declarations of war. It is commonly understood that Canada delayed its declaration until 10 September in order to emphasize its independence from British foreign policy, but there was little doubt Canada would be involved as a belligerent. Privately, Mackenzie King was personally committed to having Canada support Britain, but domestic political considerations (mainly resistance in Quebec) and a desire to influence British foreign policy led to less categorical public pronouncements. Granatstein, *Canada's War*, 1–17.

12 James Walvin, *The People's Game: A Social History of British Football* (London: Allen Lane, 1975), 137–8. Footballers signed up in great numbers and rapidly established themselves as the backbone of the Physical Training system. Within the month, many clubs also resumed limited competition. Tony McCarthy, *War Games: The Story of Sport in World War Two* (London: Macdonald & Co., 1989), 33–45. On the cancelling of the British National League (ice hockey), see 'English Season Cancelled,' *New York Herald Tribune*, 8 September 1939, 29. Like soccer, the ice hockey season soon resumed, but only for the 1939–40 season, after which it was suspended until after the war.

13 Limited military recruiting had been authorized on 1 September, but overseas deployment still seemed far in the future. In the first few weeks of September there was no shortage of volunteers, to the point that recruiting was suspended on 24 September, except for the army. Professionals, university graduates, youths under 18, and married men with more than two children were discouraged from signing up. J.L. Granatstein and J.M. Hitsman, *Broken Promises: A History of Conscription in Canada* (Toronto: Oxford University Press, 1977), 134.

14 George Strickler, 'Hockey and Olympics Are Periled by War,' *Chicago Daily Tribune*, 4 September 1939, 29. McLaughlin was probably unaware that at the outset of the war Canada had fewer than 10,000 regulars.

15 Mayer understood Washington to be awaiting a decision from Ottawa. Charles Mayer, 'Si la ligue National n'opérait pas ce serait un coup pour

le hockey amateur,' *Le Petit Journal* (Montreal), 10 September 1939, 55. Mayer's assumption that amateur hockey would benefit from stoppage of the professional game did not take into account the number of amateurs that would enlist.

16 Bill Roche, 'NHL Clears Decks to Carry on Next Winter,' *Globe and Mail* (Toronto), 8 September 1939, 17.

17 'Hockey League Plans to Carry On Despite War,' *New York Herald Tribune*, 8 September 1939, 29.

18 Hy Turkin, 'Hockey Sked Okay; War's Fever Cools,' *Daily News* (New York), 14 October 1939, 29.

19 Stevenson, *Canada's Greatest Wartime Muddle*, 18; Granatstein and Hitsman, *Broken Promises*, 138–9.

20 Granatstein and Hitsman, *Broken Promises*, 140.

21 Ibid., 142.

22 Stevenson, *Canada's Greatest Wartime Muddle*, 18–19; Granatstein and Hitsman, *Broken Promises*, 143.

23 Granatstein and Hitsman, *Broken Promises*, 145. As married men were also to be a lower priority for call-up, a spate of July marriages resulted as well. For a description of the call-up procedure, see Stevenson, *Canada's Greatest Wartime Muddle*, 18–21ff.

24 Letter from Smythe to Maple Leafs players, 17 July 1940, Archives of Ontario (AO), Conn Smythe fonds (F223), vol. 75, Military Training (1931–1941) file.

25 Ibid.

26 Herb Goren, 'War Menace Affects Hockey,' *New York Sun*, 10 September 1940, Madison Square Garden, Scrapbook #35 (Season 1940–41). Concerned about fifth columnists gaining access to the United States, on 6 June 1940 the U.S. government announced that as of 1 July Canadians would require passports to enter the country. This caused an administrative crisis in the Passport Office at External Affairs, as they hurried to hire staff and arrange special eight-page passports for the estimated 500,000 Canadians who travelled to the States each year. John Hilliker, *Canada's Department of External Affairs. Volume 1: The Early Years, 1909–1946* (Montreal and Kingston: McGill-Queen's University Press, 1990), 232.

27 Andy Lytle, 'Governors Clearing Decks,' *Toronto Daily Star*, 5 September 1940, 14. It is assumed that Calder was negotiating with the DNWS, although no record of such meeting could be found in the department's extant files (Library and Archives Canada [LAC], RG44). There does not seem to have been any formal policy outlining such exceptions, and since the DNWS also controlled the information agencies like the CBC, it may

have been inclined to support hockey given the popularity of hockey broadcasts, which were beginning to be used by government departments to communicate with the public. See *Imperial Oil Made a Promise* (promotional booklet, summer 1943), LAC, Canadian Broadcasting Corporation fonds (RG41), vol. 218, Canada/USSR Hockey file.

28 'Hockey Players Unaffected by War Situation,' *New York Herald Tribune*, 13 September 1940, Madison Square Garden, Scrapbook, #35 (Season 1940–41). Furthermore, a tentative deal was reached between the NHL and the Canadian Amateur Hockey Association (CAHA) allowing the NHL to sign amateurs upon payment for each called-up player of $500 to the CAHA, $250 to the International Ice Hockey Association, and another $250 if the player stayed with the team. If he did not, he was still eligible to be reinstated as an amateur.

29 Jim Hurley, 'Moguls Plan Ice Season in Spite of War Threat,' *Daily Mirror* (New York), 11 September 1940, 36. The Manager of the New York Americans, Red Dutton, claimed that the Canadian government 'made a concession to hockey players ... giving them permission to play until spring,' but that they could be called up at any time. Players were allowed to do 30-day training in summer and were exempted from drill three times a week 'as demanded of others by Canadian military authorities.' Harry Cross, 'Canadian Hockey Players in U.S. Win Ottawa's Permission to Finish Season,' *New York Herald Tribune*, 9 January 1941, 28.

30 J. Lewis Brown, 'Hockey Despite Hitler,' *National Home Monthly*, December 1940, 18.

31 For another example, see 'People Need Relaxation,' *Globe and Mail* (Toronto), 17 September 1942, 19.

32 For an overview of the financial challenges brought by the war, see Robert B. Bryce, *Canada and the Cost of World War II: The International Operations of Canada's Department of Finance 1939–1947* (Montreal: McGill-Queen's University Press, 2005), esp. chapters 2 and 4.

33 Copy of letter from Smythe to G.R. Cottrelle, 20 July 1940, Bank of Canada Archives (BCA), Foreign Exchange Control Board of Canada (FECB), vol. 143, Hockey Players file. Smythe wrote to Cottrelle in the latter's capacity as president of Maple Leaf Gardens, but may have wanted his advice on how to approach the government. Cottrelle had been appointed Oil Controller of Canada the previous month.

34 The FECB plan was announced 2 October 1940. Smythe had two reasons for wanting the plan: (1) to support Canada's foreign exchange and (2) to concentrate the administration of cross-border permissions in Calder's office at the NHL, which would help prevent the emergence of an 'outlaw'

league. See J. Andrew Ross, 'The Paradox of Conn Smythe: Hockey, Memory, and the Second World War,' *Sport History Review* 37, 1 (May 2006): 23–4. The administrator of the program, Alan Gibbons, later wrote that this type of arrangement was not typical of FECB policy, but was illustrative of the range of action that was taken by the board. See Alan O. Gibbons, 'Foreign Exchange Control in Canada, 1939–51,' *Canadian Journal of Economics and Political Science* 19, 1 (February 1953): 43; and Bryce, *Canada and the Cost of World War II*, ch. 5.

35 Dick Cullum, 'Americans Can Play Hockey,' *Esquire Magazine*, February 1941, 61.

36 Letter from Rodney Adamson, MP for West York, to Conn Smythe, 27 May 1941, AO, F223, vol. 45, Governmental Correspondence 1940–41 file.

37 Canada, House of Commons, *Debates*, 30 May 1941, 3325.

38 Ibid., 2 June 1941, 3382. Church's assertion that no nickels were made was fairly bold, considering the Gardens was a publicly traded corporation that paid regular dividends. He also made positive reference to the 'manager of the arena,' who was of course Conn Smythe.

39 Ibid., 3382–3. 'As usual' being a comment on the lagging government war effort, Church was suggesting that hockey players were willing soldiers, if only the government would draft them.

40 Frank Selke, acting managing director of Maple Leaf Gardens remembered that this 'Federal Inquiry of 1941' was prompted by those who 'thought professional hockey should not be played, and that the Gardens should be closed down, to save much-needed electricity for wartime purposes.' After he showed them how much the Gardens generated in dividends and for charity, he claimed they told him to 'go ahead as before.' Frank J. Selke with H. Gordon Green, *Behind the Cheering* (Toronto: McClelland and Stewart, 1962), 66.

41 Under section 4 of the NWS Regulations a man in an age class liable to be called had to obtain permission. The 21–24 age classes were the first liable for call-up. The boards were in major regional centres in Canada, generally corresponding to the Military Districts.

42 'US Puck Teams Lose Western Talent,' *Winnipeg Free Press*, 13 September 1941, 22. The players were Bill Reay, 23, and Eddie Bruneteau, 21, of Omaha Knights (Detroit Red Wings farm team); Sammy Lavitt, 19, Hugh Millar, 20, and Johnny Arondeus, 20, going for Red Wings tryouts; and Bob Whitelaw, 24, Red Wings defenceman. Reay, Bruneteau, and Whitelaw were members of the Royal Winnipeg Rifles, and said they were 'sitting tight' waiting to hear from Detroit.

43 'Army Comes First,' *Winnipeg Free Press*, 13 September 1941, 22.

44 Ibid.
45 Ibid.
46 Ralph Allen, 'Mostly Incidental,' *Globe and Mail* (Toronto), 13 September 1941, 14. Allen joined Conn Smythe's Sportsmen's Battery the day after the attack of 7 December 1941 on Pearl Harbor.
47 'Why Pick on Hockey Players,' *Evening Citizen* (Ottawa), 16 September 1941, 22.
48 'Saskatchewan to Bar,' *Winnipeg Free Press*, 15 September 1941, 10; 'Saskatchewan Divisional Board Firm Stand on Hockey Question,' *Evening Citizen* (Ottawa), 16 September 1941, 11. Gillanders said the players could not be 22 or 23 and subject to immediate call, must sign a declaration to keep the board informed of their address at all times, undertake to return at their own expense if called up, and indicate there is no evidence of intention or design to escape the provisions of the act. 'Certain Conditions,' *Winnipeg Free Press*, 15 September 1941, 10.
49 'Allen Kuntz and Gordie Bruce Seek Permission from Board,' *Evening Citizen* (Ottawa), 15 September 1941, 15.
50 'Famous Hockey Line of Boston May Be Ruined,' *Winnipeg Free Press*, 17 September 1941, 1, 8. The other member of the line was Bobby Bauer.
51 'Bulletin: Trainee Exemptions for Reserves Ended,' *London Free Press*, 18 September 1941, 1.
52 'No Further Applications,' *Winnipeg Free Press*, 16 September 1941, 1, 7. Col. Charles Lindbergh of flying fame and U.S. Senator Burton Wheeler of Montana were prominent and outspoken members of the isolationist America First Committee, which bitterly opposed U.S. intervention in the European war. See Wayne S. Cole, *America First: The Battle against Intervention, 1940–1941* (Madison: University of Wisconsin Press, 1953).
53 '"Should Be in Army" Rules Embury in Vetoing Passports,' *Winnipeg Free Press*, 20 September 1941, 25.
54 Ralph Allen, 'Mostly Incidental,' *Globe and Mail* (Toronto), 19 September 1941, 14.
55 'Recruiting Problems,' *Winnipeg Free Press*, 22 September 1941, 13.
56 Ibid.
57 Charles Mayer, 'Frais sur la glace,' *Le Petit Journal* (Montreal), 28 September 1941, 48.
58 'Hockey Moguls Ready for Worst,' *Evening Citizen* (Ottawa), 19 September 1941, 14.
59 'Seek Lifting Passport Ban on Hockeyists,' *Winnipeg Free Press*, 7 October 1941, 1. Calder 'seemed surprised' that his whereabouts were known, so he could not have been happy when his picture appeared on the front

page of the *Free Press* coming out of the office of a local barrister. The presence of Kilpatrick and Dutton was no coincidence. It was the first appearance Kilpatrick had ever made to a Rangers training camp in eight years, and Dutton had come in from the Americans' training camp in Port Arthur, Ontario (present-day Thunder Bay).

60 Ibid.

61 'Hockey Players in Wartime,' *Winnipeg Free Press*, 16 October 1941, 13.

62 Ibid. $21 was the amount paid to draftees under the Selective Training and Service Act of 1940, which had instituted the first peacetime draft in U.S. history.

63 'N.H.L. President Converses with Head of Manitoba Board,' *Winnipeg Free Press*, 16 October 1941, 12; 'Calder n'obtient rien au Manitoba,' *La Presse* (Montreal), 17 October 1941, 31. The word *La Presse* used was 'inutile.' Dutton met with the Saskatchewan board two days later, to no result. 'Saskatchewan War Services Board Maintains Stand,' *Winnipeg Free Press*, 18 October 1941, 23.

64 The *Tribune* article was reprinted in the *New York Times*: 'Passport Ban Stands for Hockey Players,' 17 October 1941, 30.

65 H.H. Roxborough, 'Is This a Time for Pro Sport?' *Maclean's Magazine*, 1 January 1942, 8. Other arrangements were also made between teams – Bruins prospect Terry Reardon was loaned to the Canadiens because of his passport difficulties. See Charles L. Coleman, *The Trail of the Stanley Cup*, vol. 2 ([Montreal]: National Hockey League, 1969), 426. The different regional treatments of the players is notable, but without detailed information on the rate of deferments or permissions to travel, it is hard to do more than speculate about the relative leniency of the Ontario boards as compared with those in the West. Winnipeg, Vancouver, and Regina had given none or only one passport permission, while Toronto, Kingston, and Montreal had given 22, 6, and 5, but on the other hand Edmonton had given 13 and Quebec City only 1. Whether these represent regional differences, the whims of individual boards, or the geographical concentration/dispersion of professional hockey players is difficult to determine rigorously without knowledge of how many applied and were refused. Stevenson contends that a major flaw in the system was the tendency for a mobilization board taking on the personality of its chairman, and he singles out Justices Manson of Vancouver and Embury of Regina for specific criticism. See Stevenson, *Canada's Greatest Wartime Muddle*, 25–6.

66 Canada, House of Commons, *Debates*, 11 November 1941, 4281. The leader of the opposition, Richard Hanson, had brought up the issue the week before. Ibid., 4 November 1941, 4095.

67 Ibid., 11 November 1941, 4282.

68 Ibid., 4283.

69 The committee comprised Thorson, Minister of Justice Louis St-Laurent, and Minister of National Revenue Colin Gibson. Its secretary was Alex Skelton. C.P. Stacey, *Arms, Men and Governments: The War Policies of Canada, 1939–1945* (Ottawa: Queen's Printer, 1970), 404; Granatstein and Hitsman, *Broken Promises*, 187.

70 Stacey, *Arms, Men and Governments*, 404; Granatstein and Hitsman, *Broken Promises*, 189.

71 Stevenson, *Canada's Greatest Wartime Muddle*, 20; Granatstein and Hitsman, *Broken Promises*, 189, 190. Non-essential occupations included clerk, taxi driver, typist, cashier, jewellery-maker, toymaker, soap-makers, and also those employed in entertainment-related industries and sporting goods.

72 Granatstein and Hitsman, *Broken Promises*, 190.

73 Stacey, *Arms, Men and Governments*, 399–402.

74 The *Journal* article was cited in 'Canada to Ban Permits for Hockey, Paper Says,' *New York Herald Tribune*, 21 April 1942, 30.

75 Ibid.

76 'Adams, of Wings, Threatens to Buck Any Plan to Drop Hockey during War,' *New York Herald Tribune*, 15 May 1942, 23.

77 Coleman, *The Trail of the Stanley Cup*, 2: 449.

78 That summer saw the enlistment, among others, of Alex Shibicky, Bill Juzda, Neil Colville, and Mac Colville of the Rangers; Joe Cooper of the Hawks; Nick Metz, Wally Stanowski, and Pete Langelle of the Leafs (recall the role of the latter two in the 1941 passport controversy); and Eddie Wiseman of the Bruins. In January 1942 Boston's 'Kraut Line' of Milt Schmidt, Woody Dumart, and Bobby Bauer were called up and joined the Ottawa RCAF unit.

79 Little was an executive of Anglo-Canadian Pulp and Paper Mills Ltd who had been serving as head of the Wartime Bureau of Technical Personnel. Stacey, *Arms, Men and Governments*, 404–5.

80 'Wartime Fate of Pro Hockey Hangs on Case by President,' *Evening Citizen* (Ottawa), 8 August 1942, 11.

81 Ibid. Little wanted a list of Canadians playing in the league, with their age, marital status, and eligibility for call-up.

82 'NHL Has Good Chance to Survive Big Crisis,' *Globe and Mail* (Toronto), 10 August 1942, 16; 'Wartime Fate of Pro Hockey Hangs.'

83 Granatstein and Hitsman, *Broken Promises*, 193. The authors emphasize that the new NSS regulations implied 'control over the lives of Canadians to an unheard-of degree,' but Stevenson shows how this control never

came close to being achieved due to inefficiency and a lack of administrative coordination. See Stevenson, *Canada's Greatest Wartime Muddle*, 3–4.

84 Letter from Frank Calder to Elliott Little, 7 August 1942, LAC, External Affairs fonds (RG25), vol. 3041, file no. 4198-A-40 (Status of Professional Hockey Players under United States and Canadian Selective Service Regulations). Calder wrote that the letter was 'following my conversation of Tuesday, the 4th.' If this is the case, then there is every reason to believe this memo contains the substance for Calder's arguments at the 6 August meeting. External Affairs was regularly copied on correspondence relating to its departmental purview, although its foreign missions were not always in the loop, as can be seen in the MacNamara policy misstep of the fall of 1943. Although Mackenzie King's personal opinions on hockey are not in evidence, except with reference to the Conn Smythe controversy in 1944–5, it should be noted that King also acted as Secretary of State for External Affairs for the entire period of the war, working closely with Undersecretary O.D. Skelton and, from January 1941, with his successor, Norman Robertson.

85 Letter from Frank Calder to Elliott Little, 17 August 1942, ibid.

86 Ibid.

87 Ibid.

88 The International-American Hockey League had changed its name to the American Hockey League for the 1940–1 season.

89 Sawyer's exact connections to the league are not apparent; he may have been hired for this one lobbying effort. Frank Selke wrote that AHL owners Lou Jacobs of Buffalo, Arthur Wirtz of Chicago, and AHL president Maurice Podoloff prevailed upon Sawyer, 'a top-ranking United States lawyer and statesman, to visit Ottawa on behalf of the American clubs which depended on Canadian boys.' Selke, *Behind the Cheering*, 66.

90 Letter from Keenleyside to Moffat, 21 August 1942, LAC, RG25, vol. 3041, file no. 4198-A-40. Keenleyside was also the Canadian secretary of the Permanent Joint Board of Defence.

91 Ibid.

92 It is not clear why Calder did not mention passports, but Sawyer did. Perhaps Calder recognized that only the regional NSS board chairmen were authorized to approve passport applications, but with NSS-approved contracts in hand, the players would have an easier time getting permission. Sawyer may have believed that Little had passport permission in his bailiwick, so he framed the issue in those terms.

93 Letter from Charles Sawyer to Elliott Little, 17 August 1942, LAC, RG25, vol. 3041, file no. 4198-A-40. This was significant given that the AHL was composed of only American clubs. The AHL had played an All-Star game

in February 1942 for the American and Canadian Red Crosses, but it was poorly attended and raised less than $5000. See Chuck Miller, 'Patriotic Duty: The 1941–42 AHL All-Star Game,' at http://members.aol.com/boardwalk7/4142ahl.html (accessed 22 October 2003). Despite Sawyer's promise the game was not played again until 1955.

94 Letter from L.E. Westman, for Director of NSS, to Keenleyside, 21 August 1942, LAC, RG25, vol. 3041, file no. 4198-A-40.

95 Letter from Keenleyside to Moffat, ibid.

96 Ibid.

97 'Ottawa and Washington Flash Green Light to Hockey,' *Toronto Daily Star*, 15 September 1942, 16. A draft in the External Affairs file notes, 'It is my understanding that this short statement is the one desired by Mr. Sawyer and the Canadian authorities.' The pronoun 'my' likely refers to Moffat, although the context is not clear. LAC, RG25, vol. 3041, file no. 4198-A-40. For background on McNutt and the formation of the WMC, see George Q. Flynn, *The Mess in Washington: Manpower Mobilization in World War II* (Westport, CT: Greenwood Press, 1979), 9–20.

98 Press release from National Office, National Selective Service, Ottawa, 22 October 1942, LAC, RG25, vol. 3041, file no. 4198-A-40. The procedure to follow to obtain such a permit was contained in P.C. 9011 (1 October 1942), an order-in-council that created the Labour Exit Permit (LEP). No person over the age of 16 was permitted to leave to take or seek employment outside of Canada without an LEP (in addition to their passport). However, exemptions were provided for several persons, including 'members of dramatic, artistic, athletic, or spectacular organizations departing from Canada temporarily for the purpose of giving public performances or exhibitions of an entertaining or instructive character.' P.C. 9011 – 'Order-in-Council establishing the Labour Exit Permit Order,' 1 October 1942, LAC, Department of Labour (RG27), vol. 153, file no. 611.19-2 (NSS – General Correspondence 1942–43). This effectively confirmed that players on Canadian teams did not need an LEP to cross the border to play on road trips, but that a permit was required for those playing on American teams who needed to stay longer in the United States. (Bear in mind that Canadian players still needed Special Border Permits from the FECB in order to carry currency across the border.) The regional board chairmen would still have the say on whether a player was given permission to cross the border, although it was expected that when National Selective Service took over mobilization from the DNWS a uniform policy would probably be laid down 'in line with the green-light decision for professional sport.' 'People Need Relaxation,' *Globe and Mail* (Toronto), 17 September 1942, 19.

99 'Ottawa and Washington Flash Green Light to Hockey'; 'League Members
    Cheered' and 'Gorman, Selke Pleased,' *New York Times*, 16 September
    1942, 32.
100 Mainly due to player shortages, in the next two seasons the AHL was
    reduced from ten to six clubs.
101 Coleman, *The Trail of the Stanley Cup*, 2: 451.
102 Ibid.
103 See Stevenson, *Canada's Greatest Wartime Muddle*, 6–10; Stacey, *Arms, Men
    and Governments*, 407–9; and Granatstein and Hitsman, *Broken Promises*,
    193.
104 Stevenson calls him the 'living embodiment of the concept of gradualness
    espoused by the King government.' MacNamara was to continue as NSS
    director until the end of the war, and he turned out to be more politically
    astute than Little, managing a mobilization effort that, if not the most
    efficient, effective, or military-friendly, succeeded in treading the fine
    line between sacrifice and standard of living that the politicians felt they
    could sustain. Stevenson, *Canada's Greatest Wartime Muddle*, 10. Stacey
    writes that 'the departure of Little may be considered a victory for those
    in favour of gradualness over those who favoured more drastic policies;
    also, perhaps, for the cautious civil servant over the impatient wartime re-
    cruit from industry; and also, in effect, for the civilian point of view over
    the military.' But 'as time passed, events moved in the direction desired
    by [Minister of National Defence J.L.] Ralston, Little and the soldiers.'
    Stacey, *Arms, Men and Governments*, 408–9. On the political background of
    Mackenzie King's war policies, see Granatstein, *Canada's War*.
105 Memorandum from MacNamara to C.F. Needham, Associate Director
    [Civilian], 13 March 1943, LAC, RG27, vol. 153, file no. 611.19-4 (National
    Selective Service – Memoranda 1942–45). The full phrase MacNamara
    used was the 'unfortunate publicity last fall,' but it is not clear what
    events of this nature in the fall of 1942 he is referring to. He may be refer-
    ring to the fall of 1941. At any rate, his concern with adverse publicity is
    the important point.
106 Ibid.
107 Ibid.
108 Letter from NSS Associate Director (Civilian) C.F. Needham to Keenley-
    side, 8 April 1943, LAC, RG25, vol. 3041, file no. 4198-A-40.
109 Dave Egan, 'Hard to Jubilate over Bruin Victory,' *Boston Daily Record*, 1
    April 1943, a retyped article attached to a letter [from Lester B. Pearson] to
    N.A. Robertson, 14 April 1943 (LAC, RG25, vol. 3041, file no. 4198-A-40).
    N.B. Egan was the same writer cited by the *Winnipeg Free Press* during the

passport crisis. The reappearance of his opinion leads one to ask whether he was at all representative of either prevailing American or Boston opinion. Although a complete survey is beyond the scope of this study, Egan seems to have been one of the more extreme critics. Many writers saw the issue of Canadian manpower as a Canadian issue, and were more concerned with the service of baseball players, who were Americans. Furthermore, Canadian writers themselves were very critical, and it is probably wrong to suggest that Americans writers were *more* apt to criticize. When they did, however, Canadians seemed to have taken notice.

110 Letter [from Pearson] to Robertson, 14 April 1943, LAC, RG25, vol. 3041, file no. 4198-A-40.
111 Letter from Keenleyside to Needham, 17 April 1943, ibid.
112 Ibid.
113 Ibid. The proposed meeting does not seem to have occurred, no doubt a casualty of the approaching summer.
114 After Calder collapsed at a board of governors meeting, day-to-day functions of the league were given to Mervyn Dutton, the former New York Americans manager, who still sat on the board as a governor. An executive committee of Lester Patrick of the Rangers and Col. MacBrien of the Maple Leafs provided further advice and guidance. In August the NHL also retained a local Ottawa lawyer, J.P. Ebbs, to act as their liaison with the NSS and to handle passport and border permits. Andy Lytle, 'Speaking on Sports,' *Toronto Daily Star*, 18 August 1943, 12.
115 'Hockey Seeks Standing for War Manpower,' *Christian Science Monitor* (Boston), 17 August 1943, 23; 'Hockey Group Told of Player Status,' *New York Times*, 17 August 1943, 23. McNamara told the NHL men that there was a difference of opinion among board chairmen, but that he had overruled them. Andy Lytle, 'Speaking on Sports,' *Toronto Daily Star*, 18 August 1943, 12.
116 'Hockey Group Told of Player Status,' *New York Times*, 17 August 1943, 23.
117 Letter from McNutt to MacNamara, 25 August [1943], LAC, RG25, vol. 3041, file no. 4198-A-40. Cited in Teletype EX-4108 sent by B.M. Bridge of External [Affairs] Ottawa to Canadian Minister in Washington, 20 October 1943, authored by 'NR,' presumably Norman Robertson.
118 National Selective Service Circular Memorandum Number 283, 16 September 1943, LAC, RG25, vol. 3041, file no. 4198-A-40. The memorandum was clarified by NSS Memorandum 283-1, issued 2 October 1943. A and B ratings designated 'highly essential' and 'essential' workers, respectively, while C & D referred to 'less essential' and 'non-essential' workers. See Stevenson, *Canada's Greatest Wartime Muddle*, 32 (table 1).

119 Teletype message WA-5236 from Canadian Minister [in Washington] to Secretary of State (External Affairs), 21 October 1943, LAC, RG25, vol. 3041, file no. 4198-A-40.

120 Letter from Robertson to Director of NSS [MacNamara], 25 October 1943, LAC, RG27, vol. 134, file no. 601.3-7. Robertson also noted that 'in view of the unquestionably lower physical standards of the United States Army, rejection by the Canadian Army will be no guarantee that an individual will also be unacceptable to the American Forces.'

121 Ibid.

122 Ibid.

123 Letter from MacNamara to McNutt, 30 October 1943, LAC, RG27, vol. 134, file no. 601.3-7.

124 Telegram from MacNamara to McNutt, 11 November 1943, ibid.

125 Telegram from McNutt to MacNamara, 12 November 1943, ibid.

126 Ibid., 15 November 1943. MacNamara specified four players in his telegram (Erhardt [sic] Heller of the Rangers and Douglas Bentley, George Allen and William Thoms of Chicago), but seemed to suggest there were (or might be) others ('We have no available numbers of local draft boards'). Since the hockey season was only weeks old, it is unclear why the call-up notices were coming out so early. It is possible these four players had entered the United States in the late summer.

127 Telegram from McNutt to MacNamara, 19 November 1943, LAC, RG27, vol. 134, file no. 601.3-7.

128 Letter from MacNamara to Robertson, 8 December 1943, LAC, RG25, vol. 3041, file no. 4198-A-40.

129 Ibid.

130 Letter from Robertson to MacNamara, 10 December 1943, LAC, RG27, vol. 134, file no. 601.3-7.

131 Ibid.

132 Ibid.

133 Paul Koistinen argues that even before the US Selective Service System (SSS) had been put under WMC control in December of 1942, it was a 'tightly structured bureaucratic system that had been operating for two years before WMC was fully under way [and was] beyond the commission's reach.' McNutt eliminated exemptions for men with dependents but many boards refused to go along with these and in the end Congress established the SSS as an autonomous agency. It was 'McNutt's determination to make selective service policies more rational and consistent [that] led to SSS breaking free of WMC control.' Paul A. Koistinen, *Arsenal of World War II: The Political Economy of American Warfare, 1940–1945* (Law-

rence: University Press of Kansas, 2004), 377. George Flynn's interpretation of McNutt's philosophy is quite different. He argues that McNutt's approach was 'Jeffersonian' in its emphasis on both local solutions and voluntarism, and that it was these principles that directed his delegation of power to the local and regional levels. Flynn, *The Mess in Washington*, 11–12. This difference in interpretation will not be evaluated here, but it is noteworthy that the US struggle for regimentation, centralization, and uniformity of policy and administration had a parallel in the Canadian mobilization experience. Both phenomena resist an interpretation of the war as a linear process of centralization and bureaucratization.

134 Very few records of the regional offices are still extant. Much of the draft board information is only accessible through newspaper reports.

135 However, Hextall was refused permission to enter the United States for the following season. 'Heller, Hextall Called in Draft,' *Daily News* (New York), 1 February 1944, 37.

136 'Speaking on Sports,' *Toronto Daily Star*, 20 October 1943, 14.

137 'Are Canadian Athletes Given Special Deal?' *Calgary Herald*, 20 October 1943, 4; Dink Carroll, 'Playing the Field,' *The Gazette* (Montreal), 28 October 1943, 16. For other commentary, see Panunto, 'For Club or Country?' 143–4.

138 Panunto, 'For Club or Country?' 142.

139 The CAHA Wartime Regulations allowed players engaged in military service to switch clubs during the season if moved by military authorities, and for military teams to be entered into the Allan Cup playdowns. *1940 Official Hockey Rules*, LAC, Canadian Amateur Hockey Association fonds (MG28 I151), vol. 80, 8–9. The Allan Cup was symbolic of the Canadian amateur hockey championship, having been donated in 1908 after it became clear amateurs could no longer succeed against professional teams in Stanley Cup competition.

140 The practice had also appeared in boxing. Dink Carroll, 'Playing the Field,' *The Gazette* (Montreal), 28 October 1943, 16.

141 Telegram from Adjutant General to Mailing List 'A' 'B' Ranks 7775, 8 January 1944, LAC, James L. Ralston fonds (MG27 III B11), vol. 79, Hockey, Ice – Participation of Army Personnel in Organized Ice Hockey, January 1944 file.

142 Annual Army Estimates, 1944–45: Subject: Participation of Army Personnel in Organized Ice Hockey, date-stamped 29 January 1944, LAC, MG27 III B11, vol. 79, Hockey, Ice – Participation of Army Personnel in Organized Ice Hockey, January 1944 file.

143 Ibid.

144 As the man who started the firestorm, Artillery Gunner Broda was duly sent overseas, where he spent the rest of the war in the European theatre in uniform. He was injured in Holland while fighting off pucks as a member of a Canadian Army all-star hockey team.

145 Coleman, *The Trail of the Stanley Cup*, 2: 481. Ross attacked the other clubs for lack of charity in a blistering letter to Selke. Letter from Ross to Selke, 20 January 1943, Boston Public Library Special Collections, Harold Kaese Papers, vol. 1. Other team managers with sons and daughters in the service included Conn Smythe, Mervyn Dutton, Frank Calder, Lester Patrick, James Norris of Detroit, Charles Adams of Boston, and T.P. Gorman of the Canadiens. J.R. Kilpatrick and Smythe were enlisted themselves and, along with Dutton and Frederic McLaughlin of Chicago, were also veterans of the First World War.

146 Letter from Ross to Selke, 20 January 1943.

147 'All Hawks' Profits Will Go to Charity,' *New York Times*, 22 March 1942, S1. It is not known whether this plan was carried out, but Art Ross expressed his doubts to Selke. Letter from Ross to Selke, 20 January 1943.

148 Memorandum from George G. Greene, Private Secretary to Minister of Labour Humphrey Mitchell, to MacNamara, 31 May 1944, LAC, RG27, vol. 134, file no. 601.3-7. Greene had received the text of the resolution from the Montreal club.

149 Ibid.

150 The Canadiens actually solicited the intervention of Minister of Labour Humphrey Mitchell in Ottawa, perhaps to pressure the NHL to rescind the resolution. The NSS chief enforcement officer, T.R. Walsh, opined that given the Canadiens' strong performance on the ice, he did not think they needed help to win their battles. Memorandum from Walsh to MacNamara, 6 June 1944, LAC, RG27, vol. 134, file no. 601.3-7.

151 *New York Times*, 10 September 1944, S1.

152 Pete Horeck and Johnny Harms were the rejects mentioned. '"War Comes First," Sports Officials Agree,' *Chicago Tribune*, 24 December 1944, A1–A2.

153 'Watson Joins Rangers after Army Rejection,' *New York Herald Tribune*, 7 November 1944.

154 On 12 September, the NSS issued an Interpretive Letter to the boards which stated that in a meeting in Washington between the NSS representative, the Canadian Military attaché, and a US Selective Service representative, 'it was agreed that applications to the American authorities for certificates of non-residence in the case of Canadians proceeding, or who have proceeded, to the United States, be reduced to a minimum.'

The chairmen of mobilization boards could still submit particulars to the NSS to get the US authorities to issue a certificate of non-residence if they deemed it necessary. NSS Interpretive Letter no. 12, September 1944 – Revised Draft, LAC, RG27, vol. 128, file no. 601.3-1-14 (Department of National War Services – Mobilization Division – Interpretive Letters Regarding to Mobilization Act 1943–44).

155 Letter from Manson to MacNamara, 23 September 1944, LAC, RG27, vol. 134, file no. 601.3-7.

156 Ibid.

157 Ibid.

158 Copy of letter from MacNamara to Manson, 28 September 1944, ibid.

159 Ibid.

160 Although it seemed that the most recalcitrant board chairmen were from the western Canadian boards, lest there be any perception that there was an East-West division of opinion, it should be noted that many of the same hesitations were expressed by the chairman of the Toronto board. The Maritime boards had fewer such cases to consider, and no conflicts are evident, but the lack of any correspondence on these issues from the Quebec boards, where one might expect their frequent appearance, is interesting. The recruitment system in Quebec, however, was a special case, fraught with general administrative problems. For a discussion of the difficulties of the Montreal board, which included fraud and misman-agement, see Stevenson, *Canada's Greatest Wartime Muddle*, 22–4.

161 NSS Circular no. 283-3, 18 January 1945, LAC, RG27, vol. 134, file no. 601.3-7.

162 Billy Reay of the Detroit Red Wings was one of them and the ruling stopped the former sailor from joining the Red Wings in Detroit. 'Patrick Sees No Hockey for 1946,' *New York Journal-American*, 21 January 1945. Another affected was Neil Colville, who had not served overseas and was thus prevented from entering the United States; he did, however, play four Canadian games for the Rangers. 'Rangers get Colville for Canadian Games,' *Daily Mirror* (New York), 27 January 1945, 17.

163 Richard Goldstein, *Spartan Seasons: How Baseball Survived the Second World War* (New York: Macmillan, 1980), 199.

164 Ibid., 200. 4-F was the lowest US military medical designation and ex-empted a man from the draft.

165 The American debate revolved around baseball and football, but all sports were likely to be affected.

166 Ibid., 201–2. Growing Allied success in the spring of 1945 eased the pres-sure and the 'work or fight' legislation was not passed. However, in early

1945 a few baseball players previously exempted as 4-F were suddenly found fit and drafted, simply because they were professional athletes.

167 Memorandum from T.R. Walsh to MacNamara, 19 January 1945, LAC, RG27, vol. 134, file no. 601.3-7.

168 Ibid.

169 Memorandum from Walsh to L. Prefontaine & B.G. Sullivan, Regional Superintendents, Montreal & Toronto, 24 January 1945, ibid.

170 Panunto, 'For Club or Country?' 161–7.

171 Smythe demanded that the Canadian government permit 150 men to play hockey next season, 'to pursue their business the same as everybody else.' 'Smythe Demands Fair Hockey Deal,' *New York Times*, 6 February 1945. Smythe's comments followed his even more incendiary criticism of government overseas reinforcement policy in the fall of 1944, which helped ignite the second conscription crisis. See 'Untrained Troops Hazard at Front, Smythe Complains,' *Globe and Mail* (Toronto), 19 September 1944, 1; Ross, 'The Paradox of Conn Smythe,' 26, 34n50; Stacey, *Arms, Men and Governments*, 440–1; and Hunter, *War Games*, 136ff.

4 Organizing Hockey for Women: The Ladies Ontario Hockey Association and the Fight for Legitimacy, 1922–1940

CARLY ADAMS

Understanding the Canadian Ice Hockey–Identity Relationship

Canadians are inundated with images and representations of hockey.[1] Reinforced by daily visual reminders, such as the sentimental scene on our five-dollar bill, ice hockey, and the mythology surrounding the sport, is deeply intertwined with Canada's national identity and the concept of 'Canadianness.' Drawing on the work of Benedict Anderson, Michael Robidoux argues that 'the task of defining a national identity is a creative process that requires constructing a shared history and mythology(ies) that best suit the identity *imagined* by those few responsible for responding to this task.'[2] Through an ongoing process of negotiating what it means to be Canadian, ice hockey has become an integral element of the national identity. In 1981 Peter Gzowski explained the Canadian obsession with hockey by simply defining it as the 'game of our lives.'[3] Similarly, Richard Gruneau and David Whitson argue that hockey is a part of our collective memory; it is a story we tell ourselves and others about what it means to be Canadian.[4]

However, it is the men's game and the worship of male hockey heroes that embodies the relationship between hockey and Canadian identity. Male hockey stars of the professional North American game such as Maurice Richard, Gordie Howe, and Wayne Gretzky were exemplars of particular brands of masculinity, ones that boys were supposed to emulate.[5] This relationship between Canadian identity and men's hockey positions the sport as the game of *their* lives, a game of boys and men, a timeless tradition that crosses generational boundaries to bond fathers and sons.[6] Historically, the attempts of girls and women to enter this 'sacred' territory have been viewed with derision. Through a complex process of control and compromise, women's hockey was effectively stigmatized as an inferior form of the 'real' game. What does this suggest then about hockey and its relationship to Canada's national identity? Is hockey really a part of the collective memory of *all* Canadians? Were women historically included as legitimate participants in Canada's national sport and, by extension, claims to self-identification as Canadians?

This chapter examines the early development of organized hockey for women in Ontario and, more specifically, the attempt of a specific group, the women of the Ladies Ontario Hockey Association (LOHA), to organize hockey in Ontario for working women. The LOHA between 1922 and 1940, from its formation to its dissolution into the Ontario branch of the Women's Amateur Athletic Federation (WAAF), sought to administer and control the women's game in Ontario while also offering an opportunity for women to be officially recognized as participants of Canada's revered national game. This study, focusing on women's hockey in Ontario during the interwar years, provides a historical outline of the LOHA, the decision-making leaders, the changes that took place over time, the dominant issues that faced the organization, and the toils of the LOHA in its efforts to maintain control over women's hockey in the province. The LOHA was the first governing body for women's hockey at the community level in Ontario, and as such it provided unprecedented opportunities for women to compete in organized leagues and championships. However, as a governing body, the LOHA faced many challenges and difficult decisions throughout its nineteen-year existence, including: maintaining control over women's hockey with men in advisory positions; the decision to pattern and align itself with the male hockey community in an effort to achieve recognition; negotiating a space for women's hockey through alliances with other sport governing bodies while simultaneously maintaining a degree of independence and control; attempting to circumvent the negative impact of the ten-year domination of one team on much needed membership numbers; and maintaining a positive reputation for women's hockey in light of socially prescribed notions of 'appropriate' femininity. The unequivocal acceptance of hockey as the rightful place of boys and men and the mythologies built around the men's game helped to sustain the gender polarities in hockey; as a result, while successfully offering women an organized hockey structure in Ontario throughout the 1920s and 1930s, the LOHA was unable to position women's hockey in the province as a legitimate hockey community.

The Complexities of Historical Hockey Research

Canadian women have been donning their skates and gliding across the ice in pursuit of the hockey experience since the late 1880s. However, like other facets of women's sport, many aspects of the history of women's hockey remain uncelebrated and even unknown. In contrast, men's hockey has been the focus of countless fictional, popular history, and scholarly works that have educated Canadians to appreciate not only the importance of playing the game but also the associated historical meanings intertwined with the professional, amateur, and recreational experiences. National bestsellers such as Ken Dryden and Roy MacGregor's *Home Game* combined with the engrained national mythology of the sport seemingly edify Canadian boys and men as well as girls and women about the importance of our national pastime. In contrast, our understanding of the history of women's hockey in Canada is based solely on a small number of commercial and academic publications that have had limited exposure across Canada. Brian McFarlane's *Proud Past, Bright Future: 100 Years of Canadian Women's Hockey*, published in 1994, attempted to rectify the shortcomings of ice hockey literature.[7] Although not a scholar per se, McFarlane was the first author to document women's participation in the national game. His book, coupled with the growth in women's international hockey during the 1990s, stimulated interest in the history of women's ice hockey, and soon other authors, such as Joanna Avery, Julie Stevens, Elizabeth Etue, and Megan Williams, dedicated themselves to writing histories of the women's game.[8] These publications have provided the foundation for understanding women's roles in Canada's national pastime; but the relationships between the male and female hockey communities and the impact of female-driven organizations need to be further explored.

In Search of Control

Historically, hockey has been a male preserve – the rightful place of boys and men.[9] The sport was characterized by rough, aggressive physicality, a site where men and boys learned the celebrated values of manhood. In the late nineteenth century, with the increasing popularity of the game, definitions of 'appropriate' femininity left little room for women to engage in competitive and aggressive sport. Before the First World War, only small numbers of women engaged in informal hockey games as a form of physical activity. The war brought vast changes in all areas of women's lives, including their sport participation. Women who flooded the cities seeking employment sought activities, such as sport, to fill their spare time. Ann Hall suggests that while women's sport was well established in colleges and universities before the First World War, there were few opportunities for the majority of women who could not afford higher education.[10] By the 1920s, working women sought to expand their sporting opportunities through a grass-roots movement of women's sport clubs.[11]

Working women were seeking increased control over the administration and organizational aspects of the community sports they played, including hockey.[12] Bruce Kidd suggests that by the 1920s 'most sportswomen felt they should administer their own activity as much as possible.'[13] As an example, the life of sportswoman and journalist Alexandrine Gibb embodies this philosophy of 'girls sports run by girls.'[14] Her actions and public expressions as manager of various teams and as a columnist for the *Toronto Daily Star* clearly articulated her belief that women should control their own sporting activities, and that men, although needed as advisers, should stay in the background.[15] For example, in 1937 there was a dispute within the Ontario Women's Softball Association: a majority of women were elected to its executive and the male leaders thought more men should have held positions. In response to the election results, the men threatened to walk out and leave the women on their own without any advice or support. Gibb's reaction to this incident reinforced the importance of men as advisers and encouraged the female softball leaders to find a way to keep the men involved: 'Men are very useful, they can help with advice and many men have done just that. Men have had years and years of experience in sport organization and girls have only been in the game for the past ten years. So we have lots to learn, girls. But we want a chance to learn it. If we look after our own affairs we too will gain experience and be experts ... Keep the men with you if you can, but impress on the men the importance of your learning how these things should be done.'[16] A decade earlier, in 1927, while speaking at an Ontario Hockey Association (OHA) annual meeting, Bobbie Rosenfeld supported the importance of the involvement of men, stating, 'I feel that the L.O.H.A. needs the benefit of the brains and brawn of the strong men I see present this morning to keep it off the rocks.'[17] Indeed, conventional thought assumed that male advisers were necessary to educate and support women in their quest to organize and control their own sport practices. Men had the valuable experience that female leaders wanted to gain. In mid-

December of 1922, the Toronto-based newspapers the *Globe* and the *Toronto Daily Star* reported the formation of a new governing body for the sport of ice hockey: the Ladies Ontario Hockey Association. Similar to other sports associations of that decade such as the Ontario Women's Softball Association, the LOHA followed a similar pattern with the end goal of creating an organization run completely by women, with men holding advisory positions.

The Ladies Ontario Hockey Association

The LOHA was formed on 16 December 1922 at the Temple Building on the corner of Richmond and Bay Streets in Toronto.[18] At the inaugural meeting, women's hockey was, for the first time in the province, set on an organized path by women themselves.[19] Male administrators from the Toronto Hockey League (THL) played a significant role in orchestrating this initial meeting and launching the new governing body. Newspapers reported that Frank McEwen, president of the THL, presided over the meeting with Frank Smith acting as secretary. The THL was formed in 1911 to organize amateur hockey for boys and men in the city of Toronto.[20] By the 1920s it also offered city leagues for girls and women.[21] At the initial LOHA meeting in 1922, the majority of club representatives present were from the Toronto area. The *Globe* reported that twenty-five women's teams from the THL were present and another twelve expressed their support for the organization through letters.[22] Members from clubs in London and St Thomas were also in attendance, and a letter was sent from the Ottawa Alerts hockey club expressing its interest in joining the new organization. While the THL offered competitive opportunities for women under the umbrella of the men's organization, the LOHA was a separate province-wide governing body solely for women's hockey. The objectives of the initial meeting of the LOHA were (1) to elect officers who would oversee the 1922–3 competition year, (2) to formalize the playing rules and the governing constitution, and (3) to create subcommittees that would be responsible for organizing the leagues and dealing with the operational aspects of the new hockey club.

At the meeting on 16 December 1922, the issue of whether all the offices should be held by women or a combination of women and men was discussed in great detail. While the women at the meeting wanted an executive composed completely of women, they were wary of doing this in their first year of existence. The *Globe* reported that 'the lady delegates decided that while they would prefer to have all the offices occupied by ladies, it would be best to have some of them filled by men for the first year or so. The male members of the executive were finally selected as Hon. President, President, Secretary, and two members of the committee, while the ladies will occupy the other five offices.'[23] The 1922–3 officers were: honorary president, John DeGruchy, Toronto;[24] president, Frank Best, Welland; first vice-president, Mae Maxwell, St Thomas; second vice-president, Winnie Simpson, Thornhill; third vice-president, Frank Smith, Toronto; secretary, Mr C.W. MacQueen, *Empire and Mail*, Toronto; and treasurer, Janet Allen, Toronto. Kathleen Milne, London, Miss E. Harrison of Dunnville, Alan Campbell of Bowmanville, and Mr W.M. Davis of Chesley were members-at-large. Each officer was elected for a one-year term. Although the THL was a key organizational force in establishing the new association, it had only one representative, Frank Smith, on the executive and only four of the ten officers were from Toronto. The male members of the association played a considerable organizational role, providing guidance and support, under the guise of preparing the female members to take control the following year.[25]

A subcommittee, comprised of the president and second and third vice-presidents, was entrusted with the practical task of organizing the member teams into functional leagues. Given the large geographical distance between some of the teams such as Ottawa in the east and London in the west, the goal of the group was to create smaller leagues, as compact as possible, to reduce travelling expenses.[26] A convener was appointed for each league to oversee the operations and to deal with any problems, controversies, or issues that occurred throughout season play. In an effort to decentralize the organization, the conveners were given the power to represent the LOHA on all matters. When the 23 December entry cut-off date arrived, there were eighteen teams fully paid and entered in the 1922–3 season of the LOHA.[27] The dues for the 1922–3 year were set at eleven dollars per team, which included a six-dollar annual fee and a five-dollar one-time membership fee.[28]

The 1922–3 season was considered to be a trial period for the organization. In the years that followed, many changes were made to both the administrative structure and the governing constitution of the LOHA to adapt it to the nature of the women's game. At each annual meeting new officers were elected by a vote, with all present parties casting a ballot. At the second annual meeting, in December 1923, the election resulted in a split more in favour of female leaders. Men held only

Table 1
Presidents of the LOHA

1922–3	Frank Best
1923–27	Janet Allen
1927–34	Hazel Ruttier
1934–39	Bobbie Rosenfeld
1939–40	Roxy Atkins

* Sources: *Toronto Daily Star*,
1922–40 and *Globe*, 1922–40

three positions, as the honorary president, first vice-president, and secretary.[29] At the third annual meeting, in December 1924, the membership elected an all-female executive with the exception of two honorary presidents as advisers.[30] By 1925 there was no longer any mention of male honorary presidents as part of the organizational structure, suggesting that within four years of its existence the LOHA had achieved its goal of having a women's hockey organization completely run by women.[31] Hockey player Janet Allen of Toronto was elected the first female president of the LOHA in 1923, a position she held until the organization's sixth annual meeting in the fall of 1927 (see table 1).[32]

Seeking Recognition and Approval from the Male Hockey Community

Men's hockey became organized in Ontario in 1890 with the formation of the Ontario Hockey Association.[33] Maintaining a staunch amateur ideology during its first two decades of existence, the OHA gained in popularity and influence, and teams flocked to compete under its organizational umbrella. In 1914 the OHA played a key role in the creation of the Canadian Amateur Hockey Association (CAHA). Drawing on the wisdom of male hockey leaders, the constitution of the LOHA was patterned on the OHA's constitution, with a few changes to suit the women's game.[34] These changes included increasing the number of substitutes available for each game to four, allowing clubs that played games on open-air ice surfaces to join as members, and granting eligibility to teams who represented commercial firms.[35] The change that allowed commercially sponsored teams to join the LOHA suggests not only that financial support for women's hockey was a key concern, but also that upholding the staunch ideals of amateurism espoused by the

OHA was less important in the women's game. Similarly to the OHA, the direction of the LOHA was determined at the annual meetings, with the power to run the organization between these meetings vested in the executive committee.

Despite the effort made to pattern the LOHA after the OHA, the women's association was not accepted by the Canadian hockey community more broadly. On 1 December 1923 the OHA presidential address related the events of a CAHA meeting in Port Arthur whereby a vote was taken as to whether women should be given official recognition in Canada's national pastime. In a majority vote, women were denied recognition by the leading governing body for hockey in Canada. In his presidential report, W.A. Fry of Dunnville stated: 'A special committee was appointed to investigate and report on all phases of women's activities in sport. While the participation of women and girls in many competitive sports, such as tennis, swimming, skating and field and track events is growing, my belief that hockey, for various reasons, should be an exception, led me at an executive meeting of the C.A.H.A., held in Port Arthur, to vote with the majority not to give them official recognition. In my opinion there is all the necessary scope for them in games where the personal contact element is not a factor.'[36] It is indeed interesting that by 1923 women's hockey had grown to a degree where the CAHA felt the need to address it and cast a formal vote to decide whether or not to recognize women's organizational efforts officially. The result of the vote suggests a consensual belief among Canadian male hockey leaders that hockey was an inappropriate sport for female sport enthusiasts – an expression of ideological boundaries that continued to dictate the nature and form of appropriate sport for women.

Forming Alliances: The LOHA, AAU of C, WAAF, and OHA

For its inaugural year, the LOHA affiliated with the Ontario branch of the Amateur Athletic Union of Canada (AAU of C), making it the second governing body for women's sport to do so. [37] The AAU of C, established in 1909, had representatives from every province and, according to historian Alan Metcalfe, 'was the most important and powerful organization in amateur sport.'[38] Most of the sport governing bodies across the country were affiliates. Affiliating with the AAU of C offered the LOHA a degree of legitimacy in Canada sport; however, it remained an outsider in an organization that was controlled by men and ultimately focused on male sport endeavours. Hall suggests that, for the most part, the all-male AAU of C 'paid little attention to women and did not accept female registrations.'[39] It was not until 1925 that a female branch of the national sport organization was created.

The women of the LOHA were partly responsible for the creation of a female complement to the AAU of C. An athlete, administrator, and female sports advocate, Alexandrine Gibb was ultimately the driving force behind the formation of the Women's Amateur Athletic Federation (WAAF). In 1925 the British Women's Amateur Athletic Association (WAAA) invited a Canadian team to attend an international track and field competition in London, England. Gibb was asked to choose the team and to accompany the women as the Canadian team manager. She was inspired by this trip and, more specifically, by the time she spent in close contact with the leaders of the British WAAA. Upon her return to Canada and after gaining the support of key female sports organizations in Ontario, Gibb proposed the creation of a female national body to the AAU of C.[40] The new organization offered women the chance to control, organize, and develop women's competitive sport formally. While women's sport had long been organized in university and school settings, the WAAF offered organized sport to working women who had little opportunity or means to attend an institute of higher education.

The Canadian WAAF closely aligned with and patterned itself on its British counterpart and was very different from its equivalent in the neighbouring United States, where the Women's Division of the National Amateur Athletic Federation was mostly an organization of professional physical educators.[41] In 1930 Gibb, in her column 'In the No Man's Land of Sport,' suggested that the American organization was 'interested only in the school and university girl. For them the businesswoman does not exist, and if she does, they believe that she would have no place in the athletic world.'[42] Gibb criticized the organization for its exclusion of working women, an example of the class restrictions that were often placed on women's sport in North America.

On 11 September 1925 the AAU of C approved Gibb's proposal for a national women's federation governed by women with men acting in advisory capacities.[43] Janet Allen, president of the LOHA, served as provisional president of the new organization. Like many of the early women's sport governing bodies, the WAAF modelled itself on the male-run AAU of C and developed a uniform code of eligibility for all women's sports.[44] By November 1929 the WAAF had issued over one thousand eligibility cards, mostly to track and field, softball, and basketball players.[45]

Throughout its existence the LOHA forged and maintained a close affiliation with the WAAF. At the fourth annual meeting in December 1925 the LOHA executive voted to affiliate with the Ontario branch of the WAAF.[46] The LOHA was one of three organizations responsible for the formation of the WAAF, so this affiliation was an obvious step for the hockey association.[47] This move became more significant to the council in the late 1930s as the association struggled to stay operational. In 1929 the WAAF, in an effort to increase the number of card-carrying members, passed the following amendment: 'Athletes competing in any organized women's association must hold amateur cards, and no athlete holding an amateur card will be allowed to compete with or against an athlete not holding an amateur card (schools excepted).'[48] Despite the LOHA's declaration of affiliation with the new governing body in December 1925 and the requirement of the WAAF for all athletes competing in an organized women's sport to hold an amateur card, it was not until the mid-1930s that the hockey association made it mandatory for its athletes to carry WAAF eligibility cards.

During the early 1920s the LOHA operated as one of the strongest women's sports organizations in the province. Press reports indicated that each year the association maintained a reasonable amount of money in its coffers. The consistent number of teams under the LOHA banner across the province suggests that the organization achieved a degree of acceptance and identification among women's teams as the voice and administrator for women's organized hockey in the province during its early years of existence.[49] At the fourth annual meeting in 1925, to accommodate the varying abilities of the teams across the province, to create a more level and welcoming playing field, and to bolster membership numbers, the executive officers voted to form an intermediate division within the LOHA. This division, as a complement to the senior division, offered teams with lesser skill levels the opportunity to join the organization. However, attracting teams to the new division was a challenging task given the limited resources of the LOHA for advertisement beyond the major cities where member teams already operated. In an effort to increase awareness of the LOHA across the province and to encourage female hockey clubs to join and compete in organized leagues that led to a provincial championship, the executive turned to the general membership of the OHA. In 1927 Janet Allen and Bobbie Rosenfeld, then respectively president and secretary of the

LOHA, attended the 38th annual meeting of the OHA. Their rationale for attending was to ask the male hockey representatives from across the province for help in promoting the LOHA in the towns that they represented. Both women expressed gratitude to the men on the executive for the assistance, support, and advice that had been offered to the LOHA over the years. After these opening pleasantries, whereby the women set the mood for the meeting, Janet Allen made a point of explaining how successful the LOHA had been over its first five years of existence in organizing the sport for women: 'I understand that in your Senior series you had six or seven teams last year, and when I tell you that we had seven Senior teams last year I think you will admit that we have done something for Girls hockey.'[50] Rosenfeld went beyond hockey to relate the quest of the LOHA to put women's hockey on the same organizational level in Ontario as softball and basketball: 'There is no need to tell you how ladies athletics and sports have come to the fore. At one time girls soft ball and basket ball was a novelty, but now it occupies the limelight for the simple reason that it was given the support and encouragement of the men in different towns, and it was changed from a rattling lizzie to a six-cylinder (laughter) – and it is hitting on all six too. It is not at all unusual now to see four or five thousand people watching a girls' basket ball or base ball game, and our idea is to place ladies' hockey on the same basis.'[51]

After sharing this information about the state of the sport, the women turned to the task at hand – securing an agreement for direct support and endorsement from the men. If the men endorsed and promoted the LOHA in their home communities, it would help to boost LOHA membership numbers – a top priority for the organization. Junior and intermediate teams were needed to broaden the level of play and create opportunities for smaller towns and cities to compete in a competitive environment that was relative to their skill level. Allen appealed to the men to help the LOHA in its quest to attract more teams to the association: 'I believe that if the men interested in hockey in the different centres were to try to interest the girls in their own towns in the game and would assist them in every way possible, our Association would be the better for it.'[52] Rosenfeld more forcefully told the men: 'All that is necessary is that someone should go out and say: "We are interested in ladies' hockey. If you will only flock to us we will support you." I would like very much to see every one of you go back to your home town and do that little thing – work up a little bit of enthusiasm in ladies' hockey ... We are having our annual meeting on December 3rd in Toronto, and we want each of you delegates to go back home and to try to have someone appointed to attend our meeting on that date.'[53] After the women's speech, the chairman of the meeting invited Allen and Rosenfeld to the next annual meeting and encouraged the men in the room to provide the assistance needed and do what they could for women's hockey. There was, however, no formal motion put forward or passed endorsing OHA support of the LOHA. As the LOHA had few resources to promote and expand the women's game across the province, it had to rely on female players hearing about the LOHA's annual meetings and taking the initiative to join. Allen and Rosenfeld believed that the men at the annual meeting of the OHA were the answer to their problem – this was a tangible means by which women's hockey could be promoted. In the years to follow, teams did join the intermediate league and a provincial championship was contested at both the senior and intermediate levels.[54]

'Who said ladies first?': Fighting for Survival in the 1930s

Despite the initial promise of the LOHA, the organization spent the majority of its existence fighting to survive. The Depression years significantly impacted the survival of the LOHA, as available financial reservoirs in all areas of society were drained, with funds being reallocated to essential services. It was under these broad conditions of economic strife and uncertainty that the LOHA struggled to develop a stable governing body for women's hockey in the province. Plagued by continuing problems of access to ice, declining membership numbers, and maintaining a positive reputation for the sport, the work of a few key women on the executive board who donated countless hours and endless energy sustained the provincial organization. In her 22 February 1935 column in the *Toronto Daily Star*, Gibb explained that 'the hockey rinks aren't in love with letting the girls have their choice of hours or nights either on their ice surfaces, taking what is left has become a custom.'[55] Thus, female hockey players faced unique barriers. Men's teams had their choice of ice times and women settled for the remainder. For example, in March of 1938, the semi-final round of the LOHA championships between the Preston Rivulettes and the Northern Marvels of Cobalt was scheduled to be played in Preston but the venue had to be changed. Bobbie Rosenfeld in her column in the *Globe and Mail*, 'Feminine Sport Reel,' explained: 'Everything was hunky-dory for this series to be played at Preston, ... but, the O.H.A. stepped in and ordered the semi-finals of their intermediate "A" Section to be played in Preston this weekend. Naturally it necessitated the canceling of the ladies' series. Who said "ladies first?" Anyhow in order that a winner be declared by the required date, in order that Ottawa District may be entertained, the Preston Rivulettes, seven-time Eastern Canada champions are now considering a counter offer of the Marvels to play the L.O.H.A. semi-finals there.'[56] The men's play-off series always assumed first priority at the rinks and the women were often forced to make accommodations and last-minute changes.

By the early 1930s, press reports suggested that the breadth of the LOHA's membership was declining.[57] Although teams that did compete under the LOHA umbrella were dedicated and enthusiastic about the sport, the number of teams in both the senior and intermediate division had decreased over the years. By 1934 the executive body of the LOHA had only five officers. Only seven teams from across the province sought membership and, unlike 1922 when the majority of the teams in the LOHA were from Toronto, only one Toronto team competed for the provincial title.[58]

During the summer of 1937 an unexpected financial grant to women's sport in Ontario offered the hockey association a certain degree of financial stability. In August 1937, the *Globe and Mail* reported that the Ontario branch of the WAAF had recently been the recipient of a five-hundred-dollar monetary grant from the Ontario Athletic Commission (OAC) for the purpose of fostering female sport in Ontario.[59] The Ontario branch of the WAAF decided that the money would be split among the affiliated sport organizations based on the number of members each association had within the branch. The LOHA portion of this grant was fifty dollars.[60] Given that the yearly membership fee to affiliate with the WAAF was ten dollars, the actual benefit to the hockey organization was only a forty-dollar stipend. While not a lot of money, it certainly enriched the LOHA coffers.

Despite this financial boost, it could be argued that the LOHA only survived the latter years of the 1930s because of the organization's president – Bobbie Rosenfeld. A star player of the Toronto Pats hockey club in the 1920s and later an esteemed member of the LOHA executive, Rosenfeld was elected president of the LOHA in the fall of 1934, a position she held for five years until Roxy Atkins assumed the position in 1939 (see table 1).[61] By the 1936–7 hockey season, the LOHA faced a state of crisis within the organization. Gibb, in her *Toronto Daily Star* sports column, reported that, for the 1936–7 season, Bobbie Rosenfeld acted as the association's president, secretary, and treasurer.[62] By November 1937, because of little evidence of activity within the organization, Gibb went so far as to question if the LOHA was even still alive.[63] Through her persistence and dedication, Rosenfeld managed to revive the organization and make it strong enough to govern women's hockey until the end of the decade. In November 1937 Rosenfeld called an annual meeting of the executive and the teams across the province interested in competing in the 1937–8 season. While three of the top players, Nellie and Hilda Ranscombe and Marm Schmuck from the reigning provincial champions, the Preston Rivulettes, were in attendance, there was an overall poor showing at the Toronto meeting. In response to the small turnout, Gibb lamented in her *Star* column: 'Girls who are willing to step in and rescue a drowning on ice association and emerge with it on top ... alive and kicking ... are too few these days.'[64] It was clear that if the LOHA was going to remain as the governing organization for women's hockey in the province, the leadership would fall to a small group of dedicated women. Indeed, at this meeting a small group committed themselves to saving women's hockey in the province and new officers were elected: honorary president, Dr Edwin Hagmeier of Preston; president, Bobbie Rosenfeld, Toronto; vice-president, Marm Schmuck, Preston; second vice-president, Helen Carefoot, Markdale; secretary-treasurer, Olive Hewitt, Hamilton.[65] With an insufficient number of teams interested, the LOHA decided to operate only the senior series for the 1937–8 season. The LOHA had to increase its membership numbers if it wanted to continue to operate; yet it had difficulty attracting teams. Ironically, the organization was forced to deal with the impact of the success of one team, the Preston Rivulettes, on the declining membership numbers.

'Queens of the Ice Lanes'[66] or Cold Irony: The Preston Rivulettes, 1931–1940

In 1931 a new team, the Rivulettes, joined the LOHA intermediate division.[67] Their dominating prominence of skill and superior style of play, coupled with the extensive cross-country media attention bestowed on their achievements throughout the 1930s, helped to promote women's hockey across the province; yet ironically at the same time, the success of this team posed an organizational challenge to the provincial governing body. Due to the team's late entry at the end of January 1931, it was not able to partake in league play with other area teams, who already had a fixed schedule. Consequently, the LOHA arranged for the Rivulettes' entry against the Port Dover Sailorettes, winner of the Port Dover–Simcoe league, in the first round of the play-offs.[68] The Rivulettes defeated Grimsby in two exhibition games before meeting the Port Dover Sailorettes in the LOHA play-offs. Defeating Port Dover in the quarterfinals, London in the semi-finals, and Pembroke in the finals, the Rivulettes claimed the 1931 LOHA intermediate championship title, a prelude to their dominating reign over women's hockey in Ontario.[69] The Rivulettes went on to out-skate and outplay opponents both provincially and nationally during the 1930s. By 1940 when the team retired, it had claimed ten Ontario titles and four dominion championships.[70]

By 1935, with their convincing defeat of the western champions, the Winnipeg Eatons, to win the Dominion Championship for the first time, the Rivulettes had resoundingly positioned themselves at the top of women's hockey. After five consecutive provincial championships and five seasons undefeated in the province, other teams had little hope of defeating the 'queens of the ice lanes.' Indeed, the Rivulettes maintained their reign over the province until they disbanded following their tenth season in 1940.

By 1938 the success of the Preston Rivulettes hockey club caused a significant problem within the LOHA. Teams in Ontario did not want to join the organization – which by this time had only enough teams to operate a senior division across the province – because of the unlikely chance they had of winning not only the provincial title but even individual games. Ultimately, the success of the Rivulettes was causing LOHA membership numbers to decrease. Indeed, since entering the LOHA in 1931, the Rivulettes had not lost a game in Ontario.[71] Instead of joining the organization only to be beaten by the Rivulettes, teams chose to play exhibition games against other teams with similar skill levels. In order to draw these reluctant teams into the organization, the LOHA executive voted at the 1938 annual meeting to create an 'A' and a 'B' league within the senior division. The 'B' division consisted of first-year teams and teams that were not at the same skill level as the Senior 'A' teams.[72] In justifying this decision, President Bobbie Rosenfeld in her *Globe and Mail* column related that 'it was deemed the only thing to do if the L.O.H.A. hoped to increase its number of affiliated teams, and was done in answer to the cry from centres throughout Ontario that claimed that the Preston power had become too potent to cope with.'[73] Indeed, attracting less-skilled teams to the LOHA was a viable strategy for increasing membership numbers.

The dilemma that the Rivulettes produced and faced was similar to that of another dominant women's team in Canada – the Edmonton Commercial Graduates. Gibb compared the Rivulettes to the Edmonton Grads basketball team, stating that 'like the Edmonton Grads ... [n]o team wants to play with them ... they are too powerful.'[74] Similarly to the Rivulettes in hockey, the Grads had maintained their position at the pinnacle of women's basketball since their formation in 1915. Their superior skill and ability were also elements of their demise. Elaine Chalus suggests that 'the Grads were so predictable that fans began to attend only the first home games of a series, which caused box-office receipts to drop in the late 1930s.'[75] Both the Rivulettes and the Grads were dependent on box-office income to support their travel budgets. Without this income, they had difficulty fulfilling their game commitments. Both teams achieved top honours in their sports; yet, ironically, this success, while increasing the exposure of the sport, led to an overall decline in participation at the top competitive level and was an element in the demise of both the Grads and the Rivulettes in 1940.

Celebrating Manhood versus Female Respectability

The quest to increase membership numbers and to promote the LOHA across the province were critical issues to its executive; but the association also faced a greater challenge that went beyond the organizational aspects of the game. Indeed, throughout its nineteen-year existence, maintaining a positive reputation for women's hockey was one of the utmost challenges that confronted the LOHA. By the early 1920s the game had a reputation for being a working-class women's pastime, where brawls, aggressive play, and injuries were common. More broadly, the sport of hockey has always been characterized by rough, aggressive physicality, a site where men and boys learned the celebrated values of manhood. Women, while emulating the brand of hockey revered by Canadians, the male hockey model, faced censure for copying the aggressive actions of their male counterparts. As early as the first month of the LOHA's existence, press reports made clear the social expectations of female hockey players. There was one, and only one, proscribed way that women's hockey should be played:

If the new Ladies' Ontario Hockey League is to be a permanency the officials must start the teams away on the grind under competent referees specially instructed to curb anything which savors of rough or unladylike play, and to enforce the rules of the game to the letter. Well conducted the league will attract nice people and nice players and will result in a lot of excellent outdoor exercise for the young women of various towns. Any tendency to rough play will start trouble among both the players and the spectators. An outbreak between two players on the ice would almost spell 'finis' to the game in any town on the circuit. The new league has a strong-looking set of officers, and there is no reason to believe that they do not fully appreciate their responsibilities in the new venture.[76]

This warning strongly encouraged the LOHA to enforce a specific brand of femininity. John DeGruchy, the AAU of C's chief 'women's advisor' at this time,[77] also 'favoured the cutting out of anything that would make the game too strenuous.'[78] Such period perspectives demonstrate that aggressive sports such as hockey helped to sustain the gender polarities of the Victorian era, where lines were drawn between appropriate social demonstrations of masculinity and femininity. Of course, this value structure was well supported by a network of institutions, including medicine, science, and organized religion. As present scholarship has amply demonstrated, the polar opposite to the empowered, strong man was the weak, passive, fragile, dependent woman. Victorian notions of the body and the gender order have had a lasting effect on women's participation in recreation, leisure, and sport. As R.W. Connell reminds us, men have been the main beneficiaries of these social arrangements, and this explains, somewhat, the relative dependency on men's support needed to ensure the success of the LOHA.[79]

However, as early as the 1920s, female hockey players were challenging the residual Victorian notions of women as weak and passive and, by extension, their imposed inferiority status. Fighting, stick-swinging, even deaths have been a part of the male hockey culture since the early 1900s. In chapter 5, Stacy Lorenz and Geraint Osborne, examining violence and masculinity in amateur and professional hockey before the First World War, suggest that narratives of hockey in the Canadian press described the violent nature of the sport in terms of both 'brutal butchery' and 'strenuous spectacle.' Indeed, the game's aggressive and violent features provided popular entertainment both in the arena and to newspaper readers. Men's hockey, at both the professional and amateur levels, provided the model for all elements of the game including skills, strategies, and, of course, aggression and violence. Newspaper reports from women's hockey during the interwar years suggested that, like the men's game, women's hockey was also fast, aggressive, and, at times, violent.

Deferring to the contemporary prescribed notion of femininity, the LOHA executive, during the 1923 annual meeting, attempted to curb the aggressive tendencies of the players by unanimously deciding that women's hockey would deviate from the male model through the complete elimination of body-checking in every form.[80] However, such effort to eliminate aggressive play, coupled with the social censure expressed through the media, seemed to have had little effect on changing the inherent aggressive style of the women's game. Press reports from the 1920s and 1930s suggested that the women's game was not as 'clean' as critics would have preferred.[81] Headlines such as 'Sticks and Fists Fly Freely as Girl Hockeyists Battle,' 'Girls Wanted Another Fight but Referees Stopped Them,' 'Hockey Amazons in Fistic Display,' and 'Girls Draw Majors for Fistic Display' suggest that women played a tough, aggressive form of hockey.[82] The LOHA intermediate semi-final series in February 1931 between the Preston Rivulettes and the Port Dover Sailorettes caused one reporter to proclaim, 'And, dear readers, you can believe it or not, but we discovered last evening that even women have tempers.'[83] At the conclusion of this series, the *Galt Evening Reporter* suggested that the 'management of the Port Dover club wanted to have Helen Schmuck [a player from the Rivulettes] disrobe. They thought she was a boy.'[84] By being aggressive, tough, and occasionally violent – emulating the male hockey model – women were actively resisting prevailing notions of acceptable feminine behaviour. Perhaps if they could play the game like 'them,' they would be accepted as rightful participants of the treasured Canadian pastime like 'them.' Kidd, however, argues that the perceived aggressiveness of women's hockey led to a negative reputation for the sport during the interwar years and discouraged many women from participating.[85]

Sport has always been a powerful medium for disseminating social meanings. The standards for sportsmen and sportswomen were different early on. For example, in the 1920s newspaper reports on women in the Olympic Games tended to focus on the feminine figures of the female athletes, with mention of athletic abilities often added as an afterthought. Journalists commented explicitly on the appearance of female athletes and on personal information such as their marital status to assure the reader that sports were not stripping women of their feminine attributes.[86] With respect to this process of negotiation, Kevin Wamsley argues that appropriating the performance and symbolic value of female athletes was vital to ensuring the primary position of men, as 'a feminized athlete could not challenge the celebration of manhood through sport and, thus did not displace men as the "real" athletes of the era.'[87] However, game reports suggested that unlike other sportswomen of the time, female hockey players did not showcase their femininities, thus posing a direct threat to the established male hockey culture. Interestingly, female sports leaders of the era recognized the potential consequences of this perceived threat and encouraged women to 'clean up' the sport. For example, Alexandrine Gibb, in her *Toronto Daily Star* column 'No Man's Land of Sport,' repeatedly chastised aggressive players for their 'non-lady-like' behaviour. Commenting on the Dominion Championship game in 1935 between the Preston Rivulettes and the Winnipeg Eatons, where 'tempers flared, sticks and fists flew in reckless abandon as the rival players dropped the foils,' Gibb reprimanded the behaviour of the athletes: 'Athletic girls do not often lose their tempers in any game. They have been taught that it is very bad indeed for the boys to do that, but it is practically fatal for girls ... Girls can't afford to stage shows of that kind if they want to keep in sport. It's quite exciting to see it at the time and you get a kick out of the exhibition, but when it is all over and the tempers cool out, they are usually much ashamed. They should be.'[88] Aggression and violence, although perhaps an emulation of the 'real' form of hockey, were not always accepted and appreciated in the women's game.

Indeed, a tension existed not only among critics but also among female players concerning the acceptable definitions of womanhood and appropriate female behaviour while on the ice. While some women obviously relished playing the rough game with all of its aggressive tactics, others followed a more refined definition of feminine behaviour in sport. Kidd argues that in 1925 the University of Toronto team, provincial champions of the 1923–4 season, withdrew from the LOHA, stating as the reason 'certain unsatisfactory aspects of competition.'[89] This action by the Toronto team suggests that there was a tension among women between acceptable definitions of womanhood.

More Questions than Answers

By 1940 the LOHA could no longer maintain its existence as an independent governing body for women's hockey. After more than a decade of dedicated service to the organization, Bobbie Rosenfeld retired as president in the fall of 1939. Roxy Atkins, also president of the Ontario

Branch of the WAAF, was elected the new president, a post she would only hold for one year. Atkins and the executive reintroduced the intermediate division to expand competition and appealed to the past president of the OHA, George Dudley, for help in promoting the intermediate group to teams in Mount Forest, Dundalk, Durham, Flesherton, Walkerton, Collingwood, Shelbourne, Meaford, and Owen Sound – all were playing exhibition matches outside the organizational structure of the LOHA.[90] However, the efforts to attract teams to play in an intermediate division were seemingly unsuccessful. By October 1941 news reports suggested that both the senior and intermediate divisions had folded and the LOHA had 'closed shop.'[91] The LOHA amalgamated with the Ontario branch of the WAAF, a move that was facilitated by Atkins, president of both organizations. News reports in the early 1940s suggested that women's hockey continued in the province; however, there were no organized leagues and no provincial championships.[92]

Elizabeth Etue and Megan Williams attribute the demise of women's hockey by 1940 to the effects of the Depression, the Second World War, and the rise of professional hockey.[93] Certainly, these factors and their related social and economic implications influenced the women's game. Women continued to play in some leagues and tournaments, but the momentum from the 1920s and 1930s had disappeared.[94] Specifically in Ontario, it was perhaps more than broad social and economic factors that forced the LOHA to the margins, unable to gain a stable position within the hockey world. The organization was constantly struggling merely to survive so that it could promote an organized system for female hockey competitors. The men's game had the established organizational strategies of experienced male hockey leaders from the professional and amateur game, supported by the enduring mythologies created and perpetuated around Canadian hockey. One could not have existed and thrived without the other. For supporters or participants, hockey may be a part of the collective 'imagined' memory of many Canadians. But undoubtedly there are many groups of Canadians, both male and female, who have not contributed to the creation of this national identity.

Women's hockey in the 1920s and 1930s was a fast, aggressive, competitive sport. It challenged traditional notions of women as weak, passive, and fragile. While athletes and leaders such as Bobbie Rosenfeld and Hilda Ranscombe were emblematic of the female hockey community, in female hockey circles they were not household names in the way legendary male hockey stars of the time were. Female hockey organizations such as the LOHA were never able to draw on a mythological element of the women's game as a self-existing promotional ingredient. Female hockey players were not a part of the Canadian hockey folklore. What was missing that prevented women from inclusion in the Canadian hockey mystique? A simple explanation is that spectators and hockey enthusiasts were not drawn to women's hockey by a national medium such as the revered 'Hockey Night in Canada' on the CBC. There was no national, professional equivalent in women's hockey that was broadcast across the nation on the radio. Similarly, although by the 1920s there were regular feature columns on women's sport in national newspapers, community-level women's hockey did not receive consistent coverage unless a particular team had succeeded in making it to the provincial or national championships.

The enduring collective memory of hockey as something quintessentially Canadian began as a shared experience of male hockey participants and enthusiasts. The stories of 'famous triumphs' in hockey revolve around the men's game, linking male hockey traditions with nationally perceived concepts of the sport. During the 1920s and 1930s, except in towns where female teams had achieved top honours, such as the Rivulettes from Preston, Ontario, recognition for women who played hockey was not widespread. This selective and sparse attention to women's hockey leads, then, to broader questions about hockey and how it has contributed to Canadian identity. In relation to women's hockey, more specifically, why are men considered the rightful custodians of the game in our collective national memories and identities? Ultimately, the demise of the LOHA in 1940, coupled with the LOHA's struggle to exist, its continual dependency on male hockey leaders for promotion, support, and advice, and the decline in women's hockey after 1940, more broadly suggest that, despite the efforts of the LOHA, hockey remained the rightful place of male athletes with women as outsiders left to contemplate their own existence within a sporting culture that neither accepted nor admired their dedication, ability, or enthusiasm for the national sport. The contributions of the LOHA in attempting to establish women's hockey in Ontario and the lack of support for the organization within the broader hockey community reinforce the gendered nature of Canada's national identity – an identity that ultimately privileges men. In the collective imagination of Canadians, hockey during the first half of the twentieth century was a game of boys and men – a game that played little part in creating a sense of national identity for Canadian women.

NOTES

1 For the rest of the chapter ice hockey will be referred to as hockey.
2 Michael A. Robidoux, 'Imagining a Canadian Identity through Sport: A Historical Interpretation of Lacrosse and Hockey, *Journal of American Folklore* 115, 456 (2002): 209. See Robidoux's article for an examination of Canada's national identity through lacrosse and hockey.
3 See Peter Gzowski, *The Game of Our Lives* (Toronto: McClelland and Stewart, 1981).
4 See Richard Gruneau and David Whitson, *Hockey Night in Canada: Sport, Identities and Cultural Politics* (Toronto: Garamond Press, 1993), 13.
5 Ibid., 168–9.
6 Elizabeth Etue and Megan Williams, *On the Edge: Women Making Hockey History* (Toronto: Second Story Press, 1996), 158.
7 Brian McFarlane, *Proud Past, Bright Future: 100 Years of Canadian Women's Hockey* (Toronto: Stoddart, 1994).
8 For example, see Etue and Williams, *On the Edge*; and Joanna Avery and Julie Stevens, *Too Many Men on the Ice: Women's Hockey in North America* (Victoria, BC: Polestar, 1997).
9 See Gruneau and Whitson, *Hockey Night in Canada* 168.
10 M. Ann Hall, 'A History of Women's Sport in Canada Prior to World War I,' MA thesis (University of Alberta, 1968).
11 Ibid., 43. Andrew Holman suggests that this was similar in the United States; see Holman, 'Stops and Starts: Ideology, Commercialism, and the Fall of American Women's Hockey in the 1920s,' *Journal of Sport History* 32 (2005): 334.
12 For more information see Ann Hall, *The Girl and the Game* (Peterborough, ON: Broadview Press, 2002), 41–72; Bruce Kidd, *The Struggle for Canadian Sport* (Toronto: University of Toronto Press, 1996), 94–145.
13 Kidd, *The Struggle for Canadian Sport,* 109.
14 For more information on Alexandrine Gibb, see M.A. Hall, 'Alexandrine Gibb: In "No Man's Land of Sport,"' *International Journal of the History of Sport* 18 (2001): 149–72.
15 Ibid., 154.
16 A. Gibb, 'No Man's Land of Sport,' *Toronto Daily Star,* 1 May 1937, 17.
17 Minutes of the 38th OHA meeting, 19 November 1927, OHA Papers, Library and Archives Canada (LAC), M2308.
18 To date, a history of the Ladies Ontario Hockey Association has not been written. The location of the meeting minutes for this organization, if they exist, is unknown.

19 See 'Lady Hockeyists to Organise Tomorrow,' *Toronto Daily Star*, 8 December 1922, 3; 'Lady Hockeyists to Meet Tomorrow,' *Globe*, 8 December 1922, 8; 'Over Forty Teams Enter New Series,' *Globe*, 18 December 1922, 9.

20 For a list of teams in the league by 1913 see 'Here's the Schedule: Where's the Ice?' *Globe*, 16 January 1913, 12. Frank Smith founded the organization and acted as the league's secretary-general for fifty years. An attempt has been made to locate the early papers of the THL, with no success. The Greater Toronto Hockey League's (the current name of the organization) website (http://www.gthlcanada.com/frontoffice/history.html) suggests that during the 1920s the league had 8 to 12 women's teams during any given year.

21 For example, see 'T.H.L. Ladies' Series Will Have Large Entry,' *Globe*, 5 December 1923, 8. Newspaper reports suggest that the THL continued to offer women's leagues in the city of Toronto throughout the 1920s. See 'Ladies' Hockey in for a Good Season,' *Toronto Daily Star*, 17 November 1926, 11; and '"Pats" Picked to Win Ladies' T.H.L. Honors Again,' *Toronto Daily Star*, 3 March 1927, 15.

22 'Over Forty Teams Enter New Series,' *Globe*, 18 December 1922, 9.

23 Ibid.

24 The men involved with the LOHA had vested interests in sport in Ontario. For example, John DeGruchy was also the president of the Ontario Branch of the AAU of C in 1922, had been president of the Ontario Rugby Football Union for 25 years, and was president of the Canadian Rugby Union in 1925, 1930, and 1935. As with women's hockey in the United States in the 1920s, these men were well entrenched in the amateur establishment of Canadian sport and were businessmen with commercial interests and particular agendas for promoting the women's game. For more on the commercial interests of male promoters of women's hockey in the United States see Holman, 'Stops and Starts,' 335–7.

25 As an example, at the OHA annual meeting in 1927, Bobbie Rosenfeld expressed the LOHA's appreciation for the guidance offered by W.A. Hewitt. See Minutes of 38th OHA meeting, 19 November 1927, OHA Papers, LAC, M2308.

26 'Ladies' Hockey League Organized,' *Toronto Daily Star*, 18 December 1922, 25.

27 'No Body Checking in Ladies' Hockey,' *Toronto Daily Star*, 17 December 1923, 11. It is interesting to note here that there were over 25 teams in attendance at the original organizational meeting.

28 'U of T Ladies Enter Local Hockey League,' *Globe*, 12 December 1922, 10.

29 See 'Ladies to Take Complete Charge of Their Own Hockey Association,'

Toronto Daily Star, 8 December 1923, 13; and 'No Body Checking in Ladies Hockey.' The 1923 officers were: honorary president, John DeGruchy, Toronto; president, Janet Allen, Toronto; first vice-president, John Dennison, Preston; second vice-president, Eva Ault, Ottawa; third vice-president, Frank Smith, Toronto; secretary and treasurer, Mr C.W. MacQueen, *Empire and Mail*, Toronto. Executive committee: Florence Semple, Dunnville; Kathleen Milne, London; Phyllis Nichols, Preston; and Grace Webb, Galt.

30 'Miss Allen Leads Lady Hockeyists,' *Globe*, 8 December 1924, 8. The 1924 officers were: honorary presidents John DeGruchy and Elwood Hughes; president Janet Allen, Toronto; first vice-president Eva Ault, Ottawa; second vice-president Mr W.H. Legg, London; and secretary-treasurer Fanny Rosenfeld, Toronto. Executive committee: Phyllis Nichols, Galt; Edith Anderson, Ottawa; Florence Semple, Whitby; and Grace Webb, Galt.

31 See 'Intermediate Series for Ladies' Hockey,' *Toronto Daily Star*, 14 December 1925, 10. The 1925 Officers were: president Janet Allen, Toronto; first vice-president Eva Ault, Ottawa; second vice-president Grace Webb, Galt; secretary-treasurer Fanny Rosenfeld, Toronto. Executive committee: Edith Anderson, Ottawa; Eunice Servair, Grimsby; Grace Talbot, London; and Hazel Ruttier, Toronto.

32 In 1927 Hazel Ruttier of Toronto was elected the new president of the LOHA.

33 For more information on the OHA see Scott Young, *100 Years of Dropping the Puck: A History of the OHA* (Toronto: McClelland and Stewart, 1989), 7–192; and Alan Metcalfe, 'Power: A Case Study of the Ontario Hockey Association, 1890–1936,' *Journal of Sport History* 19 (1992): 5–25.

34 'Over Forty Teams Enter New Series,' *Globe*, 18 December 1922, 9. For the complete 1922 OHA constitution and rules of competition, see OHA Constitution, Rules of Competition, Laws of the Game, Canadian Hockey Yearbook (1923); and OHA Papers, LAC, M2308.

35 'Over Forty Teams Enter New Series,' *Globe*, 18 December 1922, 9.

36 Minutes of OHA annual meeting, 1 December 1923, 2. OHA Papers, LAC, M2308.

37 See Hall, *The Girl and The Game*, 43. The first women's association to affiliate with the AAU of C was the Canadian Ladies Golf Union, formed in 1913.

38 Alan Metcalfe, *Canada Learns to Play* (Toronto: McClelland & Stewart, 1987), 102.

39 Hall, *The Girl and the Game*, 47.

40 The information for this paragraph has been pulled from secondary sources. Historian Bruce Kidd in his book, *The Struggle for Canadian Sport*, relates

that few records of the WAAF remain. He states that according to Margaret Lord, 'the main files were destroyed by Irene Wall in the late 1950s. Irene Moore McInnis kept copies of the Ontario and national constitutions, only to have them stolen from a sports history display in Thorold several years ago' (290n60). For more information, see Kidd, *The Struggle for Canadian Sport*, 113–19; and Hall, *The Girl and the Game*, 45–54.

41 For more information on the Women's Division of the National Amateur Athletic Federation see Susan K. Cahn, *Coming on Strong: Gender and Sexuality in Twentieth Century Women's Sport* (New York: The Free Press, 1994), 61–8.

42 A. Gibb, 'In the No Man's Land of Sport, *Toronto Daily Star,* 18 February 1930, 8.

43 For press reports on the formation of the new organization see 'Plans Outlined for Women's A.A.U. of C.,' *Toronto Daily Star,* 26 September 1925, 13; and 'Constitution Is Drafted for Women's A.A.U. of Canada,' ibid., 16.

44 For more information on the AAU of C see Metcalfe, *Canada Learns to Play,* 102–19.

45 See A. Gibb, 'In the No Man's Land of Sport,' *Toronto Daily Star,* 1 November 1929, 14.

46 See 'Intermediate Series For Ladies' Hockey,' *Toronto Daily Star,* 14 December 1925, 10.

47 The other two organizations involved in the formation of the WAAF were the Ladies Ontario Basketball Association and the Ontario Women's Softball Association. See A. Gibb, 'In the No Man's Land of Sport,' *Toronto Daily Star,* 18 February 1930, 8.

48 This WAAF amendment to their organizational constitution was quoted in A. Gibb, 'In the No Man's Land of Sport,' *Toronto Daily Star,* 1 November 1929, 14.

49 According to press reports, the LOHA bank account had a balance of $103.33 at the end of the third season. See 'Intermediate Series for Ladies' Hockey,' *The Toronto Daily Star,* 14 December 1925, 10.

50 Minutes of the 38th OHA meeting 19 November 1927, OHA Papers, LAC, M2308.

51 Ibid.

52 Ibid.

53 Ibid.

54 No specific information can be found on the number of teams registered with the LOHA for the 1928–9 season. The intermediate championships were not covered in the major Ontario newspapers of the time.

55 A. Gibb, *Toronto Daily Star,* 22 February 1935, 13; see also *Toronto Daily*

Star, 2 March 1938, 12. Women had to wait until the men's play-offs were finished before they could schedule their own play-off series.

56 B. Rosenfeld, 'Feminine Sport Reel,' *Globe and Mail,* 2 March 1938, 15.

57 See M.J. Rodeen, 'On the Highways of Sport,' *Globe,* 3 December 1932, 8.

58 A. Gibb, 'No Man's Land of Sport,' *Toronto Daily Star,* 17 December 1934, 10.

59 B. Rosenfeld, 'Women's Federation Aids Feminine Sports Bodies,' *Globe and Mail,* 9 August 1937, 15.

60 Rosenfeld, 'Feminine Sports Reel,' 16.

61 Roxy Atkin was also the president of the Ontario Branch of the WAAF in 1939.

62 A. Gibb, 'No Man's Land of Sport,' *Toronto Daily Star,* 6 December 1937, 13. For more information on Bobbie Rosenfeld, see Joseph Levy, Danny Rosenburg, and Avi Hyman, 'Fanny 'Bobbie' Rosenfeld: Canada's Woman Athlete of the Half Century,' *Journal of Sport History* 26 (1999): 392–6; Bill Humber, 'Backtracking: Bobbie Rosenfeld,' *Athletics* (1983): 56–7; and Anne Dublin, *Bobbie Rosenfeld: The Olympian Who Could Do Everything* (Toronto: Second Story Press, 2004).

63 A. Gibb, 'No Man's Land of Sport,' *Toronto Daily Star,* 16 November 1937, 14.

64 A. Gibb, 'No Man's Land of Sport,' *Toronto Daily Star,* 6 December 1937, 13.

65 Ibid. For the first time since 1924 the association went back to the practice of having a male honorary president on the executive committee.

66 'Queens of the Ice Lanes,' and other variations such as 'Champions of the Ice Lanes' and 'Queens of the Frozen Surface,' were nicknames for the Rivulettes often found in press reports in the late 1930s. See, for example, 'Ottawa Rangers Arrive in Town,' *Galt Daily Reporter,* 25 March 1938, 6.

67 For a more extensive examination of the Preston Rivulettes Hockey team see Carly Adams, '"Queens of the Ice Lanes": The Preston Rivulettes and Women's Hockey in Canada 1931–1940,' *Sport History Review* 39 (2008): 1–29.

68 'Rivulettes in Ontario League,' *Galt Evening Reporter,* 27 January 1931, 4.

69 For accounts of the games from local papers see, 'Rivulettes Win From Port Dover Sailorettes 1–0,' *The Galt Evening Reporter,* 3 March 1931, p. 4; 'Local and Personal,' *The Prestonian,* Preston, Ontario, 5 March 1931, p. 21; 'Rivulettes Defeat London On Local Ice to Gain a Two-Goal Lead, L.O.H.A. Playdowns,' *The Galt Evening Reporter,* 6 March 1931, p. 4; 'Preston Girls Win,' *The Prestonian,* Preston, Ontario, 12 March 1931, p. 23.

70 Most frequently cited in the literature is that the Rivulettes won 6 domin-

ion titles from 1935 until 1940. But in 1936 and 1940 the Dominion Championships were not contested. See Adams, '"Queens of the Ice Lanes,"' 2.

71 For more information on the successes of the Rivulettes see Adams, '"Queens of the Ice Lanes,"' 1–29.

72 In 1938, the LOHA organized only a senior competition. The placement of teams in the A and B divisions was determined based on skill. In the past, when the LOHA operated senior and intermediate sections, the placement of teams was determined by age and skill, as in the OHA.

73 'Hockey Girls Hold Annual,' *Globe and Mail*, 28 November 1938, 20.

74 A. Gibb, 'No Man's Land of Sport,' *Toronto Daily Star*, 28 November 1938, 13.

75 Elaine Chalus, 'The Edmonton Commercial Graduates: Women's History: An Integrationist Approach,' in *Winter Sports in the West*, ed. Elise A Corbet and Anthony W. Rasporich (Calgary: Historical Society of Alberta, 1990), 75; for more information on the Grads, see also Kevin B. Wamsley, 'Power and Privilege in Historiography: Constructing Percy Page,' *Sport History Review* 28 (1997): 146–55; John Dewar, 'Edmonton Grads: The Team and Its Social Significance from 1915–1940,' in *Herstory in Sport*, ed. R. Howell (Westpoint, NY: Leisure Press, 1982), 541–7; S.F. Wise and D. Fisher, *Canada's Sporting Heroes* (Don Mills: General Publishing, 1974), 72–4, 77–8; and Cathy MacDonald, 'The Edmonton Grads: Canada's Most Successful Team: A History and Analysis of Their Success,' unpublished MA thesis (University of Windsor, 1976).

76 'Random Notes on Current Sports,' *Toronto Daily Star*, 18 December 1922, 24.

77 See Kidd, *The Struggle for Canadian Sport*, 111.

78 'Ladies Ready for Hockey,' *Toronto Telegram*, 18 December 1922.

79 See R.W. Connell, *Masculinities* (Los Angelas: University of California Press, 1995); Helen Lenskyj, *Out of Bounds* (Toronto: Women's Press, 1986), 17–34; and Patricia A. Vertinsky, *The Eternally Wounded Woman* (Chicago: University of Illinois Press, 1994).

80 'No Body-Checking in Ladies' Hockey,' *Toronto Daily Star*, 17 December 1923, 11.

81 For more on the aggressive nature of women's hockey during this period, see Kevin B. Wamsley and Carly Adams, 'Stepping In with Fists: Aggression in Early Women's Hockey,' paper presented at the annual conference of the North American Society of Sport Sociology, 2006, Vancouver, British Columbia.

82 'Sticks and Fists Fly Freely as Girl Hockeyists Battle,' *Toronto Daily Star*, 26 March 1935, 12; 'Girls Wanted Another Fight but Referees Stopped Them,'

Toronto Daily Star, 28 March 1935, 14; 'Hockey Amazons in Fistic Display,' *Toronto Daily Star,* 20 February 1936, p. 16; 'Girls Draw Major for Fistic Display,' *Toronto Daily Star,* 4 March 1937, 14.

83 'Rivulettes Play in Port Monday,' *Galt Reporter,* 27 February 1931, 4.

84 'Fee Fo Fi Fum,' *Galt Evening Reporter,* 6 March 1931, 5.

85 Kidd, *The Struggle for Canadian Sport,* 102. The rules for women's hockey during this period were not different, being patterned after the OHA's.

86 See H. Lenskyj, 'Physical Activity for Canadian Women, 1890–1930: Media Views,' in J.A Mangan and Roberta Park, eds, *From 'Fair Sex' to Feminism: Sport and the Socialization of Women in the Industrial and Pre-Industrial Era* (London: Frank Cass, 1987), 208–31.

87 K.B. Wamsley, 'Womanizing Olympic Athletes: Policy and Practice during the Avery Brundage Era,' presented at Onward to the Olympics: Historical Perspectives on the Olympic Games, Wilfrid Laurier University, 2003, p. 5.

88 See Gibb, 'Sticks and Fists Fly Freely.' For other examples see A. Gibb, 'No Man's Land of Sport,' *Toronto Daily Star,* 21 February 1936, 14; 'No Man's Land of Sport,' *Toronto Daily Star,* 9 April 1938, 13; and 'No Man's Land of Sport,' *Toronto Daily Star,* 30 January 1940, 12.

89 Kidd, *The Struggle for Canadian Sport,* 103.

90 See B. Rosenfeld, 'Roxy Atkins Heads "LOHA,"' *Globe and Mail,* 18 December 1939, 18.

91 See A. Gibb, 'No Man's Land of Sport,' *Toronto Daily Star,* 15 October 1940, 12.

92 See, for example, B. Rosenfeld, 'Feminine Sports Reel,' *Globe and Mail,* 22 January 1941, 13. Although the LOHA amalgamated with the WAAF, there is no evidence that the WAAF actually took control of organizing women's hockey in the province. Ultimately, the demise of the LOHA in 1940 had devastating effects on organized women's hockey in the province. It was not until over thirty years later, in 1975, that another governing body for women's hockey in Ontario was established – the Ontario Women's Hockey Association (OWHA).

93 Etue and Williams, *On the Edge,* 69.

94 Holman suggests that the development and decline of women's hockey was quite different in the United States, where women's hockey was at a height of popularity by 1916 and had declined by the early 1920s, just as Canadian women's hockey was gaining momentum. For more information on the American situation, see Holman, 'Stops and Starts,' 332–4.

5 Brutal Butchery, Strenuous Spectacle: Hockey Violence, Manhood, and the 1907 Season

STACY L. LORENZ AND GERAINT B. OSBORNE

Contrary to some popular opinion that hockey violence is growing worse, violence has been a central part of hockey culture for more than a century. David Seglins argues that from the game's beginnings to today, 'violent forms of hockey have been tolerated, legitimized, ritualized and at times celebrated by players, fans, organizers, commentators and the Canadian state.' Since the late nineteenth century, violence in hockey has been accepted 'as just part of the game.'[1] Lawrence Scanlan writes, 'My overwhelming impression from reading the literature, from hearing the testimony of players from the early to mid-1900s, and from poring over news clippings, is that early hockey was very much like war. The blood flowed freely.'[2] For example, in 1904, Ontario Hockey Association president John Ross Robertson warned, 'We must call a halt to slashing and slugging, and insist upon clean hockey ... before we have to call in a coroner to visit our rinks.'[3] One year later, the coroner was indeed called in when an Ontario player, Alexandria's Alcide Laurin, died as a result of a stick to the head from Maxville's Allan Loney. In 1907 the coroner was summoned again after Charles Masson of the Ottawa Victorias struck Owen 'Bud' McCourt of the Cornwall Hockey Club in the head with his stick. Both Loney and Masson were initially charged with murder, but the charges were later reduced to manslaughter. In each case, the offending player was acquitted in the courts, mainly because such violence was deemed intrinsic to the sport.[4]

The 1907 hockey season featured a number of other notable incidents of on-ice violence. Following a particularly rough match between the Ottawa Silver Seven and the Montreal Wanderers on 12 January, assault charges were brought against three members of the Ottawa team. During this game, Charles 'Baldy' Spittal, Harry Smith, and Alfred Smith were involved in separate stick attacks on Montreal players. In the first of these incidents, the *Montreal Gazette* reported that Cecil Blatchford of the Wanderers 'was smashed over the head by Spittal, a short, quick jab with the stick, that laid Bla[t]chford prone, with the blood pouring from a cut over the temple.' Next, 'Harry Smith put [Ernie] Johnson down and out with a smash across the face.' Finally, Alf Smith attacked Hod Stuart: 'Smith skated in from centre ice and smashed the Wanderer cover-point across the temple with his stick. Stuart went down in a heap ... When Stuart was lying helpless on the ice, Smith was heard to remark, "Did you get that one, Hod?" Then he skated away chuckling.'[5] No player was suspended for his actions in this game. Motions for season-long and one-week suspensions were defeated by representatives of clubs in the Eastern Canada Amateur Hockey Association (ECAHA).[6] However, Montreal police later arrested Spittal and the Smiths. The charge against Harry Smith was dismissed, but Baldy Spittal and Alf Smith were found guilty of assault. Both were required to pay a $20 fine and $19 in costs, and the judge warned that similar offences would not be treated so leniently in the future.[7]

This chapter examines media narratives of hockey violence and manhood during the 1907 season in central Canada. This season is a useful case study for examining violence and masculinity in Canadian hockey before the First World War.[8] Newspaper reports of matches involving the Ottawa Silver Seven and the Montreal Wanderers receive particular attention in this case study. The Silver Seven and the Wanderers were two of Canada's leading hockey teams; games between the two clubs attracted a great deal of public attention.[9] Media coverage of the match of 12 January 1907 was especially noteworthy, as newspapers constructed a number of important narratives of hockey and masculinity in response to the spectacular degree of violence in this particular game. A late-season rematch between the two teams prompted further discussion of the place of violent and 'strenuous' play in hockey. This essay also analyses other game reports from the 1907 season in order to place the narratives surrounding the Ottawa-Wanderer rivalry in a broader context. Finally, this chapter evaluates accounts and perceptions of the death of Bud McCourt as a result of an altercation during a match in Cornwall, Ontario, in March 1907. McCourt's fatal on-ice beating, and the subsequent manslaughter trial of Charles Masson, spurred further public analysis of violence in the sport.

Narratives of hockey in the Canadian press during the period of our case study described violence in the sport in terms of both 'brutal butchery' and 'strenuous spectacle' – sometimes on the same page of the newspaper.[10] This chapter explores the meaning of these conflicting narratives of violent and physical play in hockey.[11] It considers hockey's appeal to players and spectators in light of the complex relationship between 'respectable' and 'rough' masculine ideals. It also assesses hockey violence in the context of changing standards and perceptions of manhood in the late nineteenth and early twentieth centuries. Hockey played a significant role in the social construction of masculinity in this period. By evaluating key issues surrounding violence, gender, and class in early hockey, this research addresses important gaps in the study of Canadian sport history and the analysis of hockey and Canadian popular culture.[12] In particular, this essay begins to answer the need for careful, focused case studies that examine hockey violence in a historical context. The 1907 hockey season offers considerable insight into the cultural narratives surrounding hockey violence and manliness in turn-of-the-century Canada.[13]

Knowledge of the historical origins of hockey violence is not simply valuable for the insight it sheds on the past. It is also crucial to an adequate understanding of present-day hockey violence. In the wake of such incidents as Marty McSorley's 'clubbing' of Donald Brashear in February 2000 and Todd Bertuzzi's 'blind-siding' of Steve Moore with a punch from behind in March 2004, the National Hockey League (NHL) has faced intense criticism for its brutality.[14] The Bertuzzi case, in particular, rekindled discussions about the problem of violence in NHL hockey. One aspect of this debate that has not received sufficient attention, however, is a historical perspective on the place of violence and intimidation in the game. A historical case study such as this examination of the 1907 season provides a comparative frame of reference that serves to highlight the distinctive features of contemporary hockey violence and the social and cultural context in which it is situated.

Hockey, Class, and Manliness

With the development of industrial capitalism and the emergence of an entrepreneurial and professional middle class during the nineteenth century, men increasingly perceived their gender identity in relation to individual achievement and economic success in the marketplace. This hegemonic ideal of 'self-made manhood' was championed by a rising middle class of merchants, bureaucrats, clerks, and business and professional men.[15] Middle-class notions of manliness were also rooted in the idea of respectability. According to Christopher Anstead, 'a respectable male individual had to be industrious, sober, religious, compassionate, morally upright and responsible for his own welfare and that of his family.'[16] While this version of manly respectability carried considerable cultural authority, working-class males, in particular, challenged middle-class standards of manhood. For example, labourers in industrializing cities frequently defined their masculine identity away from work, in the realm of leisure. As a result, a distinct working-class culture developed around such activities as drinking, gambling, fighting, and blood sports; within groups such as fire companies, street gangs, lodges, and political factions; and in such places as saloons, pool halls, theatres, and brothels.[17] This culture valued masculine honour, toughness, and physical prowess; in Elliott J. Gorn's words, the working class 'inverted the bourgeois ethos with an antithetical assertion of rough male conviviality.'[18]

Although there were clear differences between 'respectable' and 'rough' masculine ideals, distinctions between middle-class and working-class notions of manhood were neither simple nor rigid. Lynne Marks's examination of gender and leisure in late-nineteenth-century small-town Ontario is especially insightful in this regard. According to Marks, many young men were involved in 'less than respectable activities that were part of a certain masculine culture, predominantly a youth culture, which to some extent crossed class lines.' She argues that historians have underestimated the cross-class appeal of a 'rough' masculinity rooted in 'physical strength, recourse to violence, danger, and a certain wildness among youth.'[19] The ideals of 'responsible, respectable breadwinner' and 'rowdy rough' coexisted in such groups as fraternal orders, fire brigades, militia companies, and sports clubs.[20] Although middle-class sports associations sought to shape the manly character of young men in accordance with respectable ideals, the members of amateur sports teams sometimes pushed the boundaries of upright behaviour. 'Definitions of manly respectability were contested,' Marks writes, 'and even the most middle-class sports clubs, like their counterparts among the fraternal orders, were part of a larger masculine leisure culture and as such accepted a certain level of manly roughness.'[21]

Kevin B. Wamsley and David Whitson offer a similar perspective on gender and class identities in their analysis of the Arthur Pelkey–Luther McCarty boxing match, held in Calgary, Alberta, in 1913.[22] Manslaughter charges were brought against Pelkey following McCarty's death during the fight – the first time a boxer was killed in the ring in Canada. The trial revealed that the kinds of masculinity demonstrated in rough sports like boxing, lacrosse, and hockey were widely respected among influential, middle-class men in the community. Though criticized by moralists and social reformers, boxing champions were respected, popular exemplars of a rough version of masculinity that embraced toughness, force, and violence. According to Wamsley and Whitson, boxing's celebration of aggressive manhood appealed to middle-class businessmen and professionals, as well as working men.[23] The testimony given by witnesses at Pelkey's trial 'spoke explicitly to codes of masculinity, understood within the sporting community, that identified violent confrontations within sporting contests as legitimate and valuable social interactions between consenting men.'[24]

The emergence of modern hockey was tied to conceptions of middle-class amateurism and 'respectable' middle-class masculinity. Before the First World War, organized hockey in Canada was played, developed, and controlled mainly by the male, urban, English-speaking middle and upper-middle classes. Amateur sportsmen, social reformers, and muscular Christians regarded hockey as a 'manly' sport that instilled moral virtue and developed valuable character traits.[25] At the same time, however, some organizers, players, and fans embraced elements of 'rough' masculinity within the game. Alan Metcalfe highlights this dilemma when he notes that '"manliness" was a concept that defied simplistic definition – one man's manly behaviour became another man's "roughness" and "brutality." The line between acceptable and unacceptable behaviour was thin indeed, depending on the social and educational background of the individuals, local conditions, and the importance of a particular contest. Thus it was extremely difficult to determine when actions on the ice actually constituted "brutal" as opposed to "manly" behaviour.'[26]

Hockey also came to occupy a prominent position in Canadian popular culture at a time of significant change in society's notions of manliness and masculinity. During the late nineteenth century, a version of aggressive masculinity that E. Anthony Rotundo calls 'passionate manhood' became the most influential masculine ideal in North America.[27] Anchored in concepts of physicality, martial spirit, eugenics, and Social Darwinism, this passionate standard of masculinity exalted combativeness, competitiveness, and toughness, and placed a high value on bodily strength and athletic skill.[28] In addition, the ascendancy of passionate manhood was connected to a revaluation of what Rotundo refers to as 'primitive masculinity' – a growing tendency to look at men as creatures of impulse and instinct, even as 'animals' or 'savages,' and to regard this 'brutish' side as a pure expression of manliness.[29] As frustrations with the new bureaucratic world of male white-collar work and concerns about cultural feminization and 'overcivilization' spurred efforts to revitalize manhood in new ways, sport became one of the most important vehicles for countering effeminacy and conferring manliness.[30] Moreover, this reshaping of conceptions of manhood during the 1880s and 1890s helped make the roughness and violence of sports like hockey acceptable – even necessary – in the manufacturing of manly character. Rugged sports, in particular, effectively cultivated the characteristics of physical prowess and martial spirit that were at the core of passionate manhood.[31]

Violence in hockey addressed a social need in helping Canadians to define and develop a meaningful masculinity. Although the persistence of physicality and aggression in hockey seemed to contradict the ideals of respectability at the heart of middle-class manliness, this affinity for violence is understandable in the context of both a developing model of masculinity rooted in 'passionate manhood' and a 'rough' masculine leisure culture that cut across class lines. The new standard of active, muscular manhood glorified physical struggle and violent action. 'Primitive' elements in sports like hockey helped to counter the fear that overcivilization was making men weak, effeminate, and over-sophisticated. At the same time, the cross-class appeal of an aggressive masculinity based on force and danger helps to explain the popularity of 'strenuous,' even 'brutal,' hockey among middle-class players and spectators. Like working-class men who favoured more elemental touchstones of masculine prowess, many middle-class men were attracted to the excitement of a fiercely contested, hard-hitting hockey game.[32]

Ottawa-Wanderer Game: Montreal Narratives

Media narratives of the Ottawa-Wanderer game of 12 January 1907 shed considerable light on the place of violence and roughness in hockey during the early twentieth century. Accounts of the match in the Montreal press expressed outrage at the attacks carried out by the visiting team. Newspaper headlines communicate this narrative most clearly. The *Montreal Gazette* stated on its second page, 'WANDERER WON BRUTAL CONTEST – Champions Cut Down by Ottawa, Stuck to Task and Downed Assailants. – BUT LITTLE GOOD HOCKEY. – Occasional Skill Shown in Battle Where Strength Was Requisite Quality.' The game was called 'as disgraceful an exhibition of rough and brutal play as has been seen here – at least, in recent years,' and smaller section headlines included 'BLA[T]CHFORD CUT DOWN' and 'STUART THE NEXT VICTIM.'[33] The *Montreal Star*'s coverage was even more prominent and sensational. The two-column, front-page headline read, '"THEY SHOULD EACH GET SIX MONTHS IN JAIL," IS THE OPINION AS TO SATURDAY HOCKEY BRUTALITIES – Old Players Say it was the Worst Exhibition of Butchery they Ever Saw – Mr. Recorder Weir Would have had them Arrested – Police Magistrate McMahon of Westmount Prepared to Apply the Law.'[34] Inside the paper, the four-column headline across a lengthy, illustrated game story screamed, 'Butchery, Not Hockey, At The Arena Saturday Night.'[35]

As these headlines suggest, Montreal media coverage of the contest combined censure and sensationalism. For example, the *Montreal Star* summed up the game's key incidents in a special box on the front page as follows:

> The three inexcusable and intentional assaults of the match were:
> The one by Spittal on Blatchford, in which Blatchford did not hurt Spittal in any way, yet the latter deliberately tried to split his head by bringing down his hockey stick upon it with all the force his two hands could command.
> Blatchford was carried off senseless, the blood which dripped down in his wake marking the progress of his body to the dressing room.
> The one by Alf. Smith on Stuart. Stuart had a little altercation near the timekeepers, when Alf Smith deliberately skated across and hit him a lateral blow with his stick across the temple, laying him out, and sneering at the prostrate man afterwards. Stuart was laid out like a corpse for a few minutes. All day yesterday he was deaf in one ear as the result.
> The one by Harry Smith on Johnson: This was, as far as could be seen, as little provoked as any of the other assaults. It was a deliberate blow across the face and came near to breaking Johnson's nose. It did not break it, but the jar to the brain laid him out.[36]

In an editorial titled 'Hockey or Manslaughter?' the *Star* described the match as a 'brutal exhibition of rough play and deliberate fouling,' and called for the police to treat assaults in hockey just like crimes on the street:

[T]he police authorities have a responsibility in the case. They know now that a hockey match is likely to result in breaches of the law, and there should be competent police officers present to put under immediate arrest any player who is guilty of an assault. An assault should be no more condoned in a rink crowded with ladies and gentlemen than on St. James street; and the arrest should be as prompt, as public and as certain as if such assault were committed on St. James street in the presence of a squad of policemen. Hockey thuggism will have to be stopped even if we send the hockey thugs to penitentiary.

The editorial page also featured a drawing of a hockey player armed with a sword, axe, knife, and gun, accompanied by a caption that stated, 'The Ottawa hockey team may not be able to play hockey, but it can show the excited populace the latest fancy designs in attempted murder.'[37]

Together, the *Star*'s headlines, stories, and opinions created a narrative of shocking, even criminal, violence. These dramatic depictions of on-ice atrocities not only provided a critique of violent hockey, they also helped the newspaper to engage and attract readers. The *Montreal Star* was one of Canada's leading 'people's journals' – an influential group of innovative, inexpensive daily newspapers that challenged many of the practices of conventional journalism during the late nineteenth and early twentieth centuries.[38] These more independent and profit-oriented dailies were aimed at a much wider readership than that of the established party newspapers. The people's press was designed to appeal not simply to businessmen, professionals, and party supporters, but also to clerks, working-class men, and women and children from across the social spectrum. As a result, publishers of the new dailies de-emphasized the editorial page and politics, while devoting more space to a variety of news, special features, and entertainment. In particular, the people's journals moved away from traditional news coverage in favour of more sensational reports on crime, gossip, disaster, scandal, and sports. Moreover, as newspapers everywhere became engaged in the quest for popularity, they adopted the industry's most successful innovations, whatever their source. As a result, even 'quality' papers like the *Montreal Gazette* tried to reach a mass audience by borrowing extensively from the approaches and techniques of the people's journals.[39]

In light of these changes in the newspaper industry, it is not surprising that reporters sometimes sifted and shaped information to make roughness in hockey seem more scandalous and interesting. Hockey brutality may have been repugnant – especially when perpetrated against the home team – but it still demanded readers' attention. For instance, the *Star*'s detailed summary of the Ottawa-Wanderer match in its sports section began with the following satiric account of the Silver Seven's trip home:

> The professional Butchers' Association of Ottawa organized an excursion to Montreal on Saturday, and had a most successful and pleasant outing.
>
> After a most entertaining exhibition of their skill and prowess, attended by about seven thousand people in the Montreal Arena, situated in the model Town of Westmount, they returned to Ottawa well satisfied with the work done.
>
> On the train going home, speeches of congratulation were made to the winners of the spirited exhibition and prizes were awarded to the following gentlemen.
>
> 1. Mr. Spittal, Champion Meat Chopper for the artistic manner in which he cut down Cecil Blatchford of the Wanderers ...
>
> 2. Mr. Harry Smith, for beating Johnson into unconsciousness ...
>
> 3. Mr. Alf. Smith, for the elegant way in which he chopped down Hod Stuart with a lateral blow on the temple ...
>
> The chairman regretted that he could not bestow any medals on Mr. Pulford, as the exhibitions of scientific ferocity of the other gentlemen were far ahead of his. He came to the conclusion that Mr. Pulford could not have been very well, but expressed the hope that he would soon recover to exhibit at many more matches some of that bloodthirstiness for which he has been known in the past, and which made him a shining example for other members of the team.[40]

Although the writer censured the players' actions through this ironic appraisal, he also implicitly acknowledged that violence created fan interest by situating the 'butchery' within an entertaining and sensational story that would appeal to readers. There is also a tone of playfulness and exaggeration in this account that blunts the force of the reporter's criticism: a truly reprehensible crime likely would not have been analysed in the same way.

At the same time, even this sarcastic *Star* writer acknowledged a more acceptable – but still vicious – standard of roughness in hockey. 'There have been many rough hockey matches in the past, but at them both sides mixed it up, in the heat of battle, and the fouls that were committed were committed because the men lost their temper under the strain of a hard fought match,' the reporter pointed out, 'but on Saturday the brutality was all one sided, and men deliberately skated the width of the rink to knock out another man.'[41] Thus, in this observer's judgment, if both teams had perpetrated the violence, spontaneously, as a result of the stress of competition, the 'brutality' would not have been unusual; in fact, it would have fit the established pattern of many previous matches. Presumably, this type of brutality also would have been viewed more favourably by this particular journalist.

The *Star*'s satiric commentary continued the following day, this time in the form of a cartoon that drew parallels between hockey and the public games of ancient Rome. A caricature of the emperor Nero lamented the fact that the Romans had no hockey players to provide entertainment in the arena. The caption stated, 'VAIN REGRETS. Shade of The Arch Butcher Nero (weeping.) Alas! Alas! Why was that Ottawa Hockey Club not in existence in my time? Ye Gods! What a sight it would have been to set them on the Christians!' At the same time, a sign beside the crying emperor continued the 'butcher' analogy while placing the game back in its modern context: 'HOCKEY BULLETIN – Ottawa vs. Wanderers. A Brutal Contest. Champions Cut Down By Cowardly Butchers From Ottawa. Wanderer Players Taken To Hospital In Ambulance. – A Bloody Contest At Arena. – Montreal Butchers Association To Enter Action Against Ottawa Hockey Club For Butchering Without A Licence. – Ottawa Players Just Short Of Being Murderers.'[42] Again, the criticism of violent hockey within this cartoon is accompanied by a degree of sensationalism that serves as a reminder that 'butchery' also helped sell newspapers.

Ottawa-Wanderer Game: Ottawa Narratives

The narratives created by Ottawa newspapers presented a very different view of the events in Montreal. The *Ottawa Evening Journal*, in particular, offered a narrative of 'strenuous spectacle' that contrasted with the narrative of 'brutal butchery' espoused by the Montreal press. Like the *Montreal Star*, the *Ottawa Evening Journal* was a successful people's journal.[43] However, although both newspapers used violence to engage the interest of readers, the *Evening Journal* did not view the Ottawa-Wanderer game in the same way as its Montreal counterpart. While the *Star*'s portrayal of hockey brutality blended horror and fascination, the

Ottawa newspaper presented the sport's rougher elements as part of an absorbing, aggressive, masculine display. The *Evening Journal*'s two-column headline on page two declared, 'OTTAWAS LOST TO WANDERERS – Game was Decidedly Strenuous and Several Players Were Badly Cut Up. – Cup Holders Failed to Score When Ottawas Only had Three Men on the Ice. Officials Off Color. Great Crowd in Attendance.'[44] The reporter who composed the game story revelled in the match's intense physicality:

> Talk about strenuous hockey. You haven't seen the real thing unless you were fortunate enough to be at the Ottawa-Wanderer game on Saturday night in Montreal. It was a hummer from start to finish and will go down into history as one of the hardest fought games on record. There was tripping, slashing and hard body checking in plenty, and it was very evident that both teams had it in for each other. Knocks were exchanged at every opportunity, and these opportunities came often.

The writer emphasized the game's appeal to spectators, along with its violence:

> For people with weak hearts to go to many such matches it would be a straight case of suicide ... The excitement was intense throughout the entire match and at times the crowd would rise to its feet when some mix-up occurred and hoot and cheer by turns. An official of the Arena said he had never seen more feeling shown or a more excited crowd in the spacious rink ... When the match had finished many pools of blood could be seen on the ice.[45]

According to the *Evening Journal*, fans were keenly interested in fierce, physical, and potentially dangerous hockey. Rather than being outraged by rough play, these spectators – and readers – were drawn to the 'strenuous' aspects of the sport.[46]

Although the *Evening Journal* recounted the violent incidents that would lead to criminal charges, its reporting lacked the lurid description and sardonic indignation of the Montreal media coverage. For instance, the Ottawa newspaper described Spittal's attack on Blatchford in a way that suggested there was nothing extraordinary about it: 'Blatchford came down with a rush and skated into Pulford, who had fallen, and got Harvey over the neck with his stick. Spittal saw this and retaliated, giving Blatchford a wicked clip over the head which made a nasty cut and the blood spurted over the ice. He was able to resume in about ten minutes with his head bandaged up.' The game story also emphasized that the injuries inflicted by the Silver Seven were not serious, as the Montreal players later returned to action: 'Johnson was laid out. He was given a check across the face. It was 15 minutes before play resumed. Johnson came out with his nose covered with plaster. It was thought at first that it was broken.' At the same time, the *Evening Journal* expressed an undertone of admiration for the rugged tactics employed by the Ottawa players. 'Alf. Smith made a rush that looked good to score and Hod Stuart, who had been keeping shy of Alf, came out and attempted to give Smith the body,' noted the reporter. 'Ten minutes later, when he came to, Hod was a sadder and wiser youth. He had got a lovely crack over the head, but it was accidental, and Smith was not sent to the side ... Hod kept far away from Smith after this little affair.' Moreover, the fundamental distinction between the two teams – and the primary reason for the complaints coming out of Montreal – was that the Ottawas could take their lumps in manly fashion, while the Wanderers were soft and weak. 'The Ottawas were guilty of several offenses that could have been well cut out, but they got their share of the bumps,' stated the *Evening Journal*. 'The only real difference is they can take all kinds of knocks and never quit, while if a Wanderer player got any kind of a jab he had to be hurried to the dressing room for a breathing spell.'[47] This willingness to administer and withstand physical punishment was a core element of the cross-class, masculine leisure culture that embraced hockey during this period.[48]

Another important dimension of the *Evening Journal*'s reporting was the emphasis placed on the role of the referee. The newspaper attributed many infractions to incompetent officiating, rather than any malicious intent on the part of the Ottawa players. 'If the Ottawas has [*sic*] played a less rough game and kept on the ice instead of decorating the fence so often, there would be a different tale to tell to-day,' acknowledged the *Evening Journal* reporter. 'But then there is a good deal of reason in the methods pursued by Ottawas, as they were getting sent to the side for the most trivial offenses, in fact, at times players and spectators alike wondered what they had been ordered to the side for.' In addition to calling a series of unjustified penalties, the referee allegedly missed – or ignored – 'many a nasty jab' handed out by the Wanderers. In light of the poor quality of the officials, the growing frustration of the Ottawa players was understandable. As the *Evening Journal* pointed out, 'This naturally worked up hard feeling and left the players in anything but a good frame of mind.' Thus, the disillusionment that resulted from inept officiating served as a logical explanation for the Ottawas' subsequent rough play: 'There is no real justification for rough work, but when the officials practically make the game a farce by ordering off half your team for trivial offenses, men naturally become reckless and do many things they would not do if getting fair treatment. This was the case with the Ottawas. They thought they were getting a raw deal from the officials and well knowing that they could not beat their opponents and the officials, too, became disgusted and sailed in with a dash that threatened to put all the Wanderer team on the hospital list.'[49] Finally, rather than condemning the Ottawas for their reckless violence, the *Evening Journal* actually praised them for their steadfast play when competing short-handed as a result of penalties. 'The way the men played against such odds and with the crowd hooting and calling all kinds of "nice" things at the Ottawas, shows what kind of stuff the local boys are made of,' boasted the newspaper. 'It was an exhibition of pluck that won admiration from even the people who a moment before were calling loudly for the Wanderers to put the Ottawas out of business.'[50]

The *Ottawa Citizen* also cited the high calibre of the game, while implying that rough and aggressive play contributed to its quality. The *Citizen*'s sports page featured the two-column headline, 'WANDERERS AND OTTAWAS IN TERRIFIC MATCH – Senators Played Very Rough Hockey and Were Beaten Four Goals to Two. – Hod Stuart, Bla[t]chford and Johnston Badly Injured. Ottawas Heavily Penalized.'[51] The game report began, 'When the big gong at the Arena sounded Saturday night for the last time, fourteen tired, worn-out athletes skated or rather dragged themselves off the ice amidst one long, continuous roar from seven thousand hockey enthusiasts who had witnessed one of the roughest and most exciting struggles on record.' In addition, the *Citizen* – like the *Evening Journal* – claimed that the referee treated Ottawa unfairly. 'All the blame for the unruly tactics employed fell on the shoulders of Ottawa, and the Senators, during the greater part of the second half, were forced to play three or four men against seven,' the *Citizen* reported.[52]

However, in contrast to the *Evening Journal*, the *Citizen* combined its narrative of rough, exciting hockey with moderate criticism of excessive violence. The *Citizen*'s ambivalent treatment of hockey violence therefore reflected both its roots as a Conservative party organ and its experimentation with more sensational reporting during the late nineteenth and early twentieth centuries.[53] 'It was a remarkable match in many respects and Ottawa would probably have gone home victorious if they had played clean hockey,' acknowledged the *Citizen* writer. 'They didn't do so, but went at the Wanderers hammer and tongs in the second half, knocking them out one after another. Wanderers, on the other hand, retaliated, but did not utilize nearly such rough tactics as those which the Ottawas brought into play.' The *Citizen* referred to the Silver Seven's style of play as 'disgraceful,' and noted, 'Many of those who accompanied the Ottawas were greatly disappointed with the result, claiming that the Senators could have won if they had played clean hockey instead of attempting to butcher Stuart.' Finally, the newspaper stated, 'The rough work commenced with the beginning of the final period, and subsequently the match was more like a prize-fight than a battle between the giants of the hockey world.'[54]

Coverage of the Ottawa-Wanderer game and its aftermath also constructed what could be described as a 'squealing' narrative. Manly players were expected to react to rough play 'like men.' This meant accepting a certain degree of violence, tolerating pain and injury, and persevering through difficulty and danger. As a result, when complaining – or 'squealing' – about Ottawa brutality seemed to become excessive, the manliness of the Montreal players and their supporters was called into question. A member of the Ottawa executive expressed this view when he told the *Ottawa Citizen*, 'The Ottawa players received just as many blows as the Wanderers; they were black and blue after the match, but, unlike the Wanderers, they didn't lie down. Ottawa took their taps like men and the Wanderers should be the last ones on earth to put up a squeal.'[55] The *Ottawa Free Press* conveyed a similar message, reporting, 'Ottawa supporters claim a moral victory, and – the truth must be told – a general satisfaction to see their favorites make the home team "lay down" as they expressed it after the game.'[56] Meanwhile, the *Toronto Telegram* offered a parallel criticism of the Montreal press. 'Saturday night when Wanderers went up against Ottawa, and got the worse of it, Montreal papers executed a squealing specialty,' claimed the *Telegram*. 'There is not the slightest doubt in the world that Ottawa plays anything but a parlor game, but the idea that Wanderers are the Alice-sit-by-the-fire team that knows no wrong is enough to make old Rameses shake with boyish laughter.'[57] The fear of a perception of unmanly squealing also made representatives of the Wanderer club reluctant to criticize publicly the conduct of the Ottawa players – and, in particular, to pursue suspensions for the attacks. 'It was thought that perhaps Wanderers would take the matter up themselves with the league, but there is no prospect of this,' reported the *Montreal Gazette*.

'They will let the matter rest on the report of the officials, and avoid all cause for a charge of squealing.'[58]

The spectre of squealing later played an important part in the dismissal of charges against Harry Smith. Smith had been arrested for allegedly assaulting Ernie Johnson, but when he appeared in court, 'there was not a man amongst all the witnesses called who would positively testify that he saw Smith hit Johnson with deliberate intent.'[59] Perhaps the most interesting testimony came from Johnson himself. Reluctant to violate hockey's manly 'code,' Johnson not only declined to speak out directly against Smith, he refused even to acknowledge that he had been injured during the game. According to the *Montreal Star*'s summary, Johnson told the court, 'There was a scrimmage, he was struck by a blow coming from somewhere, he couldn't tell where, and delivered by someone, he couldn't tell who. He never lost consciousness, he did not fall on the ice because the blow knocked him out, and it was simply to keep the blood from running onto his clothes that he remained prone on the ice. The scar at present to be seen decorating his beak-like nose was not from the blow in question, but had been received the year before.' At the same time, the judge in the case asserted that a certain amount of roughness was to be expected – and accepted – in hockey. He believed that the Smith-Johnson incident fell within this normal scope of violence. As the *Star* reported, 'It was during a game, where all players must expect to receive their share of hard knocks, there was a scrimmage and a rough check. Apart from that no witness had shown that the blow had been delivered maliciously for the purpose of deliberately striking the opponent. He therefore discharged the accused.'[60]

The conflicting 'Montreal' and 'Ottawa' perspectives on these issues clearly reflect a 'home team' bias. Accounts of the 12 January game and its aftermath were filtered through the lens of local boosterism. As a result, it is not surprising that newspapers generally supported their own city's team, while criticizing opponents from other communities.[61] However, the different narratives of hockey violence surrounding the Ottawa-Wanderer match were not simply the products of civic rivalry or isolated examples of local perspectives. These narratives also spoke more broadly to different ways of experiencing and enjoying hockey; to various tensions within public perceptions of the sport; and to a more widely held ambivalence about violence in the game. For example, a newspaper story that portrayed violence as 'butchery' and 'manslaughter' would make sense to readers only if excessive violence was sometimes perceived as a problem in hockey. Similarly, a reporter's depiction of rough play as 'strenuous' action would resonate with readers only if violent hockey was often interpreted as exciting and admirable. At the same time, dramatic accounts of on-ice mayhem and descriptions of spectacular displays of masculine aggression were part of a broader move towards sensationalism and entertainment in news coverage – a move being made by quality dailies and people's journals alike. Thus, accounts of the Ottawa-Wanderer game provide exaggerated examples of complex narratives that were woven into hockey coverage on a daily basis. Stories of 'brutal butchery' and 'strenuous spectacle' were part of the usual cultural experience of hockey, and their more subtle and typical forms can be discerned in regular media coverage of the sport.

Hard and Fast, but Clean

While the degree of violence in the Ottawa-Wanderer game was exceptional, stickwork, rough play, and fighting were far from unusual elements in turn-of-the-century hockey. Descriptions of slashing, tripping, hacking, hard checking, brawls, cuts, broken noses, and other injuries were regular features of hockey reporting by 1900.[62] In fact, on the same day that coverage of the Wanderer-Ottawa match began, there were a number of other central Canadian newspaper accounts of violent play in recent hockey matches. For example, another game in Montreal on Saturday, 12 January, between the intermediate squads of the Victorias and the Shamrocks, featured a great deal of body checking, a player thrown out of the game for excessive roughness, and a brawl involving most of the players on the ice. The *Montreal Gazette* reported that the match was largely 'a question of who could do the most deliberate bodying. This was at first passed unnoticed, and the roughness went on increasing until no opportunity for administering a deliberate jab was missed by players on either side.' According to the game summary, 'Savage, of the Vics, was repeatedly ruled off for bodying, while in the second half Ryan, Shamrock cover-point, was benched for the rest of the game for rough play.' The contest reached its zenith when a fight erupted between the two clubs:

> Sticks were dropped and fists used for an exciting two minutes of the match between Intermediate Victorias and Shamrocks on Saturday afternoon. Bad feeling had been brewing between the teams from the start of the match and it culminated towards the end of the second half, when Browne, of Victorias, received a jab on the face in front of Shamrocks' goal.

In an instant the players had rushed up to the scene of trouble and paired off, blows being exchanged by all except a couple of Victoria defence men. The combatants cooled down after a couple of minutes, and 'Doc' Brown, of Montreal, who acted as referee, sent three Shamrock men to the fence.[63]

The *Toronto Star* also carried reports of 'brutal' and 'rough' hockey in its 14 January 1907 edition. Next to a detailed summary of the 'dirty work' in the Ottawa-Wanderer game, the *Star* ran a story headlined 'ROUGH HOCKEY IN AQUATIC LEAGUE.' According to the *Star,* some of the games in this Toronto-based association 'were nothing more or less than slugging matches.' For example, during a game on Friday, 11 January, involving the Toronto Rowing Club and Parkdale Canoe Club, a 'man from the penalty bench struck an opponent who was going down the board a punch that put him out,' while another player 'was knocked senseless by a cross-check and his face was seriously damaged.'[64] In addition, the Toronto newspaper picked up a story from the *Winnipeg Telegram* that attempted to downplay the extent of the violence – and unmanly complaints about rough play – in a recent game between the Winnipeg Strathconas and a Brandon team. 'The Strathconas are indignantly denying the lurid report in a local contemporary regarding the game at Brandon last week, in which the locals appeared to be "squealing" in regard to their treatment, accusing the Wheat City team of playing a dirty game,' stated the article. 'The Strathconas say they had a hard game at Brandon, but they have also seen many other games much harder.'[65] Finally, the *Toronto Star* noted, 'Owen Sound report a regular old-fashioned Donnybrook in their recent game at Markdale on the 7th.'[66]

Newspaper readers were exposed to a number of different perspectives on hockey violence in the early twentieth century. These narratives expressed the tensions and ambivalence that were evident in coverage of the first Ottawa-Wanderer match. Reporters, players, and team officials seemed to favour 'decidedly strenuous' but 'clean' hockey. They tried to distinguish between this preferred brand of 'hard' and 'fast' hockey, and an excessively violent version of the game they called 'dirty' or, sometimes, 'rough' hockey.[67] However, these distinctions were not easy to draw. The problem, of course, was that hard and strenuous hockey was marked by a great deal of physical, even violent, play. Body checking, collisions, slashing, intimidation, blood, and bruises were frequently applauded by hockey observers. The fact that 'rough' hockey could sometimes be 'clean' and at other times was considered 'dirty' also demonstrates the ambivalence towards violence that was central to perceptions of the sport. As Seglins notes,

> Indeed, assaultive behaviour, tripping, checking and fighting did enjoy a high degree of legitimacy as expected parts of the game. For leagues and referees, there was a tenuous balance to be struck. On the one hand, the spectacular, entertaining and exciting rougher aspects of play that boosted ticket sales had a high degree of legitimacy among the players and fans who expected strong, aggressive, masculine hockey. On the other hand, the leagues were concerned with prohibiting serious injuries to hockey players as well as ensuring the respectability and reputation of hockey teams and the sport in general.[68]

Following the death of Bud McCourt late in the 1907 season, the *Cornwall Freeholder* also made a perceptive comment about spectator interest in violent hockey. 'The public are not blameless,' stated the *Freeholder*. 'They encourage good, hard play as they call it, but which really means doing anything disreputable that escapes the eye of the referee.'[69]

These strains and contradictions were important dimensions of hockey reporting during the 1907 season. For instance, the *Ottawa Citizen*'s summary of a match between the towns of Arnprior and Renfrew described the essential elements of 'good, clean hockey': 'The game was without a doubt the fastest played in the Ottawa Valley league this season ... Both teams upheld their good reputation for manly playing, and while the game was well above the standard, there was an entire absence of rough work and it was, nevertheless, one of the keenest battles on record ... The players went at it with a vim and the checking was heavy and close, though no rough tactics were employed on either side.' The *Citizen* reporter observed, 'Three of the Arnprior men were in the box at one time but only for petty offenses ... McMillan and Dontigny were both accidentally knocked out in the latter half and had to be carried off the ice.'[70] In sum, the game was a 'keen battle' that featured 'heavy' checking, numerous penalties, and players being knocked unconscious during play – but it was not 'rough.' The *Citizen* generated a similar narrative in its description of a Federal Hockey League contest involving the Ottawa Victorias and Cornwall: 'Outside of three or four Stanley cup matches ... nothing more exciting has been pulled off in Dey's arena than the Victoria-Cornwall Federal league fixture of Saturday night ... The game was hard and, at times, rough, but the long list of penalties was due to close checking and tripping rather than to deliberate dirty work. True, three of the Cornwall boys were laid out, two from heavy body-checks, and one from a blow with the puck; but all this was incidental to one of the hardest matches ever seen in the Federal league.'[71] Public perceptions of high-quality hockey were also evident in a 'Hard, Fast Match in the Lower Ottawa League,' featuring teams from Vankleek Hill and Lachute. 'The exhibition of hockey put up was fast and brilliant,' declared the *Citizen*. 'The game was not rough. It was, however, exciting and strenuous at all times.'[72]

A game in Ottawa's City League between the Ottawa Seconds and the Rialtos also illustrates a high degree of tolerance for violence in hockey as expressed in press reports. According to the *Ottawa Evening Journal*, the match was fast, exciting, and entertaining, mainly as a result of its intense, physical nature: 'The checking was pretty stiff and there was some tripping, but little really rough play. The officials ... handed out quite an extended list of penalties, but the offences were not of a serious nature. Play at times was decidedly strenuous and heavy bodying was a feature of the play. Three of the Rialto forwards were slightly injured. All were struck in the face. Arial received a nasty crack over the nose and Billy Dunning had some teeth loosened. The officials did not stand for any rough work.' Further contradicting claims of clean play, the *Evening Journal* reported that, when no one scored in the first overtime period, 'The rink authorities refused to allow the teams to play after the extra 20 minutes, as they thought that rough work might result.'[73] The game therefore ended in a tie.

Clean, fast-paced hockey was widely praised by sportswriters. When the Kenora Thistles travelled east in January 1907 to play the Montreal Wanderers for the Stanley Cup, the *Montreal Gazette* lauded the western champions' style of play. 'They are in Montreal representing a fine type of manhood; what is more, the finest type of hockey, fast and clean, looking for the puck, not the man; aiming at the goal, and not with vicious intent to hurt or maim,' commented the *Gazette*.[74] The two Kenora-Wanderer Stanley Cup games were described in Montreal newspapers with such phrases as 'speedy and clean'; 'a ripping fast match'; 'brilliant, not at all rough'; 'exceptionally clean'; with 'plenty of smart, snappy hockey.' Nevertheless, while there appeared to be 'no foul play of a serious nature,' press reports did acknowledge that the contests included hard collisions, some 'rough work,' and a great deal of 'stiff' checking.[75] Following an exhibition match between the Thistles and the Ottawa Silver Seven, the *Ottawa Citizen*'s summary of the 'brilliant battle' between Kenora and Ottawa also highlighted the links between manliness and 'strenuous' hockey. The *Citizen* stated, 'There was not an unpleasant incident from beginning to end, in fact it was in many respects an ideal game. Not that the play itself was not strenuous or the teams determined, but the men had no hard feelings and deserved unlimited credit.'[76] Likewise, when the Montreal Wanderers journeyed to Winnipeg in March 1907 to try to reclaim the Stanley Cup from Kenora, the *Montreal Star* noted the tension between 'clean' and 'rough' hockey: 'It was a clean game ... There was some close checking, but in most instances it was strictly within rules. Early in the game Stuart had his splints knocked off and injured his finger, but he played throughout [the] game without wincing. Once he collided with the fence and was dazed for a moment, but he came back gamely and continued play. Not a man was seriously injured in the game ... [T]here was no wanton roughness and altogether it was creditable hockey.'[77]

An ECAHA match between the Ottawa Silver Seven and the Montreal Victorias was described in similar terms. The *Montreal Gazette* stated that the 'brilliant' contest was 'fast, clean' and free of 'foul play.'[78] The *Ottawa Citizen* agreed: 'The game was clean, brilliant and exciting from beginning to end.'[79] Similarly, under the headline 'OTTAWAS BEAT THE VICTORIAS – In One of the Most Brilliant and Sensational Games of the Season. – There was no Dirty Play and Both Teams Put up Very Speedy Hockey,' the *Ottawa Evening Journal* reported, 'It was an ideal match from every point of view. Both teams played fast, hard hockey, but there was little rough play and the few penalties that were handed out were for minor offences. Not a player was injured, nor was a foul blow of any kind struck.'[80] However, players were penalized for slashing and cross-checking, and the *Montreal Gazette* mentioned the following incident: 'Baird chased Hale across the ice, smashing out with his stick until Hale finally dropped. This was the worst of the fouls, but Hale was not hurt, and there were no nasty results.'[81]

In addition, the *Ottawa Citizen*'s reports on the contest gradually revealed more roughness than the newspaper's initial assessment. In its first game story, the *Citizen* acknowledged,

Kirby proved a capable referee and Percival did fairly well, although he penalized Baird and Pulford in the second half for nothing more than good stiff body-checks. Davidson, Howard and Bowie also used their elbows and sticks on the Ottawas in close quarters, jabbing them in the face and body. Neither Kirby nor Percival saw these little tricks, but Victorias pulled them off in a tricky manner as usual, escaping punishment.[82]

The next day, in its 'Sporting Gossip' column, the *Citizen* offered more details about the 'brilliant' game's subtle savagery:

> There was no apparent foul work in Saturday's match between Ottawa and Victorias, at least none could be observed by the referee or judge of play. After the battle, however, when the Ottawa players, after being showered congratulations, took off their uniforms at the Windsor, there was plenty of evidence that the wearers of maroon and white had not been so gentle and lamb-like after all. Harry Westwick and Alf Smith were black and blue around the shins. Their pads had not saved them to any great extent, and Westwick's ankles were painfully swollen. Davidson and Howard had used their sticks freely on the visiting forwards, but did so in such a smooth way that they escaped detection. Russell Bowie is another artist in the line of jabbing an opponent with his stick, and in spite of the fact that they were pretty roughly handled in rough quarters, Ottawa did not retaliate.[83]

Thus, even 'clean' contests included a significant amount of stickwork and physical play, and only the most violent acts seemed to constitute 'dirty' hockey.

When the Silver Seven and the Victorias met again three weeks later in Ottawa, the game threatened to cross the line between strenuousness and butchery on several occasions. Police officers present at the match even interceded during one particularly heated altercation. The *Ottawa Evening Journal*'s headline captured all the key elements of the contest: 'VICS WERE EASY FOR OTTAWAS – Locals Outplayed the Montrealers at Every Stage of a Fast, Hard Game – Play was Decidedly Rough at Times. Police Had to Interfere During a Row. Howard Injured. One of Largest Crowds on Record in Attendance.'[84] The *Evening Journal*'s game story, which was also picked up by the *Montreal Star*, stated, 'The pace set at the start was a fierce one, both teams rushing and attacking in great style, and it could soon be seen that the play was going to be decidedly strenuous. Heavy bodying, tripping and slashing were in evidence at all stages of the game, and much of it escaped the notice of the officials, although they handed out quite a lengthy list of penalties. The officials were not in any way to blame for not seeing many of the offences, as both the Ottawas and Vics are well up in the art of giving a nice jab or trip when the officials are busy in some other quarter.' 'Howard was the only man to be really injured,' added the *Evening Journal* reporter, 'although several of the players received nasty bruises and slight cuts.'[85]

Maintaining a consistent position on the teams' first meeting – and on its narrow definition of excessively violent hockey – the *Evening Journal* observed, 'The rough play came as a surprise after the remarkably clean game between the Vics and Ottawas in Montreal, but after all there was little really dirty play.' Nevertheless, despite the absence of 'dirty' tactics, the newspaper reported,

[o]n one occasion it looked very much as if the whole two teams were going to get into a free fight. Davidson had repeatedly been checking Harry Smith very hard, and just before half time Smith rushed down the ice and was sent into the boards with a crash by Davidson. Smith immediately landed the Vic man with his stick and the latter retaliated; then the two mixed it up. Several of the other players rushed over and started to separate the men, and the players of both teams were pretty roughly handled before things were straightened out.

Two police officers intervened in the melee. However, they apparently left the fans dissatisfied by failing to arrest any of the players:

Detective McLaughlin and Constable McLeod, who were seated on the side, jumped on to the ice and rushed over to where the trouble was, but the men had been separated before they reached them. The officers warned the players that if there was any repetition of the offence they would summon the players. The crowd arose to its feet expecting to see some arrests follow, but were disappointed. The greatest excitement prevailed for a time.[86]

Moreover, according to the *Evening Journal*, only Harry Smith's insistence that a cross-check administered to his head by a Victoria player was unintentional prevented the police from laying assault charges:

When spoken to this morning by a Journal representative Chief of Police de la Ronde said that no summons would be issued in the case. He further said, however, that if Harry Smith had not explained that the blow given him by Davidson was accidental the Victoria player would have been taken from the ice and locked up by Detective McLaughlin. This officer threatened to take this step, but Smith interfered on Davidson's behalf and protested that Davidson had not struck him deliberately.[87]

Just as Ernie Johnson had been unwilling to speak out against Smith, Smith himself would not turn against Davidson.

Finally, newspaper narratives revealed a perception that quality hockey required various types of 'legitimate' violence. For example, hard checking was considered crucial to sound defensive hockey. When the *Montreal Gazette* described an Ottawa player as being 'at his best,' the writer added, 'His work was not gentle – he is a big fellow and of a strenuous temperament – but it appeared to be fair.'[88] Similarly, the *Ottawa Citizen* commented that in a game between Pembroke and Renfrew, 'the checking was hard, but fair and the defences of each team used their bodies with telling effect on the light forwards.'[89] In addition, the *Citizen* praised the members of an Ottawa City League team for their body-checking prowess: 'New Edinburgh are the greatest body-checkers in the league. The average player, as a rule, utilizes a cross-check or a trip to put an opponent off his feet, but the boys in red, white and black used their bodies on Rialtos every time ... [I]t was not unusual to see Rialto men banged into the sides or hoisted over the embankment by a legitimate shoulder-to-shoulder check.'[90]

At times, fighting was also described in ways that suggested it was a routine part of the game. For example, the *Ottawa Citizen* stated in its report on the New Edinburgh-Rialto match that 'Rance Dunning and Morley Neate had a lively tussle on one occasion. The two had been handing one another bouquets all evening, and finally they met near Rialto's goal. They sparred, clinched and fell, Neate jabbing and upper-cutting Dunning as the latter lay beneath him. Referee Ellis put both men off, but they clashed again and again, when they resumed, dividing honors when it came to rough-house work.'[91] Nor did fighting seem to be unusual in a Montreal industrial league. According to game reports of 1 March 1907, one Manufacturers' League contest featured 'a free fight on the ice' and teams involved in another game 'developed a tendency for fistic exhibitions.'[92] Likewise, the Montreal *Star*'s summary of a Sault Ste Marie–Calumet match stated, in a rather off-hand manner, 'A few fist fights, much clashing [slashing?] and tripping, and very little scientific hockey characterized the game.'[93] The story was similar a week later, when Sault Ste Marie faced Calumet again: 'Vigorous checking kept bad blood up, and resulted in a scrap which caused the police and spectators to rush on the ice in the second half ... Roy Brown was jabbed in the eye by "Tuff" Bellefeuille's stick, and Lalonde and Bellefeuille exchanged swats until the police interfered.'[94]

The Ottawa-Wanderer Rematch

Media narratives of the second meeting of the season between the Ottawa Silver Seven and the Montreal Wanderers, scheduled for Saturday, 2 March, in Ottawa, also demonstrate the tensions surrounding the cultural experience of hockey during this period.[95] First, newspaper coverage of the rematch focused on the high level of spectator interest in the game. When several hundred tickets became available to the general public two days before the contest, a huge crowd gathered outside an Ottawa drug store to purchase admission to the game. In a front-page article, the *Ottawa Evening Journal* stated, 'No more exciting scenes have been witnessed in Ottawa for many a long day than those of the early hours of this morning, when thousands of people fought for tickets for the Ottawa-Wanderer hockey match.' The report continued: 'The police made several attempts to form the crowd in line and used their batons freely, but there was nothing doing. The crowd simply pushed them aside ... Never have so many lovers of the game contracted the hockey fever so badly as the crowd this morning.'[96]

The violence of the first Ottawa-Wanderer meeting did not dampen enthusiasm for the second game. In fact, the excitement and controversy surrounding the contest of 12 January appears to have fuelled intense interest in the 2 March rematch.[97] The *Ottawa Evening Journal* informed readers,

> Never in the history of the Capital has there been such a demand for seats for any sporting event as the Ottawa-Wanderer game, and this morning several thousand people were lined up where the plan was to be opened at a leading drug store. Hundreds of boys and speculators stayed up all night to get first position and at midnight quite a crowd had gathered in front of the store, and by 4 a.m. several hundred people were fighting to get near the door. By six a.m. the crowd had grown to immense proportions, and about a dozen policemen were sent to the scene but they could do nothing. The street was blocked and people were fighting madly to reach the front.[98]

People smashed store windows and stole merchandise, and several youths were injured or 'had to be taken out of the crowd in a fainting condition.'[99] As a result, ticket sales were moved from this drug store to the arena, where more windows were broken in the rush for advance seats that afternoon.[100]

In Montreal a large crowd gathered in front of the *Montreal Star*'s downtown office on the night of the game while the Ottawas and the Wanderers were facing off in Ottawa. These followers of hockey had assembled to listen to the progress of the game as telegraph bulletins were received by the newspaper. According to the *Star*, 'The plan of having a member of the Star editorial staff read out the report of the match as it came direct from the rinkside at Ottawa over a direct wire again proved to be exceedingly popular, and the four or five thousand people gathered literally hung upon the speaker's lips.' Public interest in the game was confirmed by the size and enthusiasm of the group surrounding the newspaper building: 'There have been many great crowds in front of that office on various occasions, but the crowd on Saturday night beat everything that was ever seen, not barring election nights. It extended on St. Catherine past Metcalfe street, and across Peel street down as far as the lane that runs back of Alexander's. It was a most excited and enthusiastic crowd also. In fact, never, either in the case of hockey or lacrosse matches, has a crowd at a bulletin board in Montreal shown so much excitement.'[101]

The Wanderers won the match by a score of 10–6 and claimed the Eastern Canada Amateur Hockey Association championship.[102] In contrast to the first Ottawa-Wanderer game, coverage of the rematch in Montreal and Ottawa newspapers was remarkably similar in content and tone. On the whole, media reports in both cities constructed a narrative of 'strenuous spectacle' around the contest. The only notable occurrence of excessive violence was a clash in which Ottawa's Harry Smith cut Montreal's Hod Stuart with his stick. By combining speed and skill with hard hits and physical play, the match achieved the precarious balance between strenuousness and roughness that was essential to the most exciting hockey.

The headline introducing the *Montreal Star*'s coverage read, 'Wanderers' Win Stunned Ottawa – Champions Played Opponents Off Their Feet in Stirring Hockey Struggle and Retained Title of Leadership in League.' The *Star* reported, 'It was a hard, rough match. The ice was heavy and on the slower surface it was easier than usual to reach the man, consequently there was a great deal of bodying and the boards often crashed from the impact of a victim. Apart from the incident in which Harry Smith figured and some of Baird's tricks, it was not a dirty game to the extent that some of the previous meetings have reached. The Ottawa men played hard, but their opponents stuck with them and it is probable that they gave as much as they took.' The *Star* also praised the determination of Stuart in the face of the Silver Seven's efforts to intimidate him. 'Ottawa seemed to want to get at Hod Stuart. They did land Hod, and that gentleman left a gory souvenir in Dey's Rink to mark where he fell,' wrote the Star reporter. 'He was "got at" early, probably after half a minute's play, but that nerved Stuart to his work, and he played the best game of this season, fully earning the high compensation given for his services.' In addition, the newspaper noted that police officers were present at the game in an attempt to deter the type of violence that occurred in the January meeting of the two clubs. 'However, no officer was needed,' commented the Star writer, 'and the game was played to a strenuous, but not unduly rough, finish.'[103]

Despite the fact that the Ottawa club lost the game, the Ottawa Evening Journal celebrated the quality of the match even more enthusiastically than did the Montreal Star. The Evening Journal's headlines summarized the essential ingredients of an outstanding hockey game: 'WANDERERS CAPTURE CHAMPIONSHIP; DEFEATED OTTAWAS IN HARD GAME – Victory of the Montreal Team Came as One of the Biggest Surprises in Sporting Circles in Years. – One of the Fastest Games Ever Witnessed in the Capital. Wanderers Had Best of Play Nearly all the Way. Plenty of Tripping and Slashing, but Little Really Dirty Play. Great Crowd in Attendance. Police and Firemen Stationed at Rink. Score 10 to 6.' The contest featured speed, excitement, and keen competition. 'People who paid big prices for their tickets had the satisfaction of knowing that they saw one of the greatest games of hockey ever played in Canada,' claimed the Evening Journal. 'It was a battle royal between the giants of the hockey world, and everyone wanted to witness the struggle.' Like the Montreal Star, the Evening Journal commended Stuart for persevering in the face of danger: 'Hod Stuart seemed to be the object of the Ottawa's "love" taps and he received several, but he generally returned the compliment. Stuart was laid out shortly after play started with a nasty cut, but returned to the game in a few minutes with a big square plaster over his forehead. Hod played the game of his life and was responsible for several of the Wandere[r] scores by his brilliant rushes. He also saved the situation several times by his beautiful checking.'[104]

Above all, the Evening Journal highlighted the appeal of rough, physical hockey to fans. 'The play was of the kind that kept everyone keenly excited, being fast and hard at all stages, with plenty of heavy checking and bodying and all kinds of tripping and slashing,' enthused the Evening Journal writer.[105] 'The penalty list was quite a heavy one, although the offenses in the majority of cases were not very glaring. That the play was rough no one will question, but there was little really dirty work.' Finally, the newspaper noted that 'the officials were fair in their decisions and quick to act in case of rough play ... Some nasty trips and slashes escaped their notice but that is to be expected in such a strenuous and fast game.'[106] In sum, these media narratives revealed that the formula for compelling hockey involved an exhilarating combination of speed, competitiveness, and physicality. A few days later, however, this volatile mixture of 'nasty' and 'strenuous' play exploded in Cornwall, Ontario, and another debate over violence in hockey began.

Bud McCourt and Charles Masson

The death of Bud McCourt as a result of injuries sustained in a Federal Hockey League game between Cornwall and the Ottawa Victorias on Wednesday, 6 March was the most serious incident of violence during the 1907 hockey season. McCourt was killed by a blow from a hockey stick during a chaotic melee that involved several players from each team. Although there were contradictory accounts of the precise role played by various participants in the events leading up to the Cornwall player's death, no one seems to have disputed the fact that Charles Masson skated across the ice and, using his stick, struck a deliberate blow to McCourt's head. Masson's motivation appears to have been to stop McCourt from clubbing another player with his own stick, although at least one observer claimed that McCourt and Ottawa's Charles Chamberlain were 'scrapping' with their fists when Masson hit McCourt. Other witnesses said that McCourt had already slashed Chamberlain over the head when Masson intervened; still other accounts indicate that McCourt was mixed up with Arthur Throop, who also received a severe head wound during the stick fight and had to leave the game. In addition, doctors testified that, before being battered by Masson, McCourt had sustained an earlier blow to his skull, likely from the stick of either Chamberlain or Throop. Meanwhile, after knocking out McCourt, Masson was hit across the head by Cornwall's Zion Runions. In the end, the jury in Masson's manslaughter trial returned a not-guilty verdict after just half an hour of deliberations, mainly because McCourt had received so many shots to the head in the skirmish leading to his death that it was not clear whether Masson alone was responsible for the decisive strike.[107]

Newspaper accounts of the McCourt-Masson incident generated several important narratives relating to violence in early-twentieth-century hockey. First, media coverage of the game further contributed to the notion that hockey was dangerous, violent, and unruly. The wild melee that led to McCourt's death reinforced readers' perceptions that stick swinging, blood, and brawls were standard elements of hard-fought hockey. The fact that a player was killed as a result of an intentional blow delivered by an opponent during a game was the most powerful contributor to this narrative. However, as the *Montreal Star* reported, several other players also sustained injuries during the 'general row' that broke out: 'Many players were hurt at this time, Throop, Chamberlain and [Alfred] Young of Ottawa were amongst them, while McCourt and [Aeneas "Reddy"] McMillan of Cornwall also received injuries. That more did not prove serious was a wonder, for during that brief period of less than half a minute, players with uplifted sticks were striking right and left. One of the witnesses who took part in the fight, and who by his own evidence said that he hit Masson, gave as his reason that "he saw everyone in it and thought he might as well have a hand, too."'[108] Similarly, the *Ottawa Citizen* stated, 'So many sticks were flying that it was impossible to tell which was which.'[109] As many as six different blows were delivered to players' skulls. McCourt suffered two significant wounds, while at least four Ottawa players – Throop, Young, Chamberlain, and Masson – reportedly returned from the game with lumps, cuts, or stitches on their heads, apparently as a result of Cornwall sticks.[110] The *Montreal Star* concluded that more than one player could have died in the fray. 'There was a general fight after the first blow, and in the row players of both teams were cut down,' declared the *Star*. 'That only one was killed seems to have been an act of some special Providence.'[111]

Despite the seemingly obvious level of deliberate brutality in this particular game, another narrative interpreted the entire episode as a 'tragic accident.'[112] According to this view, the events that occurred during the Cornwall-Victoria match were certainly 'unfortunate'; however, in the context of hockey culture, such incidents were understandable, and perhaps even inevitable. For instance, immediately after McCourt's death, the *Ottawa Evening Journal* reported, 'The general feeling in Cornwall is that the fatality is a most unfortunate affair and the result of hot-headedness and unpunished rough play rather than viciousness ... The general opinion is that a strict referee would have checked the rough play and kept the game clean.'[113] Although Masson's attack on McCourt had been severe enough to kill him, another early report from Cornwall asserted, 'It is plain that he [Masson] did not strike a blow maliciously.'[114]

Perhaps the clearest statement of this viewpoint was offered by police magistrate Daniel Danis, the judge who made the decision to reduce the charges against Masson from murder to manslaughter. According to the *Montreal Star*, Danis concluded, 'Under these circumstances, I cannot believe that any jury or any court would hold this young man guilty of murder. There was certainly no evidence of any intention to do anything more than the usual injury that is generally committed in this game. There is a great deal in this young man being very unfortunate. It was certainly an accident in many respects.'[115] A similar impression was conveyed by the *Montreal Star* when the jury at Masson's manslaughter trial arrived at a decision of 'not guilty': 'The verdict was a popular one and one that was generally expected. Nearly every one in Cornwall was hoping that Masson would be set free for the general feeling was, that if he did strike the fatal blow that caused "Bud" McCourt's death, the act was not one of malice and that there was more than one other player in the match in question who might have been, only for good luck, in just such an unfortunate position. That many hard blows were exchanged in the game is certain for some of the players themselves admitted that they had been guilty of raising their sticks for other purposes than when engaged in chasing the pucks.'[116] McCourt's teammates seem to have agreed, as several members of the Cornwall club were reportedly among the first to congratulate Masson after he was released from custody.[117] Thus, even though Masson hunted his victim down and delivered a severe blow that likely caused McCourt's death, he could credibly claim, within the conventions of hockey, that he acted without 'malice,' and merely intended to inflict 'the usual injury' that was accepted within the sport.

Another significant aspect of the McCourt-Masson case was the discussion that it generated around the issue of what constituted 'rough' hockey. As players, referees, journalists, and lawyers attempted to distinguish between 'rough' and 'strenuous' play, it became evident that many of those involved in hockey tolerated extremely high levels of 'acceptable' violence – a situation that is not surprising in light of public reluctance to regard Masson's attack on McCourt as 'vicious' or 'malicious.' Concerns about accusations of cowardly 'squealing' were likely on the minds of players and team representatives as well. The consensus of newspaper reporters – who rarely downplayed the sensational elements of any scandal – was that the Cornwall-Victoria contest was extremely rough, with the level of violence becoming more threatening as the game went on. 'The first half of the match was ragged and rough,' declared the *Ottawa Evening Journal*. 'Tripping and cross-check-

ing was freely indulged in by players of both teams, and the roughness steadily increased throughout the first half.'[118] However, players,
team personnel, and officials involved in the game were reluctant to
acknowledge that the match was 'rough' or violent. For example, according to a *Montreal Star* reporter, Reddy McMillan, captain of the
Cornwall team, 'said that the game had not been a particularly rough
one. He said that there had been lots of tripping, and that the Ottawa
players were using the butt end of the stick in checking their covers.
There was also a lot of holding and interference. McMillan said that
Throop had jabbed the butt of his stick into the faces of several players,
and to such an incident he attributed the couse [*sic*] of McCourt's rush
after Throop.'[119]

The line between 'rough' and 'strenuous' hockey was probed in detail at the coroner's inquest presided over by Dr C.J. Hamilton. During
this inquiry, referee Emmett Quinn was involved in an exchange with
Hamilton that echoed the tensions that were evident in the hockey narratives examined throughout this chapter:

> To questions by Dr. Hamilton, Mr. Quinn said that the game had been a
> strenuous one.
>> 'What do you mean by strenuous?'
>> 'There was plenty of hard checking.'
>> 'Was it a rough game?'
>> 'Not very. There was lots of tripping and minor fouls.'[120]

Quinn's opinion was shared by many witnesses. E.A. Pilon, the judge
of play, stated, 'The play up to the time of the accident was hard, but
not rough.'[121] John Hunter, goaltender for the Cornwall Hockey Club,
told the coroner that 'he did not consider this particular match a rough
one. He did not know of any match this winter in which some player
was not hurt by sticks.' George Airey, the Cornwall trainer, claimed that
the game 'was not very rough,' and that he 'did not think that there
was any bad blood between the players.' Finally, James Dingwall, the
county attorney and prosecutor for the Crown, showed his frustration
with these kinds of responses while questioning Charles Chamberlain
of the Victorias:

> 'Was it a rough match?'
> 'No, not up to that time.'
> 'What do you call rough? Here we have had witness after witness come

up and say it was not a rough match, yet all the players show cuts and marks and McCourt was killed.'
'Well, it was not rough up to that time.'[122]

Dingwall was perplexed by the witnesses' answers; to him this was a clear case of 'brutal butchery.' However, in the context of the narrative of 'strenuous spectacle,' the distinctions being drawn in the courtroom between 'hard' and 'rough' hockey made perfect sense. They also demonstrate, once again, the high threshold for 'normal' violence in hockey during this period.

Conclusion

This study has analysed contradictory media narratives of rough and aggressive hockey in relation to gender and class identities in late-nineteenth- and early-twentieth-century Canada. It has examined hockey violence in the context of media and spectator interest, and considered the meanings of hockey within the wider history of manhood and masculinity in North America. During the 1907 season, central Canadian newspapers created hockey narratives that combined elements of 'brutal butchery' and 'strenuous spectacle.' Hockey as 'brutal butchery' expressed outrage and concern, while revealing a degree of popular fascination with the game's violent possibilities. By contrast, hockey as 'strenuous spectacle' represented the sport as a stirring public display of masculine force and aggression. The Ottawa Silver Seven–Montreal Wanderer rivalry provided a particularly vivid forum for the expression of these complex narratives. Newspaper descriptions of games involving different teams in a variety of leagues reflected similar concerns and perceptions related to roughness in hockey. Finally, accounts of the death of Bud McCourt and the trial of Charles Masson revealed the same kinds of tensions surrounding the issue of hockey violence.

Ideals of respectable, middle-class masculinity and rough, working-class masculinity coexisted within accounts of fast, skilled, rugged, hard-hitting hockey.[123] Excitement and entertainment were equated with both speed and violence; admiration for precise and diligent work was expressed alongside approval of 'stiff' checking and jarring collisions. 'Manly' hockey was expected to be fast and clean, with no 'foul' or 'dirty' tactics. Yet, tripping and slashing were regarded as legitimate parts of the game, heavy body checks were applauded, and a high level of violence was expected under the strain of a closely contested match.

Even being knocked unconscious by an opponent could be considered 'incidental.' At the same time, the danger, physicality, and competitiveness of 'decidedly strenuous' hockey cultivated and reinforced standards of passionate manhood and primitive masculinity. In the culture of hockey, 'keen battles' were welcomed, and the ability to absorb pain and punishment without complaint was widely respected. As a result, both middle-class and working-class fans expected players to 'take their taps like men' and to refrain from unmanly 'squealing.'

This historical case study also reveals that contemporary hockey violence is not unique. Violence has been central to 'manly playing' since hockey's earliest days and has always garnered the attention of the media and most fans, regardless of their class origins. A proper understanding of contemporary debates and incidents, such as those involving Marty McSorley and Todd Bertuzzi, requires not only an appreciation for the current state of violence in the sport, but also an acknowledgment of its deep historical roots. By enhancing our awareness of the kinds of violence accepted in the game's formative era, this analysis of media narratives of violent and physical play during the 1907 hockey season helps us to understand more clearly the long history of accepted brutality within the sport. In addition, by demonstrating that the elimination of violence would strike at the core meanings of hockey, this chapter helps to explain why the hockey establishment has been so resistant to cracking down on rough play.

The justifications for violence that were articulated in the context of the Ottawa-Wanderer rivalry and the Charles Masson case continue to be voiced in contemporary discussions of hockey violence. Similarly, the admiration of robust, rugged hockey expressed in 1907 newspaper accounts is still prominent in the culture of hockey today. The game reports and trial coverage examined in this case study suggest that stick-swinging incidents and aggressive hits have been regarded as ordinary aspects of 'strenuous hockey' for at least a century. Injuries that resulted from violent play were downplayed or ignored; even death from a deliberate stick attack could be rationalized as an unfortunate accident. Like McSorley and Bertuzzi, a number of early-twentieth-century hockey players used their sticks or fists to inflict severe, intentional blows on their opponents – yet, within the conventions of hockey, all these players could credibly claim that they had not acted 'maliciously,' and that they had merely intended to deliver the usual 'hard knocks' that are accepted within the sport. At the same time, lenient punishments for such assaults confirm that the criminal-justice system and hockey leagues themselves have tolerated significant levels of savagery within the sport. The outcome of the three 1907 assault cases involving members of the Ottawa Silver Seven and the verdict in the manslaughter trial of Charles Masson made powerful statements that such violent acts were simply part of the game. Similarly, Todd Bertuzzi's plea agreement, his reinstatement by the NHL, and his selection to the 2006 Canadian Olympic men's hockey team indicate that the threshold for 'normal' violence in hockey continues to be extremely high – and that our willingness to accept on-ice brutality has not diminished much in the last hundred years.

NOTES

A portion of this chapter was published as Stacy L. Lorenz and Geraint B. Osborne, '"Talk About Strenuous Hockey": Violence, Manhood, and the 1907 Ottawa Silver Seven–Montreal Wanderer Rivalry,' *Journal of Canadian Studies* 40, 1 (2006): 125–56. The authors would like to thank the *Journal of Canadian Studies* for granting permission to republish this work. Parts of this chapter were also presented at the North American Society for Sport History conference in Green Bay, Wisconsin, in May 2005, and Glenwood Springs, Colorado, in May 2006, as well as the 'Canada and the League of Hockey Nations: Critical Perspectives on Hockey in Canada and Beyond' conference in Victoria, British Columbia, in April 2007. Finally, the authors wish to acknowledge the helpful suggestions made by reviewers from the *Journal of Canadian Studies* and University of Toronto Press.

1 David Seglins, '"Just Part of the Game": Violence, Hockey and Masculinity in Central Canada, 1890–1910,' MA thesis (Queen's University, 1995), 41, 135. For a useful analysis of key issues surrounding violence and masculinity in hockey, both historically and in the present, see Richard Gruneau and David Whitson, *Hockey Night in Canada: Sport, Identities and Cultural Politics* (Toronto: Garamond Press, 1993), 175–96.
2 Lawrence Scanlan, *Grace Under Fire: The State of Our Sweet and Savage Game* (Toronto: Penguin Canada, 2002), 30.
3 Roy MacGregor, 'Canada's Troubled Game Suffers Yet Another Blow,' *Globe and Mail*, 10 March 2004, A1.
4 John Barnes, *Sports and the Law in Canada* (Toronto: Butterworths, 1983), 108–12; Barnes, *Sports and the Law in Canada*, 2nd ed. (Toronto and Vancouver: Butterworths, 1988), 305–8; Barnes, 'Two Cases of Hockey Homicide:

The Crisis of a Moral Ideal,' paper presented to the North American Society for Sport History, Banff, Alberta, 1990; Seglins, '"Just Part of the Game,"'
97–113, 124–33; Stacy Lorenz, 'On-Ice Violence Has Been a Part of Hockey
for Almost 100 Years,' *Edmonton Journal,* 28 December 2004, A16. For an
analysis of legal issues surrounding sports violence and criminal liability,
see Barnes, *Sports and the Law in Canada,* 3rd ed. (Toronto and Vancouver:
Butterworths, 1996), 251–69.

5 *Montreal Gazette,* 14 January 1907, 2.

6 *Montreal Star,* 19 January 1907, 22; *Montreal Gazette,* 19 January 1907, 4.

7 *Montreal Star,* 1 March 1907, 3. See also *Ottawa Evening Journal,* 18 February
1907, 1; 28 February 1907, 1; *Montreal Star,* 18 February 1907, 1; 28 February 1907, 6; *Ottawa Citizen,* 1 March 1907, 8. This game and its aftermath,
including the court cases involving Smith, Smith, and Spittal, are examined in Seglins, '"Just Part of the Game,"' 76–7, 113–24. At least three other
assault charges were brought against Canadian hockey players in the early
twentieth century as a result of violent incidents during games. Although
four of these six cases ended in a conviction, punishment was lenient,
ranging from a $3 penalty to a $20 fine. No player served jail time for
knocking an opponent senseless with his stick. See Seglins, '"Just Part of
the Game,"' 145.

8 Case studies have a long and impressive record as a sound methodological
approach in the social sciences. They are particularly noted for their ability
to initiate the process of discovery. While researchers are limited in the
generalizations they can draw, case studies are nonetheless especially useful for intensively examining and understanding a single case, engaging
in theoretical analysis, and generating insights and hypotheses that may
be explored in subsequent studies. See J.C. Mitchell, 'Case and Situational
Analysis,' *Sociological Review* 31 (1983): 187–211; Diane Vaughn, 'Theory
Elaboration: The Heuristics of Case Analysis,' in *What Is a Case? Exploring
the Foundations of Social Inquiry,* ed. C. Ragin and H. Becker (Cambridge:
Cambridge University Press, 1992), 173–202; R. Gomm, M. Hammersley,
and P. Foster, 'Case Study and Generalization,' in *Case Study and Method:
Key Issues, Key Texts,* ed. R. Gomm, M. Hammersley, and P. Foster (Thou-
sand Oaks, CA: Sage, 2000), 98–115; R.K. Yin, *Applications of Case Study Research,* 2nd ed. (Thousand Oaks, CA: Sage, 2003); and R.K. Yin, *Case Study
Design and Research,* 3rd ed. (Thousand Oaks, CA: Sage, 2003).

9 In 1907 the Ottawa Silver Seven and Montreal Wanderers participated in
Canada's most prestigious league, the Eastern Canada Amateur Hockey
Association, commonly known as the Eastern Canada Hockey League. Os-
tensibly an amateur organization, the ECAHA was moving towards open

professionalism between 1904 and 1910. In 1907 it permitted 'declared' professionals to play in the league. See Alan Metcalfe, *Canada Learns to Play: The Emergence of Organized Sport, 1807–1914* (Toronto: McClelland and Stewart, 1987), 168–72; Gruneau and Whitson, *Hockey Night in Canada*, 72–7; and John Chi-Kit Wong, *Lords of the Rinks: The Emergence of the National Hockey League, 1875–1936* (Toronto: University of Toronto Press, 2005), 38–47.

10 This essay draws upon ideas and methods utilized in other historical studies of sports media narratives. See, for example, Michael Oriard, *Reading Football: How the Popular Press Created an American Spectacle* (Chapel Hill and London: University of North Carolina Press, 1993); Michael Oriard, *King Football: Sport and Spectacle in the Golden Age of Radio and Newsreels, Movies and Magazines, the Weekly and the Daily Press* (Chapel Hill and London: University of North Carolina Press, 2001); David B. Welky, 'Viking Girls, Mermaids, and Little Brown Men: U.S. Journalism and the 1932 Olympics,' *Journal of Sport History* 24, 1 (1997): 24–49; Welky, 'Culture, Media and Sport: The *National Police Gazette* and the Creation of an American Working-Class World,' *Culture, Sport, Society* 1, 1 (1998): 78–100; Mark Dyreson, *Making the American Team: Sport, Culture, and the Olympic Experience* (Urbana and Chicago: University of Illinois Press, 1998); and Pamela Grundy, *Learning to Win: Sports, Education, and Social Change in Twentieth-Century North Carolina* (Chapel Hill and London: University of North Carolina Press, 2001).

11 Because of the inconsistencies, tensions, and contradictions evident in early-twentieth-century meanings of 'violent' and 'rough' hockey, we do not attempt a precise definition of such terms here. One of the goals of this essay is to grapple with the various meanings of 'physical,' 'hard,' 'strenuous,' 'clean,' and 'dirty' hockey expressed in 1907 newspaper narratives.

12 Studies of hockey before the First World War include Don Morrow, 'The Little Men of Iron: The 1902 Montreal Hockey Club,' *Canadian Journal of History of Sport* 12, 1 (1981): 51–65; Morris Mott, 'Flawed Games, Splendid Ceremonies: The Hockey Matches of the Winnipeg Vics, 1890–1903,' *Prairie Forum* 10, 1 (1985): 169–87; Michel Vigneault, 'La diffusion du Hockey à Montréal, 1895–1910,' *Canadian Journal of History of Sport* 17, 1 (1986): 60–74; Metcalfe, *Canada Learns to Play*, 61–73, 168–72; Barnes, 'Two Cases of Hockey Homicide'; Seglins, '"Just Part of the Game"'; Gruneau and Whitson, *Hockey Night in Canada*, 31–92; Daniel Mason and Barbara Schrodt, 'Hockey's First Professional Team: The Portage Lakes Hockey Club of Houghton, Michigan,' *Sport History Review* 27, 1 (1996): 49–71; Daniel S. Mason, 'The International Hockey League and the Professionalization of

Ice Hockey, 1904–1907,' *Journal of Sport History* 25, 1 (1998): 1–17; Michael
A. Robidoux, 'Imagining a Canadian Identity through Sport: A Historical
Interpretation of Lacrosse and Hockey,' *Journal of American Folklore* 115, 456
(2002): 209–25; Daniel S. Mason and Gregory H. Duquette, 'Newspaper
Coverage of Early Professional Ice Hockey: The Discourses of Class and
Control,' *Media History* 10, 3 (2004): 157–73; J.J. Wilson, 'Skating to Arma-
geddon: Canada, Hockey and the First World War,' *International Journal
of the History of Sport* 22, 3 (2005): 315–43; and Wong, *Lords of the Rinks*.
Surprisingly, there is very little published, scholarly work on the history of
violence in hockey.

13 There were certainly other narratives that brought notions of violent play
and appropriate masculinity together in the years before the First World
War. For example, this essay does not assess how discourses of femininity, race, ethnicity, nationalism, amateurism, or professionalism may have
shaped perceptions of violence during the late nineteenth and early twentieth centuries. In addition, because this research is based on English Canadian newspapers, we must be cautious about applying its conclusions to
French Canada or to French Canadian narratives of hockey and manhood.
As complements to this case study, examinations of such narratives would
be welcome avenues for future research.

14 Rod Mickleburgh, 'Judge's Warning Rejected by NHL,' *Globe and Mail*, 7
October 2000, A1, A9; Iain MacIntyre, 'Bertuzzi Likely to Face Wrath of
League,' *Vancouver Sun*, 9 March 2004, E3; Elliott Pap, 'Outrage: Bertuzzi
Faces Police Investigation, NHL Suspension for Attack on Moore,' *Edmon-
ton Journal*, 10 March 2004, A1. Periodically, incidents of extreme hockey
violence have generated both pubic discussion and legal action. For
example, the vicious stick-fighting incident between Chico Maki and Ted
Green in 1968 was comparable to that of McCourt and Masson. Although
he did not die, Green had his head fractured and suffered a brain injury.
Both players were charged with assault and acquitted by Canadian courts.
Justin Reiner, 'Excessive Violence in Sports Part II: The Hackbart Rule –
Who Got It Right and Does It Even Matter?' *Texas Entertainment and Sports
Journal* 12, 1 (2003): 9–12.

15 E. Anthony Rotundo, *American Manhood: Transformations in Masculinity
from the Revolution to the Modern Era* (New York: BasicBooks, 1993); Michael
Kimmel, *Manhood in America: A Cultural History* (New York: The Free Press,
1996); Kevin B. Wamsley, 'The Public Importance of Men and the Importance of Public Men: Sport and Masculinities in Nineteenth-Century Canada,' in *Sport and Gender in Canada*, ed. Philip White and Kevin Young (Don
Mills: Oxford University Press, 1999), 24–39; Andrew C. Holman, *A Sense*

of Their Duty: Middle-Class Formation in Victorian Ontario Towns (Montreal and Kingston: McGill-Queen's University Press, 2000); Nancy B. Bouchier, *For the Love of the Game: Amateur Sport in Small-Town Ontario, 1838–1895* (Montreal and Kingston: McGill-Queen's University Press, 2003).

16 Quoted in Bouchier, *For the Love of the Game,* 26. See also Elliott J. Gorn, *The Manly Art: Bare-Knuckle Prize Fighting in America* (Ithaca: Cornell University Press, 1986), 140–1; Lynne Marks, *Revivals and Roller Rinks: Religion, Leisure, and Identity in Late-Nineteenth-Century Small-Town Ontario* (Toronto: University of Toronto Press, 1996), 32–3; and Steven A. Riess, 'Sport and the Redefinition of Middle-Class Masculinity in Victorian America,' in *The New American Sport History: Recent Approaches and Perspectives,* ed. S.W. Pope (Urbana and Chicago: University of Illinois Press, 1997), 174.

17 Gorn, *The Manly Art,* 133–5, 141–3. See also Peter DeLottinville, 'Joe Beef of Montreal: Working-Class Culture and the Tavern, 1869–1889,' *Labour/ Le Travailleur* 8, 9 (1981/2): 9–40; Marks, *Revivals and Roller Rinks,* 81–91, 116–21, 212–13; Kevin B. Wamsley and Robert S. Kossuth, 'Fighting It Out in Nineteenth-Century Upper Canada / Canada West: Masculinities and Physical Challenges in the Tavern,' *Journal of Sport History* 27, 3 (2000): 405–30.

18 Gorn, *The Manly Art,* 133. See also Wamsley and Kossuth, 'Fighting It Out,' 409–11.

19 Marks, *Revivals and Roller Rinks,* 90.

20 Ibid., 108–25, 137–9, 211–13.

21 Ibid., 123. See also Bouchier, *For the Love of the Game,* 27–8, 106–7, 125–30, 133, 136–7; and Colin D. Howell, *Northern Sandlots: A Social History of Maritime Baseball* (Toronto: University of Toronto Press, 1995), 4–6, 14–15.

22 Kevin B. Wamsley and David Whitson, 'Celebrating Violent Masculinities: The Boxing Death of Luther McCarty,' *Journal of Sport History* 25, 3 (1998): 419–31.

23 Ibid., 420–1, 426–9.

24 Ibid., 427.

25 Metcalfe, *Canada Learns to Play,* 10, 13, 61–73, 96–8; Gruneau and Whitson, *Hockey Night in Canada,* 31–56, 193–6; Seglins, '"Just Part of the Game,"' 13–14, 18–31, 73–5; Mason and Duquette, 'Newspaper Coverage of Early Professional Ice Hockey,' 158–9.

26 Metcalfe, *Canada Learns to Play,* 69.

27 Rotundo, *American Manhood,* 5–6.

28 Ibid., 222–83; Kimmel, *Manhood in America,* 120, 181–8; Riess, 'Sport and Middle-Class Masculinity,' 184–91; Varda Burstyn, *The Rites of Men: Manhood, Politics, and the Culture of Sport* (Toronto: University of Toronto Press,

1999), 45–75; Donald J. Mrozek, 'The Habit of Victory: The American
Military and the Cult of Manliness,' in *Manliness and Morality: Middle-Class
Masculinity in Britain and America, 1800–1940*, ed. J.A. Mangan and James
Walvin (New York: St Martin's Press, 1987), 220–41; Kristin L. Hoganson,
*Fighting for American Manhood: How Gender Politics Provoked the Spanish-
American and Philippine-American Wars* (New Haven and London: Yale
University Press, 1998); Angus McLaren, *Our Own Master Race: Eugenics in
Canada, 1885–1945* (Toronto: McClelland and Stewart, 1990); J.A. Man-
gan, 'Social Darwinism and Upper-Class Education in Late Victorian and
Edwardian England,' in *Manliness and Morality*, ed. Mangan and Walvin,
135–59.

29 Rotundo, *American Manhood*, 227–32.

30 Gorn, *The Manly Art*, 187–9, 192–3; Rotundo, *American Manhood*, 239–40,
248–52, 257–62; Howell, *Northern Sandlots*, 15, 97–119; Seglins, '"Just Part
of the Game,"' 24–31; Kimmel, *Manhood in America*, 81–122, 137–41, 157–81;
Riess, 'Sport and Middle-Class Masculinity,' 184–5; Hoganson, *Fighting for
American Manhood*, 12, 34; Burstyn, *The Rites of Men*, 50–4, 62; Wilson, 'Skating to Armageddon,' 315–21.

31 On the connections between violence and masculinity in boxing and football, see Gorn, *The Manly Art*; and Oriard, *Reading Football*.

32 David Seglins, and Daniel S. Mason and Gregory H. Duquette, claim that
divisions between working-class and middle-class views of violence, masculinity, and hockey were sharper than we suggest here. See, especially,
Seglins, '"Just Part of the Game,"' 49–54; Mason and Duquette, 'Newspaper Coverage of Early Professional Ice Hockey,' 158–61, 167–70. While this
study acknowledges that such class-based perceptions of hockey violence
existed, it argues that there was considerable common ground between
middle-class and working-class understandings of violence and physicality in hockey. In particular, we suggest that Seglins and Mason and
Duquette underestimate the extent to which violent and physical play in
hockey appealed to a cross-class masculine culture that valued 'roughness'
and toughness among men.

33 *Montreal Gazette*, 14 January 1907, 2. See also ibid., 4.

34 *Montreal Star*, 14 January 1907, 1.

35 Ibid., 10.

36 Ibid., 1.

37 Ibid., 4.

38 See P.F.W. Rutherford, 'The People's Press: The Emergence of the New
Journalism in Canada, 1869–99,' *Canadian Historical Review* 56 (1975):
169–91; Paul Rutherford, *The Making of the Canadian Media* (Toronto:

McGraw-Hill Ryerson, 1978); Rutherford, *A Victorian Authority: The Daily Press in Late Nineteenth-Century Canada* (Toronto: University of Toronto Press, 1982); Mary Vipond, *The Mass Media in Canada* (Toronto: James Lorimer and Co., 1989); Minko Sotiron, *From Politics to Profit: The Commercialization of Canadian Daily Newspapers, 1890–1920* (Montreal and Kingston: McGill-Queen's University Press, 1997); and Stacy L. Lorenz, '"In the Field of Sport at Home and Abroad": Sports Coverage in Canadian Daily Newspapers, 1850–1914,' *Sport History Review* 34, 2 (2003): 133–67.

39 Lorenz, '"In the Field of Sport,"' 135–45.

40 *Montreal Star,* 14 January 1907, 10.

41 Ibid.

42 Ibid., 15 January 1907, 16.

43 Rutherford, *A Victorian Authority,* 57, 133, 194, 237; Lorenz, '"In the Field of Sport,"' 138–9.

44 *Ottawa Evening Journal,* 14 January 1907, 2.

45 Ibid.

46 See also Seglins, '"Just Part of the Game,"' 54–7, 80; and Gruneau and Whitson, *Hockey Night in Canada,* 180–1.

47 *Ottawa Evening Journal,* 14 January 1907, 2.

48 Rotundo, *American Manhood;* Marks, *Revivals and Roller Rinks;* Wamsley and Whitson, 'Celebrating Violent Masculinities.'

49 *Ottawa Evening Journal,* 14 January 1907, 2. On the tendency to blame referees for on-ice violence, see Seglins, '"Just Part of the Game,"' 77–8.

50 *Ottawa Evening Journal,* 14 January 1907, 2.

51 *Ottawa Citizen,* 14 January 1907, 8. Although the Ottawa franchise was not officially known as the 'Senators' until the 1908–9 season, this nickname was frequently used in 1907.

52 Ibid.

53 Rutherford, *A Victorian Authority,* 4–5, 71, 74, 200, 237; Lorenz, '"In the Field of Sport,"' 140, 142–3.

54 *Ottawa Citizen,* 14 January 1907, 8.

55 Ibid., 18 January 1907, 10. For other examples of 'squealing,' see Seglins, '"Just Part of the Game,"' 65–6.

56 *Ottawa Free Press* story reprinted in *Montreal Star,* 14 January 1907, 10.

57 *Toronto Telegram* story reprinted in *Ottawa Evening Journal,* 16 January 1907, 2.

58 *Montreal Gazette,* 15 January 1907, 2.

59 *Ottawa Evening Journal,* 18 February 1907, 1.

60 *Montreal Star,* 18 February 1907, 1.

61 See Lorenz, '"In the Field of Sport,"' 148–52.

62 Metcalfe, *Canada Learns to Play*, 69; Seglins, '"Just Part of the Game,"' 41–2.

63 *Montreal Gazette*, 14 January 1907, 2.

64 *Toronto Star*, 14 January 1907, 11.

65 *Winnipeg Telegram* story reprinted in *Toronto Star*, 14 January 1907, 11.

66 *Toronto Star*, 14 January 1907, 10.

67 See also Mason and Duquette, 'Newspaper Coverage of Early Professional Ice Hockey,' 161–2.

68 Seglins, '"Just Part of the Game,"' 80.

69 *Cornwall Freeholder*, quoted in *Ottawa Evening Journal*, 11 March 1907, 2. See also *Ottawa Citizen*, 8 March 1907, 6.

70 *Ottawa Citizen*, 19 January 1907, 8.

71 Ibid., 28 January 1907, 8. Reports of International Hockey League (IHL) games carried by local newspapers in IHL communities appear to have constructed similar narratives. See Mason and Duquette, 'Newspaper Coverage of Early Professional Ice Hockey,' 161–7. For example, Mason and Duquette cite a 1905 story in a Houghton, Michigan, newspaper that stated, 'The game was a clean and fast one, and though several of the Calumet men were injured in the game, there was little rough play' (164).

72 *Ottawa Citizen*, 30 January 1907, 8.

73 *Ottawa Evening Journal*, 9 March 1907, 2.

74 *Montreal Gazette*, 18 January 1907, 4.

75 Ibid., 18 January 1907, 4; 22 January 1907, 4; *Montreal Star*, 18 January 1907, 10; 22 January 1907, 10. The fact that these games occurred only a few days after the violent Ottawa-Wanderer match also seems to have heightened reporters' emphasis on 'clean' play.

76 *Ottawa Citizen*, 24 January 1907, 8.

77 *Montreal Star*, 25 March 1907, 12.

78 *Montreal Gazette*, 28 January 1907, 2.

79 *Ottawa Citizen*, 28 January 1907, 8.

80 *Ottawa Evening Journal*, 28 January 1907, 2.

81 *Montreal Gazette*, 28 January 1907, 2.

82 *Ottawa Citizen*, 28 January 1907, 8.

83 Ibid., 29 January 1907, 8.

84 *Ottawa Evening Journal*, 18 February 1907, 2.

85 Ibid.; *Montreal Star*, 18 February 1907, 3.

86 *Ottawa Evening Journal*, 18 February 1907, 2. See also *Montreal Star*, 18 February 1907, 3.

87 *Ottawa Evening Journal*, 18 February 1907, 1.

88 *Montreal Gazette*, 28 January 1907, 2.

89 *Ottawa Citizen*, 23 January 1907, 8.

90 Ibid., 15 January 1907, 7.

91 Ibid. This Ottawa City League match between New Edinburgh and the Rialtos also featured a brawl involving spectators, players, and officials, following a disputed ruling on a near-score by the Rialtos. The *Ottawa Evening Journal* reported, 'This incident created quite a row and the crowd jumped on the ice and a number of scraps occurred. The umpire was handled in no gentle manner by some of the Rialto supporters, who were decidedly sore over the decision.' See *Ottawa Evening Journal*, 15 January 1907, 2. The *Ottawa Citizen* noted, 'Rialtos claimed a game in the second half, alleging that Arial's shot had gone true. Umpire Easdale said no, however, and was assaulted by one of the spectators, who struck him a cowardly blow on the head. Neate was also given a stinging crack on the face by the same spectator.' See *Ottawa Citizen*, 15 January 1907, 7.

92 *Montreal Star*, 1 March 1907, 3.

93 Ibid., 2 March 1907, 14.

94 Ibid., 11 March 1907, 3. Mason and Duquette argue that coverage of International Hockey League (IHL) games in major Canadian newspapers – such as these *Montreal Star* reports on matches involving Sault Ste Marie and Calumet – highlighted and exaggerated the extent of the violence in IHL hockey. This overemphasis on violence in the IHL was part of a broader struggle over the meanings of hockey as this upstart professional league challenged middle-class, amateur control of the sport. See Mason and Duquette, 'Newspaper Coverage of Early Professional Ice Hockey.'

95 The Ottawa-Wanderer rematch would either settle, or set up, the championship of the ECAHA. If the undefeated Wanderers won the game, they would capture the league title. If the Ottawas avenged their earlier defeat in Montreal, the two clubs would be tied in the league standings, with just one loss each. They would then play a two-game, total goal series, with one game in each city, in order to determine the league champion. The winner of the Wanderer-Ottawa match-up would also earn the right to challenge the Kenora Thistles for the Stanley Cup. See *Ottawa Evening Journal*, 4 March 1907, 2.

96 Ibid., 28 February 1907, 1. See also ibid., 1 March 1907, 2.

97 Seglins, '"Just Part of the Game,"' 56–7.

98 *Ottawa Evening Journal*, 28 February 1907, 2. See also *Montreal Star*, 28 February 1907, 3. The *Ottawa Citizen* claimed that the 'mob of excited hockey enthusiasts' numbered almost 3000. See *Ottawa Citizen*, 28 February 1907, 8.

99 *Ottawa Evening Journal*, 28 February 1907, 2.

100 Ibid., 1, 2. See also *Ottawa Citizen*, 1 March 1907, 8.
101 *Montreal Star*, 4 March 1907, 3. On telegraph re-enactments of hockey games in this period, see Gruneau and Whitson, *Hockey Night in Canada*, 84; Morrow, 'The Little Men of Iron,' 61–3; Lorenz, '"In the Field of Sport,"' 147–8.
102 *Ottawa Evening Journal*, 4 March 1907, 2.
103 *Montreal Star*, 4 March 1907, 3.
104 *Ottawa Evening Journal*, 4 March 1907, 2.
105 According to Daniel Mason and Barbara Schrodt, when the Montreal Wanderers played the Portage Lakes Hockey Club in Houghton, Michigan, in 1904, Houghton's local newspaper, the *Daily Mining Gazette*, described the game in remarkably similar terms. The *Mining Gazette*'s account of the match stated that 'the game had all the features which go to make hockey the most exciting sport in the world. There was slashing, body checking, terrific shooting, marvelous speed, injuries to players, combination plays.' See Mason and Schrodt, 'Hockey's First Professional Team,' 61.
106 *Ottawa Evening Journal*, 4 March 1907, 2.
107 *Montreal Star*, 7 March 1907, 1, 3, 6R; 9 April 1907, 1; 10 April 1907, 6R; 11 April 1907, 6R, 12; 12 April 1907, 2; *Ottawa Evening Journal*, 7 March 1907, 1, 2; 8 March 1907, 1, 12; 14 March 1907, 2; 15 March 1907, 1; 16 March 1907, 7; 10 April 1907, 1; 11 April 1907, 2; 12 April 1907, 8; *Montreal Gazette*, 11 April 1907, 1; 12 April 1907, 1; *Ottawa Citizen*, 15 March 1907, 1; 10 April 1907, 1, 11; 11 April 1907, 1; 12 April 1907, 9. For accounts of McCourt's death and Masson's trial, see Barnes, *Sports and the Law in Canada*, 2nd ed., 307–8; Barnes, 'Two Cases of Hockey Homicide,' 51–72; and Seglins, '"Just Part of the Game,"' 124–33.
108 *Montreal Star*, 12 April 1907, 2.
109 *Ottawa Citizen*, 8 March 1907, 8.
110 Ibid., 7 March 1907, 8; 8 March 1907, 8; *Ottawa Evening Journal*, 8 March 1907, 12. See also Barnes, 'Two Cases of Hockey Homicide,' 55–8; and Seglins, '"Just Part of the Game,"' 131–2.
111 *Montreal Star*, 14 March 1907, 1. See also ibid., 12 April 1907, 2.
112 Seglins, '"Just Part of the Game,"' 128.
113 *Ottawa Evening Journal*, 7 March 1907, 1. For other examples of statements blaming the referee – interestingly, the same official, Emmett Quinn, who had been in charge of the violent Ottawa-Wanderer game earlier in the season – see *Montreal Star*, 7 March 1907, 1; 8 March 1907, 6R; and *Ottawa Citizen*, 7 March 1907, 8.
114 *Montreal Star*, 9 March 1907, 8.

115 Ibid., 16 March 1907, 5. See also *Ottawa Citizen,* 16 March 1907, 2; *Montreal Gazette,* 16 March 1907, 1.

116 *Montreal Star,* 12 April 1907, 2.

117 Ibid.

118 *Ottawa Evening Journal,* 7 March 1907, 2. See also *Ottawa Citizen,* 7 March 1907, 8; and *Montreal Star,* 7 March 1907, 1.

119 *Montreal Star,* 8 March 1907, 16.

120 Ibid., 14 March 1907, 1.

121 *Ottawa Citizen,* 14 March 1907, 10.

122 *Montreal Star,* 14 March 1907, 1.

123 Warren Goldstein makes a similar observation in relation to baseball during the 1860s. According to Goldstein, 'The potential for disorder and violence was said to attract "roughs," while the promise of manly displays of nerve and skill spoke to the "respectable" patrons. This analysis was correct but it was incomplete. These differential appeals also spoke to conflicting tendencies within every member of the baseball fraternity, no matter how "respectable," no matter how "low."' See Warren Goldstein, *Playing for Keeps: A History of Early Baseball* (Ithaca and London: Cornell University Press, 1989), 80.

6 Chinook Country Hockey: The Emergence of Hockey in Pre–Second World War Southern Alberta

ROBERT S. KOSSUTH

The late nineteenth and early twentieth centuries have been charac-terized as a relatively volatile period of change and accommodation for Canadian sport where various groups attempted to influence how sport ought to be experienced. Individuals and groups who represent-ed differing views of how and for whom sport should be organized asserted their beliefs on issues ranging from who should control sport to the place of female athletes at all levels of physical recreation. These differences often resulted in incidents of confrontation and conflict.[1] In addition, historians who have examined these and other developments within Canadian sport have often focused primarily upon specific re-gions, primarily in the central provinces, and have relied heavily upon the experiences of people from large urban centres. This central Cana-dian, urban focus has been both necessary and illuminating and has successfully demonstrated that in most instances the history of sport in Canada emerged in Quebec/Ontario, specifically the City of Mon-treal.[2] Of course, the roots of organized hockey can also be traced to Montreal.[3] However, the tendency to privilege this urban and central Canadian experience can leave the erroneous impression that the his-tory of sport in Canada, including hockey, represented a homogeneous – urban, middle-class, and male – experience. Clearly this is not the case. In order to understand how hockey assumed its dominant place in the Canadian sports-scape more fully, it is necessary to search the periphery of sport in smaller communities throughout Canada and explore how 'others' experienced this facet of the human experience. I suggest that the hockey experiences of men and women, boys and girls, on the prairies of southern Alberta have much to tell us about the way the game has been constructed in Canada, particularly outside the country's major urban centres. To expand our understanding of these developments it is necessary to look beyond what happened in Calgary or Edmonton to more distant communities such as those in southern Alberta, including Lethbridge, Medicine Hat, Pincher Creek, and Fort Macleod. Beyond that, even more remote southern Alberta settlements such as Granum, High River, Nanton, Cardston, Taber, Stavely, and Blairmore can provide further insight into the often intensely local experience that hockey provided. Finally, this outside-in examination will attempt to provide evidence that the game did not exist in the same manner or extent throughout this region during the period under consideration, but demonstrated ebbs and flows in popularity and importance that were dependent upon a variety of physical and social forces that influenced people's lives.

The prairie region of southern Alberta has been referred to as 'Chinook Country'[4] after the warm mountain winds that periodically blow in to melt the snow and ice during winter. This natural weather phenomenon has played a role in the hockey history of the region. According to Gary W. Zeman, one of the reasons that professional hockey in Alberta could not survive during the 1920s and 1930s was the lack of artificial ice, particularly in Calgary and Edmonton, which left league schedules at the mercy of the unpredictable weather.[5] Rink owners in Calgary did consider installing equipment to make artificial ice, as had proved successful on the west coast, where the Patrick family established a hockey dynasty (see chapter 7).[6] But in smaller centres where the resources simply did not exist, there was no serious contemplation of such an extravagance. For small communities, including Cardston, Granum, Rosemary, and Scandia, the step of moving off the frozen lakes and sloughs and constructing outdoor and, in some cases, covered rinks during the 1920s and 1930s represented a massive community undertaking.[7] Generally, a variety of specifically local factors influenced whether or not a community embraced hockey or viewed the sport as merely a brief distraction during the winter months. What follows is an examination of how hockey existed in rural and small-town southern Alberta. In addition to a brief examination of how hockey first emerged in this setting, this chapter will explore several common issues specific to the sport existing in this region before 1939, including: the impact of the natural environment; issues of class, amateurism, and professionalism; gender and the place of men and women on and off the ice; and the relative influence of hockey within the broader sport and recreation landscape. Ultimately, the question that must be addressed is whether we can apply present assumptions about the primacy of hockey among Canadian sports to the actual experiences of the men and women who played the game for several months each year on the southern prairies of Alberta.

Sport in Alberta before the Puck Dropped

Before launching into a focused examination of the history of hockey in southern Alberta, it is first necessary to provide some historical context as to the relative place of the game within the broader sports culture of the region. Canadians today might assume that hockey would have been among the first sports adopted by early pioneer settlers in the West, given the widespread belief that the prairie climate is ideal for the sport. This assumption, however, is not necessarily accurate, particularly in the southern regions of Alberta. In the broader context, if one examines the history of sport in Canada, it is quite evident that pastimes such as curling, cricket, snowshoeing, lacrosse, and baseball, among others, were organized well before hockey arrived on the scene by the late 1870s.[8] Indeed, hockey did not appear in any serious manner in rural southern Alberta before the 1890s. As well, it is important to recognize that the game originated within an already established sports environment.

Examinations of the sporting history of Alberta suggest that a number of sports and recreations enjoyed widespread popularity before the turn of the twentieth century. Baseball, for example, was king in Medicine Hat during the late 1880s.[9] Evidence of the citizens of Fort Macleod and Lethbridge playing baseball,[10] football,[11] cricket,[12] tennis,[13] curling,[14] polo,[15] lacrosse,[16] and golf[17] in the late 1880s and early 1890s suggests the existence of a broad sporting culture before the arrival of hockey. Thus, it should be recognized that hockey represented only one of a number of sports that captured the public's attention. As a result, caution must be taken when suggesting that the sport held any form of universal appeal in southern Alberta. More accurately, it should be recognized that while hockey was a popular winter sport for many young men, a number of factors served to delay, or in certain cases prevent, its growth during the early twentieth century.

One town where hockey did not flourish was Cardston, a predominantly Mormon community located close to the American border. According to Gary Bowie and James Day, not only was the inconsistent weather a factor in the popularity of hockey in southern Alberta, but also the game did not resonate with the large Mormon population that migrated from the United States at the turn of the twentieth century.[18] Hockey was never well established before the Second World War, and did not achieve the popular following enjoyed by American sports such as basketball and baseball.[19] Baseball in Cardston was the summer passion, while basketball ruled the winter. Interestingly, it was a ladies team who first brought attention to Cardston by winning the 1904 Provincial Basketball Championship.[20] By 1913 young men in Cardston also began to play basketball, and in 1916 a new school and gymnasium provided an ideal facility to promote the sport. By 1920 the high school boy's team had won the provincial basketball title.[21] Despite a clear interest in supporting sports generally, however, the people of Cardston showed little interest in hockey.[22] It was not until 1920 that the town built a rink suitable for hockey; and by the late 1930s there was little evidence that organized hockey had made any serious inroads into the community.[23] Therefore, as this example shows, one must be aware that hockey did not become immediately popular in every community in the early years of settlement in southern Alberta, but often took some time before becoming well established.

Establishing Hockey in Small-Town and Rural Southern Alberta

The manner in which the sport of hockey made its way to the towns and rural settlements of southern Alberta can likely be equated with the way the game spread throughout the Canadian west.[24] As with other sports and physical recreations, hockey arrived with the people who, along with their various vocational experiences, brought with them the sports and games learned in their youth.[25] Although he suggests that hockey games had been contested in Calgary as early as 1886,[26] Gary Zeman maintains that the first organized game of hockey played in the city occurred on 4 January 1893, when the Town Boys and the Tailors played at Calgary's outdoor Star Rink.[27] That same year, teams representing policemen, firemen, bankers, railroad men, and ranchers competed in Calgary, with contests arising primarily as challenge matches and not as part of a formal league.[28] That the first recorded game of hockey in the territory occurred in Calgary is not a surprise given the relative size and regional prominence the city had assumed by last decade of the nineteenth century.[29] In the southeastern corner of the Alberta district of the Northwest Territories, Medicine Hat was among the first communities to build a rink suitable for organized hockey in December of 1895.[30] Over the next half-decade, interest in the game grew in that community. An example of hockey's rapid growth and wide-spread popularity in this community is found in the report of a match played by young women from the town in March 1897, a contest that raised considerable interest even though no spectators were allowed to witness the event.[31] Despite the expanding interest in hockey in large provincial centres such as Calgary and smaller regional municipalities such as Medicine Hat at this early juncture, this did not represent the experience of other prairie communities, some of whom did not adopt the game as readily.

When evidence is sought to determine when organized hockey matches first took place in the smaller communities in southern Alberta, few accounts can be found until the turn of the twentieth century. The foothills community of Pincher Creek is reported to have played a match against the nearby settlement of North Fork in February 1898.[32] The following year the Town of Macleod organized its first team,[33] playing its inaugural game against Pincher Creek in February 1900.[34] Finally, Lethbridge played its first home match against Pincher Creek in January 1902.[35] This last match occurred a year after Pincher Creek's initial challenge to hockey players in Lethbridge.[36] These early challenge matches set the stage for senior men's inter-town hockey in subsequent years.

The Crow's Nest Pass Hockey League formed as a result of these early challenge matches, a development that marked the first inter-town hockey league south of Calgary. Play began some time between 1900 and 1903, between teams representing Medicine Hat, Pincher Creek, McLeod, and Frank, Alberta, and Fernie, British Columbia.[37] In 1906 Pincher Creek once again took the lead and proposed the formation of a new southern Alberta league to replace the Crow's Nest Pass league. Impetus to form an all-Alberta league likely arose from the designation of Alberta, which had previously been a part of the Northwest Territories, as a province within the Canadian confederation in 1905.[38] This proposal represented the beginning of a long-term trend that saw the formation, reformation, and dissolution of inter-town leagues in the south through the early decades of the twentieth century. However, this league instability does not mean that hockey could not remain viable at this time; rather, it highlights the often mercenary nature of the game, whereby towns, teams, and players were constantly seeking competition and situations that would best suit their various interests. As well, the organization of teams and leagues did remain somewhat precarious in these early years in part because of the unreliable weather, relatively small populations from which to draw local players, and the ongoing concern over the availability of appropriate rink facilities.

Weathering the Early Years

The climate of southern Alberta impacted the way hockey was organized and the quality and length of the hockey season. The influence of the Chinook winds often led to the postponement of games, even in the middle of winter. For example, the community of Nanton formed a skating rink association in November 1903 to provide a facility adequate for playing hockey. Yet no games took place on the new Nanton rink until February 1904 due in part to the warm winter weather of 1903 and early 1904.[39] This weather-related concern created an unenviable task for local rink caretaker Walter Rounds, who 'would no more make a sheet of ice than a Chinook would arrive.'[40] The availability and quality of ice was of concern for hockey enthusiasts throughout Canada in the years before artificial ice became commonplace. However, the inevitable yet unpredictable arrival of warm Chinook winds in the dead of winter was a unique concern for those who attempted to organize hockey in the southern prairie region of Alberta.

Issues surrounding weather, although unique in their cause in southern prairies, were also present in other regions of the country (see chapter 1). Yet despite the various climate-related concerns of the winter months, the sport of hockey continued to grow in Canada after the turn of the twentieth century. According to Alan Metcalfe, 'nearly every community contained a commercially operated ice arena where games were played from January until early March.'[41] Although issues such as population density and ease of transportation certainly played their part in how hockey came to be organized, the climate, particularly in southern Alberta, certainly impacted the viability of league play. By 1929, by which time inter-town leagues such as the Crow's Nest Hockey League (Blairmore, Coleman, Fernie, Macleod, and Pincher Creek) were well established, the official season lasted just two months – 2 January to 27 February – although exhibition games could be played as early as November weather permitting.[42] Yet even with this relatively brief schedule, mid-season games were not guaranteed. For instance, a 17 January 1929 contest for which the Fernie, British Columbia, team travelled to play in Pincher Creek was cancelled due to lack of ice. Clearly, the climate played an important role in the way hockey was organized and experienced in this region before the widespread availability of artificial ice facilities in the second half of the twentieth century.

Apart from the impact of the climate, the distinct demands of rural in comparison to urban work patterns likely also played a role in shaping the development of hockey in southern Alberta. According to Donald G. Wetherell, 'Before 1945 Alberta was largely a rural society. Between 1921 and 1941, about sixty per cent of the population lived on farms or in rural villages, and seasonal change was more significant for such people than it was for those who lived in cities or large towns.'[43] Because of the greater availability of free time during the winter months, young men, particularly those who worked on farms in the summer, had the time to travel in order to participate in sport and recreational pursuits. Paul Voisey's examination of life in Vulcan and surrounding districts suggests that when men were not required to be in the fields for seeding and harvest, they enjoyed a rich and varied social and recreational life.[44] Young farmers, many of whom were bachelors, had little to do during the winter, and most would leave the farm to avoid the isolation of their solitary lives.[45] This reality of rural life, may, in part, explain why large numbers of young men decided to live and play hockey in towns during the winter, before people drawn to the spectacle of competitive games. This availability of players to form competitive teams likely influenced local enthusiasts' decisions to construct rink facilities. Although some larger communities built skating rinks in the first decade of the 1900s, Wetherell suggests that 'in many communities, public skating rinks were not built until after World War I, although everywhere local creeks, lakes, and sloughs provided an important focus for unorganized skating.'[46] Therefore, one must recognize that both environmental and social factors influenced how hockey developed in rural southern Alberta. And, as interest in hockey grew, attempts to control the sport, often instigated by groups from larger urban centres, continued to affect the way hockey was experienced in the rural south.

Amateur Hockey and the Quest for Town Glory

In the late nineteenth and early twentieth centuries hockey remained primarily an activity limited to middle-class sportsmen in Canada.[47] Attempts by members of this socio-economic cohort of Canadian society to apply an amateur ideology to sporting activities led to the formation of national and provincial bodies in a variety of sports to ensure that competition would not be tainted by professionalism.[48] However, this ideological goal often ran counter to practical benefits associated with an enhanced regional visibility and the possibility of economic growth that communities sought to acquire through association with successful sport teams. At about the turn of the twentieth century, the difficulty of balancing the pragmatic town-boosting goals of civic leaders with the principled stance of maintaining sport as a purely avocational activity forced many communities to navigate a fine line that sought, on one hand, to avoid the negative associations of gambling and game fixing commonly associated with professionalism, while at the same time to accrue the positive social and economic benefits from fielding a championship-calibre team.[49]

In the very early years of the twentieth century, as hockey teams and leagues were being formed in southern Alberta, the opportunity to use success in sports such as hockey to build a reputation for a new community became apparent. The clearest example of this boosterism in Alberta was and remains the rivalry between the cities of Calgary and Edmonton. For smaller communities, the chance of besting a team from one of these cities provided a clear avenue to place their community on the map. For example, in a 1903 match, St Albert defeated the Edmonton Nationals 12–1, resulting in an accusation by the Edmonton team that their opponents were professional players.[50] In these years before the creation of a province-wide body to regulate the game, hockey represented a visible means to create and reinforce community pride, particularly for those recently settled towns and villages during the period of settlement between the late nineteenth and early twentieth centuries.

The Alberta Amateur Hockey Association (AAHA) was formed on 29 November 1907 in Red Deer.[51] By 1910, included among the towns and cities represented by this governing body were Lethbridge, Macleod, Pincher Creek, and Taber, which constituted the organization's southern division. The AAHA took a somewhat less aggressive approach to managing the amateur game than its senior counterpart the Ontario Hockey Association (formed in 1890), which adopted a stricter definition of amateurism. According to Alan Metcalfe, the 'western provinces were not as enthusiastic in their support for a rigid definition [of amateurism].'[52] At the annual meeting of the AAHA in 1910, for example, representatives from twenty teams met to discuss concerns facing amateur hockey.[53] One of the ongoing contentious issues that received attention at this meeting was the question of residency requirements for players in order to determine eligibility. According to Gary Zeman, one issue that consistently caused difficulty for the AAHA was the influx of ringers or imports that invariably resulted in heightened animosity between teams and communities.[54] These problems associated with eligibility arose from the weak rules governing how long a player needed to have resided in the community for whom he played. This residency requirement represented a particular concern in rural locales considering the number of seasonally employed, itinerant young males.[55] At the aforementioned 1910 AAHA meeting, new rules were introduced stipulating that a player needed only to have resided in a community for ten days in order to establish residency. In addition, at the local level, a player's eligibility did not necessarily hinge upon his past amateur status. For example, the 1910 Lethbridge league rule number 6 stated, 'The dead past shall be dead, and a man's history has nothing to do with his amateur standing in the City League.'[56] Thus, the leniency of both provincial and local rules relating to eligibility and amateur status meant that leagues and teams were unlikely to be deterred from employing ringers and imports, and as a result, their presence became increasingly commonplace on the province's men's amateur sides.

One example that illustrated the difficulties faced by smaller rural communities who attempted to compete at the highest level by importing players was the Granum Elks hockey team of the late 1920s. The problems that arose during the 1928–9 season provide some insight into the way small-town hockey squads attempted to balance players' amateur eligibility with the necessity of icing a team strong enough to compete. According to Bert Kellicut, a member of Elks team during the late 1920s and early 1930s, organized hockey did not exist in Granum until 1925, when the Granum Elks Lodge led a community effort to build a rink.[57] By 1927 the team was competing in the Foothills League against representatives from Claresholm, Macleod, and Pincher Creek.[58] Although the league had adopted AAHA rules, it seems that the issue of bringing in players and paying them for their services was openly discussed and acknowledged. For example, in a November 1927 *Claresholm Local Press* article, an argument to secure 'a couple of men' possibly from the Crow's Nest League was presented as a means to keep up with opposing clubs who were also hiring outside talent.[59] In an earlier edition of the same Claresholm newspaper, note had been taken of the resignation of AAHA president A.B. King over the qualification dates for residency requirements. Comment on King's decision pointed out that 'while most teams may be technically amateur, very

few of them could endure an investigation without revealing embar-
rassing details relating to their financial dealings.'[60] This sentiment concerning the difficulty of remaining truly amateur is echoed by Kellicut,
who recalled that 'in 1928 all the teams hired a few outside players.
They improved the standard of hockey played.'[61] Thus, it seems that
the Foothills League of the late 1920s was amateur in name only and
that all the league's teams were faced with the problem of adhering to
the AAHA rules while also remaining competitive.

By the 1929 Foothills League season, according to Kellicut, 'nearly all
the players were paid to play. Granum had about 11 or 12 on its payroll.
This was par for all the teams in the league.'[62] The difficulties for the
Granum Elks started with problems financing the team for the season
and ended when several of their top players had their amateur cards re-
voked during a playoff game versus Blairmore.[63] Kellicut, a participant
in this contest, reveals that several Elks players were suspended mid-
way through the playoff contest, although the newspapers remained
silent about the incident. It is clear that several serious issues surrounding amateur hockey in southern Alberta arose during the 1929 season.
A late season recap of the Granum Elks' campaign hinted at the problems that arose over the course of the season. In addition to concerns
regarding the arbitrary manner in which the AAHA's amateur rules
were enforced, the commentary concluded that 'hockey has been a disastrous experience in most Southern Alberta towns this winter.'[64] The
1929 season was the last in which the Granum team would compete at
the top amateur level; and with the onset of the problems precipitated
by Great Depression, the town's attempts at competing at the top level
of hockey ended.

Along with those in Granum, hockey supporters in other smaller
communities in southern Alberta also found it difficult to adhere to
the strictures of amateur hockey. The community of Stavely similarly
wrestled with AAHA officials during the 1929 season. In a column titled 'Amateurism or Profes'lism [sic],' the problem of players not being
officially recognized as amateurs, when it was widely acknowledged
that few if any players in the league were not professional, was again
raised.[65] Ultimately, getting an amateur card became an exercise that
was considered by players and officials on some teams to be based on
a team's relationship with AAHA officials, a situation that raised accusations of favouritism. This selective and disparate amateurism likely
represented one of primary reasons for the Foothills League's demise
and eventual disbanding by the early 1930s. However, myriad related

issues including the commitment of local boosters and broader economic concerns cannot be overlooked.

As a result of economic and regulatory concerns through the decade of the 1930s, hockey in the smaller communities of southern Alberta became increasingly less competitive. This change mirrors, to a degree, the decline (described in chapter 4) of the Ladies Ontario Hockey Association (LOHA), where competitive leagues began to falter and teams reverted increasingly to exhibition games. Beyond this, it became increasingly difficult to recruit players certified as amateurs and raise the funds required to ice a competitive team. The extent of this change could be seen when the Nanton Rangers Club won the Foothills Cup in 1937. It was noted that 'they are very proud of the fact that the entire team were Nanton boys.'[66] Therefore, competing at the highest level of senior amateur hockey represented a short-term undertaking for most of the small towns who viewed success on the ice as a step towards boosting local pride and the community's future prospects. With a limited number of success stories, great expense, and the difficulties that accompanied adhering to amateur rules and regulations, aspirations for elite hockey in these towns invariably retreated, although the game certainly did not disappear altogether. As in other regions in Canada, certain groups continued to participate in hockey throughout the early twentieth century, mostly in leagues tied to railroads, such as the amateur inter-town men's leagues discussed above and boys' school leagues resulting from the incorporation of the sport into the education system.[67] In contrast to the increasing organization of hockey for boys and men, the opportunities for girls and young women remained limited and were confined largely to infrequent exhibition games.[68]

Novelty Games for Girls and Women

To leave the examination of women's hockey in southern Alberta to the end of this chapter does, in the author's opinion, provide a disservice to the role women assumed in hockey from its earliest inception. Yet, as was the case with many sports in Canada, the presence of girls and women on the playing fields and in the arenas was generally more limited, met with greater resistance, and occurred later than for boys and men. Over the past several decades a degree of attention has been paid to the history of female hockey in Canada. For example, Brian McFarlane's *Proud Past, Bright Future: One Hundred Years of Canadian Women's Hockey*, points to Alberta's first women's team playing in Medicine Hat in 1893.[69] McFarlane, however, hastily points out that this game actually occurred several years later than the earliest contests between teams in eastern Canadian cities. Apart from the ever-present 'who played first' debate, similar to the continuing 'who invented the game' debate, it is clear that women faced a number of obstacles in assuming a place within the primarily male world of hockey. This difficulty, it seems, was exacerbated in smaller urban centres and rural communities, where hockey resources remained limited. According to Donald Wetherell, hockey represented the one winter sport in Alberta where opportunities for women remained scarce during the years before to the Second World War.[70] Thus, when one examines the history of women's hockey in southern Alberta before the war, several general themes must be considered, including the brief lifespan of most teams, the absence of leagues, and the novelty atmosphere that often surrounded exhibitions involving female players.

Evidence suggests that although not widely played, women's hockey was at least a known quantity in southern Alberta by the early 1900s. The aforementioned example of teams in Medicine Hat from the 1890s suggests that some female athletes were clearly engaging themselves in the sport at the very earliest stages of hockey's emergence in the West. A slightly later example of a women's game in Pincher Creek in February 1910 described the quality of play as being 'not only exciting, but a swift one, and was to many a revelation as to what ladies could do in wielding the hockey sticks.'[71] Even with this type of positive accounting of their ability to play, women's hockey remained little more than a novelty that would never approach the stability and acceptance of the male game. Unlike the formation of the LOHA in 1922 detailed in chapter 4, in Alberta the formation of provincial competitions occurred relatively late,[72] and success at the provincial level of competition was not apparent in the southern reaches of the province. Forces that acted against women's large-scale involvement in hockey at this time are not difficult to ascertain. The general assessment of women's hockey in southern Alberta suggested that although they could compete with a degree of skill, they really did not belong in the male, middle-class realm of organized sport. As a result, most examples of girls and women playing hockey fall into the category of interesting or novel exhibitions, certainly a far cry from the level of organization and relevance attached to hockey played by men and boys.

Although a social stigma remained attached to women's involvement in hockey in the early decades of the twentieth century both in southern Alberta and throughout Canada (see chapter 4), interest in games involving women, when they did occur, was generally high. One example of a February 1915 'girls' game between teams from Medicine Hat and Lethbridge demonstrates that the novelty of the game became intertwined with the existing inter-town rivalry.[73] Reports of the 6–0 win by the home team from Lethbridge suggested that the capacity crowd was witness to a grand victory by their team over its 'Gas Town' rivals. Yet no evidence exists of a return match later that year or for the remainder of the war years. The only other example that could be located of a ladies' hockey game in southern Alberta during the First World War occurred in the town of Claresholm, when a team from Carmangay played the local 'college girls' team in March of 1917.[74]

Despite the large-scale enlistment of male hockey players during the war that resulted in the disappearance of leagues and teams in cities such as Calgary,[75] there is little evidence of any organized attempts to fill this void with women's hockey. Following the war there was a brief and localized interest in the game in several communities including Nanton, where girls' hockey teams were organized during the 1919–20 and 1920–1 seasons.[76] These teams competed against sides from nearby communities such as Stavely and High River during the winter of 1920. Interestingly, these games often occurred in tandem with league games between corresponding men's teams.[77] This is the only evidence of women's hockey in this rural region approaching anything resembling a league structure. The issue of access to ice for practice and play in Ontario described in chapter 4 does not appear to have been an impediment to women's hockey in this region. Yet it may well have been, although the playing of games in conjunction with the men seems to suggest a limited willingness to share this commodity. These brief examples provide some evidence that women's hockey continued during and after the First World War. However, as with earlier examples, the existence of these teams remained tenuous and fleeting, or was seldom deemed worthy of the local press's attention. Yet in the cases of Nanton and High River, women's hockey re-emerged in the late 1930s; but as in the past, while the athletes were praised for their skills, the games were viewed primarily as novelty acts and not serious hockey.

Two brief examples gleaned from the winter of 1937 provide some insight into the state of women's hockey in southern Alberta immediately before the Second World War. In Nanton a ladies hockey club formed and played several exhibition games. One of these contests saw the 'Ladies' Hockey club defeat the Business Men's club by a score of three to two.'[78] This game did not represent the first such contest to take place in the province, as evidence indicates that in 1911 a Mount Royal (Calgary) girls' team defeated the boys 3–0, although the boys were limited to the use of one hand on their sticks.[79] Apart from the obvious issues that could have arisen from this type of contest, including the possibility of males being seriously challenged by their female opponents, the reason why these games occurred at all is not readily apparent. It is possible the 1937 Nanton contest represented an opportunity to raise money for charity or, simply, the choice of opposition reflected the unavailability of other female teams. In another inter-gender contest, the high school girls' team from High River played a boys' peewee team from the same town in February 1937.[80] This game, won by the boys, was described as 'a spirited engagement,' and the female players were assessed as being 'good skaters [needing] only experience to make up a fast and effective team.'[81] Again, no indication of the impetus behind the game is provided in the newspaper coverage. In addition to these novelty exhibition contests, the female teams from Nanton and High River did play in February 1937, but there is no suggestion that this was anything more than a one-off exhibition match.[82]

Therefore, this brief examination of women's hockey in southern Alberta, excluding Calgary, would suggest that the teams were generally short-lived, that they played only on an exhibition basis, and that while the players were generally regarded as playing the game well, the reason for any broad interest in the games stemmed from their novelty. Ultimately, it seems that little changed between the first contests in Medicine Hat in the 1890s and the years leading up to the Second World War, and there was certainly no serious challenge to the male hockey hegemony that existed over this period.

Conclusions

This examination of hockey in rural southern Alberta does not suggest that what took place during the late 1800s and early 1900s was dramatically different from the state of the sport elsewhere in Canada. Clearly, issues such as the climate and amateurism transcended any one region or province over this period. Yet there must be some worth in looking at the history of hockey beyond that which occurred in the country's large urban centres. Evidently, in the years before the Second World War, there were some marked differences in how hockey existed in a rural versus an urban setting. In the case of small-town and rural southern Alberta, it is possible to discern a variety of influences that resulted in an often less than stable environment for the game's growth. To begin, some communities such as Cardston never truly supported hockey, and instead favoured alternative winter team sports such as basketball. In other communities, the arrival of the game, or at least the presence of a critical mass of players to form a representative team, was hampered by the lack of adequate facilities and by unreliable weather. As the available evidence suggests, many smaller communities did not build rinks suitable for hockey until the 1920s and 1930s. Yet even when facilities were built and teams formed, small communities faced additional difficulties when it came to organizing and funding competitive teams. The example of Granum in the late 1920s shows the difficulties faced by some communities to compete at the highest levels. Yet even at the local level, consistent hockey participation was susceptible to a broad range of social forces ranging from the local ability to finance facilities to the availability of players. For female players these social obstacles were even more formidable, and, apart from a few exceptions, girls and women's hockey was never able to emerge successfully from the men's sporting shadows.

How then does this brief examination of early hockey in small-town and rural southern Alberta provide some insight into the place the sport has assumed in Canada today? Several salient points can be drawn from our understanding of hockey's place within southern Alberta during the first half of the twentieth century. First, it must be understood that hockey did not thrive equally throughout the country or even within regions, particularly in rural settings. In addition, the technology that has overcome concerns related to climate and ice conditions has clearly altered not only how hockey is played but also the way people experience hockey. With respect to social class, is it possible to argue convincingly that the sport is more accessible today than in the past when one considers the expense involved in participating? Hockey's roots were clearly middle class, male, and urban. To what degree has this changed? This chapter suggests that the sport has never been a game for the poor and the strides that women have made in terms of accessing hockey have only occurred quite recently. While Canadians often prefer to laud and idealize the place of hockey in Canadian culture, it is important to recognize that historically the game did not dominate or lead in the growth and development of sport within the country. We must recognize, through the examples of how hockey existed (or did not exist) outside traditional urban strongholds, that hockey has been fallible, unjust, unequal, and in certain cases absent altogether. Therefore, to fully comprehend how hockey exists today, it is necessary to look to the past and understand that as with any other cultural practice, certain groups assumed a favoured position often at the expense of others, and thus the sport should not be held up as an ideal but recognized as a flawed yet meaningful entity that has shaped and been shaped by Canadians.

NOTES

1 See, for example, Ann Hall, *The Girl and the Game: A History of Women's Sport in Canada* (Peterborough: Broadview Press, 2002); Colin Howell, *Blood, Sweat, and Cheers: Sport and the Making of Modern Canada* (Toronto: University of Toronto Press, 2001); Bruce Kidd, *The Struggle for Canadian Sport* (Toronto: University of Toronto Press, 1997); Alan Metcalfe, *Canada Learns to Play: The Emergence of Organized Sport, 1807–1914* (McClelland and Stewart, 1987); and Don Morrow and Kevin B. Wamsley, *Sport in Canada: A History* (Toronto: Oxford, 2005).
2 The City of Montreal has often been described as the cradle of sport in Canada. See Metcalfe, *Canada Learns to Play*, 21–6; and Morrow and Wamsley, *Sport in Canada*, 50–4.
3 This examination of the history of hockey is not concerned with the ongoing debate over its ultimate roots or who 'invented' the game. However, it is clear, in the author's opinion, that hockey became an organized sport in the mid-1870s when McGill University players adapted, adopted, and developed the earliest widely accepted rules for the game. See Wayne Simpson, 'Hockey,' in *A Concise History of Sport in Canada*, ed. Don Morrow and Mary Keyes, (Toronto: Oxford, 1989), 171–2; and Richard Gruneau and David Whitson, *Hockey Night in Canada: Sport, Identities and Cultural Politics* (Toronto: Garamond Press, 1993), 37.
4 The term 'Chinook' originally referred to a Native group who resided in the Pacific Northwest. However, the term is also used to describe the warm winter winds that arrive periodically in the prairies of Canada and the United States. 'Chinook Country' is a term employed primarily in literature that focuses upon southern Alberta. See, for example, Ken Liddell, *Exploring Southern Alberta's Chinook Country* (Surry: Frontier Books, 1981); and Bill Simpkins, *Chinook Country: Alberta South* (Toronto: Totem Books, 1986).

5   Gary W. Zeman, *Alberta on Ice: The History of Hockey in Alberta since 1893* (Edmonton: Westweb Press, 1985), 20.

6   *Lethbridge Daily Herald,* 'Calgary Still Talks of Artificial Ice,' 22 February 1919, 7; William M. McLennan, 'Skating and Hockey,' in *Sport in Early Calgary* (Calgary: Fort Brisbois Publishing, 1983), 111–12.

7   *Chief Mountain Country: A History of Cardston and District* (Cardston, AB: Cardston and District Historical Society, 1978), 206; Bert Kellicut, 'Early History of Sports in the Granum Area,' in *Leaving by Trail, Granum by Rail* (Granum, AB: Granum History Committee, 1977), 126; *Rosemary: Land of Promise* (Rosemary, AB: Rosemary Historical Society, 1977), 109; *Scandia since Seventeen* (Scandia, AB: Scandia Historical Committee, 1978), 109.

8   See Morrow and Wamsley, *Sport in Canada,* 50–62.

9   L.J. Roy Wilson, 'Medicine Hat – "The Sporting Town," 1883–1905,' *Canadian Journal of History of Sport* 16, (2) (1985), 17–19.

10 *Lethbridge News,* 14 June 1888, 3; and 22 August 1888, 2.

11 *Lethbridge News,* 26 March 1886, 3; and 5 September 1888, 3.

12 *Macleod Gazette,* 1 June 1886, 3; and *Lethbridge News,* 4 June 1886, 3.

13 *Macleod Gazette,* 1 June 1886, 3; and *Lethbridge News,* 27 April 1887, 3.

14 *Lethbridge News,* 21 November 1888, 3.

15 *Macleod Gazette,* 22 September 1893, 3.

16 *Lethbridge News,* 27 March 1895, 1.

17 *Macleod Gazette,* 16 August 1895, 1; and 4 October 1895, 4.

18 Gary W. Bowie and James A.P. Day, 'Sport and Religion: The Influence of the Mormon Faith on Sport in Alberta,' paper presented at the Second World Symposium on the History of Sport and Physical Education, Banff, Alberta, 1971.

19 Leroy V. Kelly, *The Range Men,* 75th anniversary ed. (High River, AB: Willow Creek Publishing, 1986), 109. In 1888 Joseph Card and one hundred and twenty-five Mormons settled near Lee's Creek. This settlement would later be named Cardston in his honour.

20 *Chief Mountain Country,* 195.

21 Ibid., 196.

22 Donald G. Wetherell with Irene Kmet, *Useful Pleasures: The Shaping of Leisure in Alberta 1896–1945* (Edmonton and Regina: Alberta Culture and Multiculturalism / Canadian Plains Research Center, 1990), 150. The popularity of basketball in southern Alberta, particularly Cardston, can be traced to the American origins of the Mormon settlers and the influence of local school teachers.

23 Ibid., 206. An examination of the *The Cardston News* for January 1937 found

no evidence of any organized hockey being played in the town, while there are several examples of groups organizing volleyball and basketball activities.

24 Simpson, 'Hockey,' 175–6, argues that during the 1890s and early 1900s settlement of the Canadian west, beginning in Manitoba with the arrival of the Canadian Pacific Railway in 1885, resulted in the movement of hockey to these new regions. For example, Simpson points to the groups of Germanic, Icelandic, and Scandinavian settlers who had no knowledge of hockey upon their arrival, yet soon represented a vibrant element of the West's hockey growth.

25 Metcalfe, *Canada Learns to Play*, 96. In a discussion of how sport in Canada emerged and expanded from its central Canadian roots (Montreal and Ontario) in the late 1800s, Metcalfe states, 'Canadian sport was transported to the Prairies by Ontario immigrants who took with them their newly acquired games.' He also notes that this central Canadian influence did not appear to the same degree in regions such as the Maritimes and British Columbia, where the British continued to exert their influence over daily life.

26 William M. McLennan, 'Skating and Hockey,' in *Sport in Early Calgary* (Calgary: Fort Brisbois Publishing, 1983), 103.

27 Zeman, *Alberta on Ice*, 2.

28 Simpson, 'Hockey,' 176.

29 By 1891 the population of Calgary had reach 3867 people, versus 1478 for Lethbridge, which was among the largest towns in southern Alberta. Twenty years later, by 1911, Calgary's population had grown to 43,704, compared to 8050 for Lethbridge.

30 Wilson, 'Medicine Hat,' 21–2. It is not clear whether or not there were less suitable rinks in existence before to this time, but it is likely that shinny occurred on ice that became available in natural situations such as rivers and sloughs.

31 *Medicine Hat News*, 11 March 1897. No reason was provided as to why male spectators were refused entry. This likely was done to protect the virtue of the female players.

32 *Macleod Gazette*, 11 February 1898, 1.

33 *Macleod Gazette*, 22 December 1899, 5.

34 *Macleod Gazette*, 16 February 1900, 4.

35 *Lethbridge News*, 30 January 1902, 1.

36 *Lethbridge News*, 17 January 1901, 1.

37 Zeman, *Alberta on Ice*, 9; *Rocky Mountain Echo*, 29 November 1904, 4. The team from Pincher Creek was unsure whether to rejoin the Crow's Nest Past League or only play exhibition games for the 1904–5 season.

38 *Lethbridge Herald,* 22 November 1906, 3. The teams mentioned to be included in the league were Pincher Creek, Blairmore, Coleman, Frank, Bellevue,
Cowley, Macleod, and Lethbridge.

39 *Mosquito Creek Roundup: Nanton-Parkland* (Nanton, AB: Nanton and District
Historical Society, 1975), 234.

40 Ibid.

41 Metcalfe, *Canada Learns to Play,* 64.

42 *Rocky Mountain Echo,* 14 February 1905, 4.

43 Donald G. Wetherell, 'A Season of Mixed Blessings: Winter and Leisure
in Alberta before World War II,' in *Winter Sports in the West,* ed. Elise A.
Corbet and Anthony W. Rasporich (Calgary: Historical Society of Alberta,
1990), 39.

44 Paul Voisey, *Vulcan: The Making of a Prairie Community* (Toronto: University
of Toronto Press, 1988), 158.

45 Ibid., 160.

46 Wetherell, 'A Season of Mixed Blessings,' 40.

47 Metcalfe, *Canada Learns to Play,* 65; and Simpson, 'Hockey,' 180–1.

48 For a detailed examination of the formation of amateur sport organizations in Canada and the issue of professionalism in sport see Morrow and
Wamsley, *Sport in Canada,* 70–87.

49 Problems that arose in baseball during the late 1800s and early 1900s
were most often blamed on professionalism and the vices of professional
players. See Colin Howell's *Northern Sandlots: A Social History of Maritime
Baseball* (Toronto: University of Toronto Press, 1995), 55–73, for an examination of the problems that arose out of professionalism during the late
nineteenth century in Maritime baseball.

50 Zeman, *Alberta on Ice,* 8.

51 Zeman, *Alberta on Ice,* 11; *Red Deer Advocate,* 6 December 1907, 6. Delegates
who attended this first meeting represented Calgary, Edmonton, Red Deer,
Strathcona, Olds, Lacombe, Crossfield, Stettler, and Didsbury.

52 Metcalfe, *Canada Learns to Play,* 72; brackets mine. In 1897 the Ontario
Hockey Association clearly placed the onus upon the individual athlete to
prove that he was innocent of any association with professionalism.

53 *Lethbridge Daily Herald,* 10 December 1910, 7.

54 Zeman, *Alberta on Ice,* 12.

55 Voisey, *Vulcan,* 160.

56 *Lethbridge Daily Herald,* 1 December 1910, 6.

57 Kellicut, 'Early History of Sports in the Granum Area,' 126. Kellicut
provided an entry on sport in this local history publication. According to
his 1997 obituary, he was born in Granum on 26 July 1905. His family had

been ranchers and original owners of the Standard Garage in Granum, where he worked as a mechanic before working for the Alberta Wheat Pool.

58 *Claresholm Local Press,* 16 December 1927, 1.

59 *Claresholm Local Press,* 25 November 1927, 1.

60 *Claresholm Local Press,* 18 November 1927, 1.

61 Kellicut, 'Early History of Sports in the Granum Area,' 126.

62 Ibid.

63 Ibid.

64 *Claresholm Local Press,* 8 March 1929, 3.

65 *Stavely Advertiser,* 31 January 1929, 1.

66 *Mosquito Creek Roundup,* 236.

67 Metcalfe, *Canada Learns to Play,* 64–65.

68 Ibid., 67.

69 Brain McFarlane, *Proud Past, Bright Future: One Hundred Years of Canadian Women's Hockey* (Toronto: Stoddart, 1994), 17. Evidence to support the occurrence this 1893 contest could not be located. It is the author's belief that the first women's hockey game took place in 1897 (see note 31).

70 Wetherell, 'A Season of Mixed Blessings,' 44.

71 *Lethbridge Daily Herald,* 15 February 1910, 8.

72 Joanna Avery and Julie Stephens, *Too Many Men on the Ice: Women's Hockey in North America* (Toronto: Polestar, 1997), 72. Avery and Stephens provide evidence of an exhibition game between the Red Deer Amazons and Lethbridge Kiwanettes in 1933. The Amazons, Avery and Stephens note, went on to win the Alberta Intermediate Championship that year. No evidence can be located to suggest that any team from southern Alberta participated in this or any other organized provincial competition in the 1920s or 1930s.

73 *Lethbridge Daily Herald,* 13 February 1915, 3.

74 *Claresholm Review Advertiser,* 9 March 1917, 5.

75 McLennan, 'Skating and Hockey,' 125. According to McLennan, by the fall of 1914 many players had joined the armed forces, leaving fewer players and teams to compete in the Calgary city leagues.

76 *Mosquito Creek Roundup,* 235.

77 *Nanton News,* 29 January 1920, 3; and 5 February 1920, 1.

78 *Nanton News,* 18 February 1937, 3.

79 McLennan, 'Skating and Hockey,' 118.

80 *High River Times,* 18 February 1937, 6.

81 Ibid. Brackets are mine.

82 *The Nanton News,* 11 February 1937, 3.

7 Boomtown Hockey: The Vancouver Millionaires

JOHN CHI-KIT WONG

Professional hockey emerged from elite-level amateur hockey at the beginning of the twentieth century. As a new model of organization in the business of hockey, professional hockey went through a period of growing pain and opportunities until the mid-1920s. Local businessmen who had the entrepreneurial spirit and/or connection with elite-level amateur hockey struck out to establish leagues across the northern part of the North American continent. In 1904 the International Hockey League, based in the northern Michigan peninsula, first proclaimed its status as a professional league. By the early 1910s several professional leagues operated in Canada, which, by that time, had claimed hockey as its 'national sport.'[1]

Among the various new enterprises, the Pacific Coast Hockey Association (PCHA) was arguably the most significant organization contributing to the growth of hockey as a Canadian cultural phenomenon. Before the PCHA's establishment in British Columbia in 1911, ice hockey was not an important institution on the West Coast of Canada, drawing little coverage in the media. Before the league's demise in the early 1920s, the PCHA had established franchises in various cities in British Columbia, Washington, and Oregon, manoeuvred itself to be one of the two leagues eligible to challenge for the Stanley Cup, and twice brought the coveted trophy to the West Coast. Among its franchises, Vancouver was the most important. Besides being the first PCHA club to win the Stanley Cup and thus legitimize elite-level hockey's presence on the West Coast, it was the only PCHA club to exist from the league's birth to its eventual merger with the Western Canada Hockey League in 1924 and the ultimate demise of the Western Hockey League in 1926.[2]

Stephen Hardy suggests the discipline of sport history can be enriched by an alternative line of inquiry to the dominant focus on social history. He has called for 'a shift in attention from the significance of consumption to the structures of production, from the broad sweep of social forces to the minute elements of decision-making.'[3] The creation of the PCHA and the decision to locate its flagship club in Vancouver occurred within a historical context, especially an economic nexus, in the development of the city, the province, and the nascent Dominion of Canada. On the West Coast and especially in Vancouver, an atmosphere of entrepreneurship and fervent speculative investment prevailed for much of the late nineteenth and early twentieth centuries, luring opportunity seekers into the area. Whereas the opening-up of the Prairies largely drew farmers to the West, Vancouver's position as a major port attracted people who wanted to take advantage of the trade and services in the western terminus. Many of these entrepreneurs, including those in the sport industry, set up businesses that catered to the growing city. These merchants of popular culture made decisions as to the type of business, its location, and strategies to distribute their products in hope of capitalizing on the new boom town. This chapter investigates the role of the business of hockey as part of the making of Canada in the early twentieth century, and argues that commercialized hockey in Vancouver provided another important cultural link between the West Coast and Central Canada, the seat of political and economic power. By the time Vancouver hosted the 1915 Stanley Cup competition, professional hockey had provided 'a common source of entertainment and national conversation [and] an opportunity to share a common passion' from coast to coast.[4]

Economic Development, Class, and the Creation of a Leisure Culture – Vancouver before 1911

Vancouver began humbly as a settlement in British Columbia, or what Martin Robin called 'the Company Province,' whose development was heavily influenced by the economic interests of large corporations. British Columbia began developing its resource-based economy well before Confederation. First the fur trade, and then mining, drew Europeans to the West Coast. More permanent settlements first appeared on Vancouver Island around the mid-1800s. Driven in part by the American westward colonization movement, British colonial officials authorized the Hudson's Bay Company to establish Fort Victoria on Vancouver Island in 1849. The Fraser River Gold Rush in 1858, however, redirected settlement towards the mainland and, as gold was found further inland, into the Cariboo, Stikine, and Cassiar regions. This movement of entrepreneurs and fortune seekers peaked with the Klondike gold rush in the Yukon Territory at the end of the nineteenth century. In these pursuits for minerals, Victoria, not Vancouver, became the early centre of political and economic activities and soon established an elite class that enjoyed 'frequent holidays, wholesome recreation and sport, gay evenings, congenial, [and] free-handed social life.'[5]

Indeed, Vancouver remained little more than a frontier settlement from the first European navigation in the late eighteenth century to the last quarter of the nineteenth century. The Spaniards first sailed past Isla de Langara (present-day Point Grey) in 1791, but they did not venture into Burrard Inlet. During the next year, a second Spanish expedition went north from Mexico again and found Captain George Vancouver and his two boats, *Discovery* and *Chatham*, in the area. From their base in Puget Sound, Vancouver and his crew navigated around Point Grey and into Burrard Inlet on 13 June 1792 seeking the fabled Northwest Passage. Instead, they met a group of natives from the village of Whoi-whoi (located at the present Lumberman's Arch in Stanley Park) who wanted to trade with the Europeans. Commerce, not armed conflict, marked the initial gathering between visitors and locals, and it would be commercial interests that dominated the development of Vancouver.[6]

After the initial exchange between Captain Vancouver and his native hosts, the area developed slowly. Mostly inhabited by natives and visited by fur traders, the Burrard Inlet area did not see major development by whites in terms of infrastructure and society until the middle of the nineteenth century, when the British government established the province of British Columbia[7] to regulate the rush for gold on the Fraser River. Colonel Richard Clement Moody of the Royal Engineers chose the village of Queensborough (present-day New Westminster) as the capital of the newly created colony to control traffic up the Fraser River. Fearing a naval blockade of the river at its mouth that would cut off river traffic to Queensborough, Moody built an alternate land route (the present-day North Road) from the village northward towards Burrard Inlet in 1859. To defend against a rear attack via this alternate route, the British set up a military reserve at the site of the future Stanley Park. Moody then let out a contract to build a road to Jericho Beach on English Bay connecting New Westminster with the military reserve. A third access route running along the Fraser River connected New Westmin-

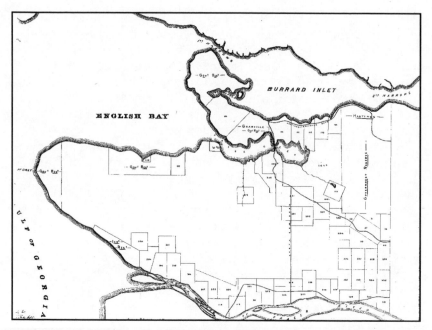

Figure 1. Map showing surveyed south shore of the Burrard Inlet, c. 1860. Moodyville (not shown) was located on the north shore of the inlet across from Hastings Mills. (City Archives of Vancouver, Map 531)

ster and Point Grey in 1863. Thus, a crude transportation system was in place accessing the future city of Vancouver by the early 1860s (see figure 1).[8]

As these routes facilitated access to Burrard Inlet, land speculation began almost at once with the elite class, people who were either in or had connection with the military and business, being the main beneficiaries. In 1860 James Douglas, governor of the colony, proclaimed the land laws of British Columbia. Walter Moberly, whose father was the Hudson's Bay Company factor, and Robert Burnaby, who was Moody's secretary, immediately filed claims on the land they had received as payment for surveying the inlet for the government. Since Moody had reserved large sections of the land for the military, Victoria politicians accused 'the military clique [of] building roads and appropriating land to enrich itself.'[9]

Despite the land grab, timber was the main industry in the early history of Burrard Inlet. A sawmill first appeared on the north shore of the Burrard Inlet in 1862. In 1865 Captain Edward Stamp organized and located his British Columbia and Vancouver Island Spar, Lumber and Sawmill Company (later renamed Hastings Mill) just east of the military reserve (Stanley Park). A settlement soon grew around the business. By 1867 there were four settlements in the peninsula. Of the four, Hastings Mill became an important centre around which sprouted a vibrant social life.[10]

Robert McDonald has argued that the production of timber products on Burrard Inlet 'was highly concentrated and ... settlement emerged out of the labour demands of industrial capitalism. Indeed, social organization can be described as a symbiotic relationship between a company-dominated clique of respectable families and a social mass drawn to the area by work in the mills, on the waterfront, and in the forests.'[11] There is evidence that recreational activities also differed along class lines in early Burrard Inlet. The upper class, mostly management and professional people of British and American stock, preferred rational recreation – activities that enriched the soul, the body, and the mind. They subscribed to the Victorian view of morality that promoted piety, sobriety, honesty, industry, and self-reliance. Mrs Ben Springer, the second schoolteacher of the village of Granville[12] and wife of Moodyville's bookkeeper, for example, organized tennis games and other social activities for her friends. Moodyville, across the inlet from Hastings Mill, was another sawmill company town whose owner established the Mechanics' Institute of Burrard Inlet, which provided books and reading room to its members. At the Hastings Mill Stamp banned liquor on the property. The working class, although ruled under a paternalistic form of industrial capitalism, sought its own recreation in saloons and company-sponsored holiday festivals. The Burrard Inlet Boat Club, for example, 'raced ... against boatmen from New Westminster as one way of escaping the social evenings organized in Granville by the Women's Christian Temperance League.'[13] A Yorkshire man, John (Gassy Jack) Deighton, took advantage of the liquor ban at Hastings Mill and established the Global Saloon outside the company boundary on 30 September 1867, and a small community, known as Gastown and later renamed Granville, quickly grew around it. Throughout the 1870s and early 1880s, Granville and Moodyville were little more than company towns with a thriving lumber export business.[14]

The fortunes of Granville rapidly changed when the Canadian Pacific Railway (CPR) chose the village over the original choice, Port Moody, as the western terminus of the trans-Canada rail line. Prime Minister John A. Macdonald's government had promised a railroad link to the province as part of the Terms of Union for British Columbia to join the Dominion of Canada in 1870. The blossoming of Vancouver as a major port, however, was largely due to the decisions made by the CPR's general manager, William Van Horne, who favoured Granville as an important transportation and trade link connecting European, Canadian, and Asian markets via the CPR rail and steamship lines. The village of Granville also helped its case by granting the CPR 6000 acres of prime real estate in the town site, consisting mostly of what is today's downtown business and waterfront districts.[15]

The trans-continental railroad agreement benefited existing settlements on the West Coast in terms of rising population and land values. Even Victoria, which would not be connected to the rail line, had an increase in population from 7000 in 1881 to 11,000 in 1885. Port Moody went through a land speculation boom when the Macdonald government first announced the town as the terminus. Town lots were selling for up to $2000 each in the early 1880s. The CPR decision's impact on Granville was unmistakable. Before the CPR decision, in 1880, the Granville population numbered around 300. Ten years later, the Canadian census listed 13,709 residents in the city, incorporated as Vancouver in 1886 – an increase of almost 4500 per cent![16]

The CPR's contribution to Vancouver as a thriving city, however, involved more than population increase, land grabs, and speculation. The company also encouraged improvement of land that would eventually increase the value of its own holdings. Leading by example, the CPR built a luxury hotel, the Hotel Vancouver, at the southwest corner of Georgia and Granville streets, which was later flanked by the new Vancouver Opera House. The Hudson's Bay Company and Bank of Montreal soon followed and relocated on Granville Street, at the end of which, near the waterfront, the new terminal would be situated. As if approving the CPR's development plan, the federal government also built the new Vancouver post office there. Spurred on by its vast holding of land in this part of town, the CPR wanted to move the business and social centre from the waterfront district near Gastown to Granville Street – a vision that did not come to fruition until the turn of the century.[17]

According to one historian, the CPR's role in the growth and development of Vancouver was even more significant in indirect and intangible ways during the boom years between 1886 and 1892. Its confidence in the future of Vancouver as a major port projected hope and optimism for those seeking opportunities. Locally, a group of citizens petitioned the provincial government to incorporate Vancouver, which received approval in April 1886, and the city council started work on improving the city proper, adding sidewalks, roads, bridges, and a sewer system. Private enterprises quickly emerged to provide electricity, water, street lighting, and public transit. Lured by the boom, people from other parts of the globe began arriving en masse, many of whom were of working age and of British stock. Yet majority of the migrant population (42.5%) came from eastern Canada, with immigrants from Great Britain forming the next largest group (29.1%). With the influx of people, only 8.7% of the Vancouver population in 1891 claimed a British Columbian origin (as compared to 36.6% in 1881). More important, the demographic profile of Vancouverites shifted towards a more ethnically homogeneous composition during the boom years.[18]

As Vancouver grew, its social life blossomed with the population. For the white population at least, social-class status defined leisure activities for the most part. Continuing its lifestyle before the construction of the CPR line, Vancouver's elite favoured rational recreation. Businessmen formed social and sports clubs such as the Brockton Point Athletic Association, in 1888.[19] Emulating the social elites in other major metropolitan areas, wealthy Vancouverites organized the Vancouver Club in 1889 and the Terminal City Club in 1899, two of the most important social clubs in the city that catered to 'the interests of business and professional men' by combining 'social and business functions.'[20] Members of these clubs and their families could also be found in later upper-class sports clubs such as the Shaughnessy Heights Golf Club and the Connaught Skating Club.[21] For working people, saloons remained important social and recreation centres. Public spaces, however, were also available to those who desired them, since a large part of the Vancouver area remained wooded despite the surge in population. Stanley Park first opened on 27 September 1888, although an access problem limited its popularity until 1895, when the local transit company extended a line to the park. Two sports fields, the Powell Street Grounds and the Cambie Street Grounds, offered local citizens opportunities in cricket, soccer, and lacrosse. An Australian visitor, Douglas Sladen, marvelled at 'a superb athletic ground where, by the influx of English and Australians, cricket is restored to its legitimate place of pride.'[22]

By the end of the 1880s, then, Vancouver began to form an identity based on its economy, demographics, and the construction of a social hierarchy. As a CPR experiment to globalize its commercial empire, the city served as a trade link that connected Canada to the Pacific markets carrying both goods and human cargo.[23] Vancouver's economy fuelled and was fuelled by speculative endeavours, and its population was increasingly white and Anglo. A young Rudyard Kipling visited Vancouver in 1889 and came under its spell and its land speculation schemes. He noted approvingly that the city was 'full of Englishmen who speak the English tongue correctly.'[24] Feeling comfortable with the city's English influence, he bought '400 well-developed pines, a few thousand tons of granite scattered in blocks, and a sprinkling of earth. That's a town lot in Vancouver. You order your agent to hold it until property rises, then sell out and buy more land out of town.'[25]

A worldwide depression in 1890 momentarily slowed but did not destroy the red-hot Vancouver economy and real estate market. Even as banks failed, land values did not succumb entirely to the economic downturn. In 1887 the site for the future Dominion Trust building at Hastings and Cambie was sold for $750. Two years later, its value had increased to $7600. In 1906 the property was again sold for $15,000. Indeed, those who were not faint-hearted and held on to their properties would reap handsome profits when the good times returned near the end of the first decade of the twentieth century. As late as 1905, one could purchase a city block near Stanley Park for merely $1500, even though access to this part of the city was greatly enhanced by a streetcar line running along Denman Street, not far from the park, and connecting this area to the downtown and English Bay. In 1910 a portion of the same lot was priced at and sold for $125,000.[26] In part, the development of mining and timber industries in the interior of the province somewhat tempered the adverse effects of economic depressions on Vancouver. In the last decade of the nineteenth century Vancouver became increasingly more integrated with the interior of the province. Besides catering to growing population, the city also served as the major resource centre to the hinterland industries and businesses. This development encouraged and created three categories of businesses within the city: externally financed and controlled corporations, externally financed but locally controlled regional businesses, and small merchants who had few employees and limited capitalization. These businesses suckled on the brief rush for gold in the Klondike in the last years of the nineteenth century and were sustained by the booming resource industry in the Kootenay region in first decade of the new century.[27]

After another economic depression hit Vancouver in 1907, the city experienced a further spurt of growth. By this time, Vancouver had well established itself as the regional centre of Canada's West Coast. Victoria had lagged far behind in terms of population and economic activities. Whereas census data showed Vancouver and Victoria had populations of 27,010 and 20,919 respectively in 1901, the gap between the two major West Coast cities grew tremendously thereafter, as evidenced in the 1911 data: Vancouver with 100,401 inhabitants and Victoria 31,660. British subjects and Canadian migrants continued to constitute the majority of this human inflow that helped push city development westward and southward in Vancouver, while transportation, in the form of additional tramlines, with New Westminster improved. Construction reached a fever pitch in 1912, with a total value of just under $20 million. Tall office buildings transformed the downtown skyline. Completed in 1910, the Dominion Trust Building, for example, reached fourteen stories and was viewed with pride by Vancouverites as evidence of the city's rising status, not only in Canada but in the world. Exaggeration or not, they were no longer satisfied comparing their city with other West Coast cities. The financing of Vancouver's growth now drew capital from Europe as the locus of businesses finally shifted from Hastings Street to Granville Street. Bank clearings rose annually from $147 million in 1906 to $444 million in 1910. Custom receipts nearly doubled between 1910 and 1911. Even local retailers viewed their businesses in a broader continental context. 'Drysdale's delivery service had the finest stable, and C. E. Tisdall's store the largest stock of sporting goods, "west of Chicago."'[28]

Accompanying the growth of Vancouver was the business of leisure. As one chronicler of the city observed: 'In the Vancouver of the early 1900's ... revelry was a subsidiary of commerce.'[29] In 1901 Vancouver held its first successful street fair featuring, among other attractions, Professor Rose, a gymnast who dove into a water tank from a one-hundred-feet-high ladder. Of course, citizens could also ride the privately financed tramline for an outing in Stanley Park or bathing at English Bay, where concerts were held on Sunday evenings at Alexander Park. Spectator sports such as lacrosse and baseball were drawing large crowds. The Vancouver Beavers Baseball Club commenced play in the Northwestern League in 1905. Lacrosse fans in Vancouver could ride the British Columbia Electric Railway Company's twelve-mile Central Park line, which terminated in Queen's Park in New Westminster, to watch the bitter rivalry between the two city clubs. Crowds as large as 100,000 filled the grounds on Saturday afternoons.[30]

The rich sporting and recreation life in Vancouver around the turn of the twentieth century indicated, in part, the growth of a middle-class population in the city. From 1900 to the beginning of the First World War, Vancouver shared in the country's prosperous 'era of wheat, tariffs and railroads.' Except for 1907–8, wages for skilled labourers in the construction, manufacturing, and transportation industries experienced a general upward trend. Increases in wages accompanied the growing influence of the middle class in civic politics as small merchants and entrepreneurs in the real estate, construction, service, and retail industries replaced the business elite in city councils. In the sport industry, entrepreneurs took advantage of economic and population growth by providing sporting contests for middle-class urbanites seeking entertainment. In 1905 private capital helped build Recreation Park, the city's first completely fenced facility, at the corner of Homer and Smythe in downtown Vancouver, for its professional baseball team. Elite-level lacrosse games were staged here as well as at the Brockton Oval in Stanley Park in front of large crowds. Given the success of lacrosse in paid attendance and victories against established eastern Canadian clubs, Con Jones, a Vancouver entrepreneur, helped organize a professional lacrosse league in 1909. In many respects, then, Vancouver at the end of the first decade of the twentieth century presented an ideal location for sport entrepreneurs.[31]

The Root and Birth of the PCHA and the Vancouver Millionaires

Commenting on the development of the resources of British Columbia's interior, Martin Robin argues that the 'Inland Empire (centring on Spokane, Washington but reaching into the Kootenay region of B.C.) built on lead, zinc, copper and silver, [and] the assault on the forests after the turn of the century ... was sponsored by free enterprisers and aided by friendly and stable governments.'[32] Near the end of the first decade of the twentieth century, the Kootenays, in southwestern British Columbia, experienced an economic upswing, drawing entrepreneurs and capital into the region. The timber industry contributed greatly to this boom. In 1905 the provincial government, under a newly elected Tory premier, Richard McBride, adopted a Special Licence System that loosened the restrictions on harvesting the province's forests. The new policy allowed for licensees to renew their now transferable permit for a period of twenty-one years and placed no limit on the number of licences an individual could possess. Near the end of 1907, when the government reversed policy, entrepreneurs had snapped up approximately 9,600,000 acres of forest. Some of these prime forest lands belonged to a late arrival, one Joseph Patrick, in the Slocan region. Patrick began his career as a clerk in a general store in Drummondville, Quebec, speculated (and failed) in the bean market, became co-owner of a successful general store, and used the sale of his share in the store to start a lumber company that expanded into the distribution and sale of lumber by-products, with an office based in Montreal. By 1907 the entrepreneurial and successful Joe Patrick had decided to pull up his roots in Quebec and move his family westward to the inviting British Columbian economy.[33]

Thanks to Joe Patrick's uncanny sense of business timing for opportunities, his fortunes had risen considerably by 1911. Under McBride's government the province had enjoyed an unprecedented period of prosperity. An agreement between the Canadian Northern Pacific Railway Company and the provincial government to construct a rail line from Yellowhead to Vancouver in 1909 fuelled the already robust economy given the railroad's potential demand for ore and timber. Depletion of traditional timber sources in the Canadian east sprouted fear of a worldwide shortage. Land speculation in British Columbia, especially in prime timber land, went into a frenzy, and attracted major capitalists from the United States, Europe, and Canada. In 1910, for example, American investments led by John D. Rockefeller of New York and M.J. Scanlon of Minneapolis totalled $65,000,000. Forecasting a continual demand for lumber, these conglomerates' strategy was to acquire more holdings through amalgamations. As the price for land moved upward, Joe Patrick sold his Patrick Lumber Company in January 1911 to an English syndicate, the British Canadian Lumber Corporation, for $440,000.[34]

According to Joseph Schumpeter, an entrepreneur can introduce innovation in a product/service, the mode of production, an organizational structure, the acquisition of resources, or the opening of markets. In these endeavours the entrepreneur is taking a risk that the innovation may not succeed. For Joe Patrick, it is not clear why he sold his successful lumber company other than that the price was more than right, for he apparently had no plans afterwards. He and his two oldest sons, Curtis Lester and Frank Alexis, held a family meeting after the sale and decided that the family would now venture into the hockey business by building facilities and creating a professional league on the BC West Coast, where organized hockey had not existed previously.

Now fifty-four years old, Joe was content to heed his sons' advice and invest the windfall into a rather uncertain and risky venture. Lester and Frank, twenty-seven and twenty-five years old respectively, were top-notch hockeyists who had starred in both amateur and professional hockey leagues in the East, but they had no previous experience running a hockey league or an arena. Still, the family decided to move to Victoria, where Lester would run a franchise. Frank, on the other hand, would be in charge of a franchise in Vancouver. Together with promoters in other western Canadian cities, the Patricks were going to bring hockey to the West Coast.[35]

Given its meteoric growth since incorporation, Vancouver made logical sense as part of the Patricks' hockey plan at first glance. As the largest city on the Canadian West Coast, Vancouver had established sporting rivalries with New Westminster, and its fans began comparing their city's sporting prowess beyond the region to the more established eastern Canadian sporting culture, especially in lacrosse competitions.[36] Yet ice hockey was not necessarily a leisure option for Vancouver's sport consumers because the climate on the coast was too mild to sustain long periods of cold temperatures, a requisite for making ice in hockey arenas in those days. The Patricks, however, already had the solution. Two years earlier the brothers had played for the Renfrew Millionaires of the National Hockey Association. After the season ended, the team accepted an invitation for a post-season tournament to be played at New York's St Nicholas Arena, which had a refrigeration system for making ice. Artificial ice-making technology had existed since the mid-1850s, and the St Nicholas Arena had used that technology to host skating events and hockey games since its opening in 1896. While hockey in eastern Canada could rely on the cold weather, the Patricks knew they had to import the new technology if they were going to introduce hockey commercially on the West Coast.[37]

Employing the ice-making technology no doubt added to the cost of putting hockey in Vancouver given the city's red-hot real estate market in 1911. The total value of buildings that received a permit to start construction stood at $17,650,092 at the end of 1911, and exceeded the 1910 total by more than 33⅓ per cent. To build an arena worthy of the growing status of Vancouver required a large tract of land in an area that would be convenient to customers. The Patrick's found a vacant plot – district lot 185, lots 1 to 5 of parcel 1 of block 64, near Stanley Park at the corner of Denman and Georgia Streets. Consisting of thirteen lots, parcel 1 extended from Georgia Street to the water's edge at Coal Har-

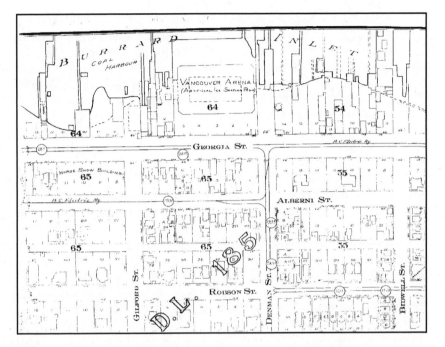

Figure 2. Map showing location of the Vancouver Arena at Georgia and Denman Streets. The BC Electric Railway had a tram line running along Georgia. Stanley Park, a popular recreation area, is about one block away to the west. Granville Street is about ten blocks to the east of Denman. (City Archives of Vancouver, Map 342-7, 1912, with permission from SCM Group)

bour and was bounded by Denman and Chilco Streets (see figure 2). A streetcar line ran along Georgia Street linking the downtown business district and beyond to this upscale West End residential area. With land values in Vancouver continuing to rise, the Patricks had to pay a premium for the location. Bearing in mind that the family would be operating two franchises and arenas, the Patricks issued public stocks to help finance the larger Vancouver arena. On 5 June 1911 the Vancouver Arena Company, Limited officially became a going concern, with a capitalization of $200,000 divided into 1000 preferred and 1000 common shares of $100 each. Preferred shareholders had 'the right to a fixed cumulative preferential dividend at the rate of ten (10) per cent per annum.'[38]

Despite the speculative nature of the city's economic environment, few people took the Patricks' offer of investment. As noted earlier, land values rose quickly in Vancouver in the early 1910s, and the arena's location was at the coveted West End area bounded by Stanley Park and English Bay. After the turn of the century, the West End had emerged as a residential neighbourhood of choice for the well-to-do, who built homes 'boasting features such as mahogany staircases, solid oak billiard tables, conservatories, and extensive garden and lawns,' and was now heavily populated.[39] It is unclear why the response was cool at best to the Vancouver Arena stock offering. Perhaps potential land speculators saw the arena as a long-term project, with a quick short-term gain out of the question. Or perhaps investors did not believe the return was high enough compared to other opportunities. Regardless of the reasons, only five people bought shares – fourteen totalling $1400, of which $520 was paid – by 9 September; and of the five, four were directors of the company. Two more investors bought a further eight shares after September, but the Patricks knew that they would have to bear the major financial burden in the Vancouver venture.[40]

Vancouver was unquestionably the anchor of the Patricks' hockey empire, and its most tangible evidence was this facility. The Vancouver arena was a marvel of its time and would probably be approved by those who compared the city to other major metropolises. It was the second largest indoor arena in North America, only New York's Madison Square Garden being bigger. Initially estimated at $175,000, its final cost grew to $226,382. The building alone cost $191,710.[41] It had an ice surface measuring '210 feet by 85 feet, which makes it five feet longer than the Montreal Arena. The building will seat over 10,000 spectators, every one of whom, owing to the admirable arrangement of the seats will have a perfect view of the play.'[42] By comparison, the Victoria's new arena seated only 4000. Not without a sense of civic pride, the *Vancouver Province* noted also that the new Toronto Mutual Street arena 'seats only 6000.'[43] Fifteen hundred people flocked to the grand opening of the new arena on 20 December for public skating. Even though the temperature was mild and it was raining outside, the arena's ice surface did not turn into puddles of water, usually a feature of natural-ice arenas throughout the country under similar conditions.[44]

As the Patricks worked on facilities in the spring of 1911, they also devised a plan to entice local sport consumers to the large arena. Since professional hockey was an unfamiliar product, the brothers decided to raid the National Hockey Association (NHA) for players in order to create instant 'brand equity.' Brand equity enhances 'name recognition or awareness, [promotes] strong mental/emotional associations, [increases] perceived brand quality, [and ultimately, creates] strong customer loyalty.'[45] Around 1910, many of the elite hockey players in Canada had turned professional, and the most recognized league in Canada was the NHA. Even the Vancouver media reported on the NHA, especially during Stanley Cup challenges, despite the fact that hockey was not a major winter sport in Vancouver; thus, some sport consumers, especially those who had migrated from the East, would have been familiar with the calibre of the players and the kind of product the NHA put on the ice. Some eastern hockey players were also top-notch lacrosse players well known to Vancouver consumers. Lured by lacrosse entrepreneur Con Jones's high salary, Newsy Lalonde, for example, played professional lacrosse for Vancouver in the summer months.[46]

Another reason to recruit NHA players was the fact that Vancouver, and for that matter the West Coast, did not have any home-grown talent capable of playing at the elite level. The lack of local talent might, at first glance, seem to hinder the task of creating a connection between the team and the community. Yet this problem would not necessarily lessen the community's identification with the team if imported players could bring glory and pride to the city, much as the NHA hockey and local professional lacrosse teams had. By the early twentieth century, supporters of professional sport had come to accept the practice of using 'players who were real stars, whose ability could not be questioned anywhere in Canada,' and the home fans could still 'take pride in the team that represents the city where they are living.' Furthermore, 'those who came from Eastern Canada [to Vancouver] ... scarcely like the allusion to Eastern players that convey[s] the impression they are of foreign blood.'[47] Interestingly, the first comment hints at the acceptance of a national identity. Given the changing view of the representational status of a team, the lack of local talent, and the desire to create credibility for the PCHA as a major league, the Patricks went east to stock their new league.

As the family tried to arrange financing and oversaw the construction of the arenas in the spring and summer of 1911, Frank and Lester Patrick began signing NHA players for the inaugural season. In the spring Lester, who had just gotten married on 7 March, went east on his honeymoon and, at the same time, to recruit players. The brothers' decision to raid the NHA could not have come at a better time. At the start of the previous season, the NHA had imposed a salary cap to cut costs after player salaries skyrocketed during the 1909–10 bidding war between the NHA and the now-defunct Canadian Hockey Association. Incensed about the salary cap, some NHA players threatened to form a players' league at the beginning of the 1910–11 season, but eventually submitted to the cut in salary. To lure NHA players to jump their contracts, the Patricks offered higher wages than the NHA clubs – a practice that Con Jones had previously used to lure eastern lacrosse players away from their teams. A number of players, unhappy with the NHA and seeking new adventure, joined the PCHA under the threat of banishment by their former employers. Locally, Lalonde was the first to be approached by Frank Patrick as the hockey/lacrosse star arrived in May to prepare for the upcoming lacrosse season. As branding goes, the players who came west consisted of some of the household names in the hockey circle. The first Vancouver team included such notables as Newsy Lalonde, Tom Phillips, and Si Griffis – all were later inducted into the Canadian Hockey Hall of Fame.[48]

Despite the heavy investment in the Vancouver arena, the Patricks did not stack the Vancouver team with star players. In terms of player personnel, they had to balance the potential revenue from a star-studded Vancouver team against the survival of the league. When their plan of persuading Edmonton and Calgary to join the PCHA failed, the Patricks had to put a third team (New Westminster) into the league to avoid a two-team league. Given the established rivalry in lacrosse between Vancouver and New Westminster, the latter's selection was a logical one. But the last-minute nature of the third team meant that New Westminster would not have a home arena, and so it had to play all its games in the Vancouver arena. Long before the days of sponsorships, licensing, and broadcast rights, attendance was the major revenue source for sport entrepreneurs. With transportation made easy by the interurban tramlines, the Patricks were gambling on the willingness of New Westminster supporters to watch their team in the Vancouver arena – if the New Westminster team was competitive. Moreover, the Patricks could not possibly make Vancouver an all-star team because of the structure of ownership (see below) and the lingering suspicion of pre-arranged outcomes in professional sports.[49]

The initial organizational structure of the PCHA represented an anomaly in the business of professional team sports at the time. Since the creation of the National League in professional baseball in 1876, professional lacrosse and then hockey followed approximately the same organizational structure as baseball. The league was composed of independently owned franchises and, depending on the stage of its development, hired a commissioner or president to oversee its daily operations. Partly because of the negative perception of professional sports – the idea that a hired man could be lured by money to win or lose – the position of commissioner or president, usually someone who had no stake in any of the franchises, helped to deflect criticism by projecting an above-board business approach and to defend the interests of the owners. In hockey and lacrosse, moreover, owners did not own their facilities given the short season. It was much cheaper to pay rent than to deal with the headaches of maintaining, marketing, and booking events for the facility year round. However, the Patricks owned both the PCHA's facilities. Since the family had to run the entire affairs of the league, it had to show the public that the games were genuine and not fixed contests. Moreover, they were keenly aware of accusations of syndicatism, as memories of cross-ownerships in professional baseball just a decade ago were still fresh. In an age of reform and trust busting, New York Giants' owner Andrew Freedman's proposal of forming a baseball syndicate under which the league, among other things, controlled player distribution to each team received much criticism and was vilified. As the *Vancouver Province* warned, the success of the league would depend on the Patricks' 'judgment in the arrangement of the three teams ... If it was good, hard close games should be seen all season and big fat gate receipts should follow.'[50]

The establishment of the Vancouver hockey club and the building of the arena, however, did more than just import professional hockey on the West Coast. The Patricks' enterprise also created a hockey culture by encouraging and cultivating interest in the sport. As the arena was under construction, Frank Patrick began promoting amateur hockey to local groups and assisted them in forming an amateur league. Obviously, additional hockey games from the amateur leagues benefited the Vancouver Arena, since it was the only facility in town capable of hosting hockey games. Seven teams sought admission into the Vancouver Amateur Hockey League and, eventually, Frank Patrick and W.P. Irving (PCHA president) selected four – all were from middle- to upper-middle-class organizations that included the Vancouver Athletic Club, the Bankers, the Columbians, and the Vancouver Rowing Club. As new adventurers, the clubs in the new league talked enthusiastically about forming a provincial organization and challenging for the Allan Cup, the amateur championship trophy, to link the city with the rest of the country in 'Canada's national winter pastime.'[51]

Linking Vancouver to the rest of Canada's winter pastime did not stop with hockey. Much in the style of the men's social clubs, the upper class in Vancouver organized the Connaught skating club in December. On the club's executive board were some of Vancouver's socially prominent families, including Sir Charles Hibbert and Lady Tupper. Frank Patrick, again, actively encouraged the formation of the club by allowing its meetings to be held in the arena, arranging a private dressing room for the lady members; 'after January 1 members will be enabled to secure afternoon tea at club rates.'[52] Furthermore, the arena also contained four curling rinks. The Vancouver Curling Club, first established in December, located its headquarters in the arena.[53]

By the end of 1911, then, the PCHA and Vancouver were poised to enter major-league hockey. Like the CPR before them, the Patricks used Vancouver (and the other two cities) to experiment with their entrepreneurial dream. They invested heavily in physical assets as both the economic climate and their desire to go major league inflated their initial capital requirements. Moreover, they presented a new model of operation in professional sport – a single-entity league with no independent franchise owners.[54] The family put up the investment, oversaw the construction of arenas, recruited the players, and basically ran the league even as the PCHA went through the customary organizing meeting to elect a board of directors at, where else, the Hotel Vancouver, the symbol of the CPR's determination to make Vancouver a major city, on 7 December. Now Vancouver had a major-league hockey team and the experiment of commercialized hockey was about to begin.[55]

Hockey, Culture, and the Stanley Cup

Frank Patrick and the Vancouver club went into their first season with uncertainty because, despite the large investments, they were not sure how the market would respond. Since newspapers of the day were usually unabashed civic boosters, however, Patrick could rely on the press to give the enterprise encouragement and promotional space – some breathing room until the club could establish itself among the local sport consumers. Indeed, on the day of the PCHA opening game in Vancouver, the *Vancouver Province* printed a lengthy article explaining the intricacies of the sport. Acknowledging that 'only a small percentage of the city's population' had seen the game, the author surmised that for 'over fifty per cent of the attendance this evening ... [the game] will be very much a novelty,' and used the two popular sports in Vancouver, lacrosse and rugby, to familiarize readers with hockey. The author was also quick to separate hockey from lacrosse by proclaiming that hockey players were much superior in their conditioning due to the nature of the sport; in particular, 'in the professional game ... the players are able to devote their whole time to the sport, or business as it is with them, [and thereby] hockey attains its highest perfection.'[56] Despite its promotion by local media, the first game's outcome, in terms of attendance, must have been disappointing to the Patricks, as less than half of the huge arena was filled. Indeed, one newspaper attributed the low attendance to the necessity of local patrons to 'master the technicalities of the sport' before the club could hope for 'crowds which will make records in the hockey history in Canada.'[57]

Although attendance at the first game was less than stellar, the first match immediately provided material contrasting the western style of play to the eastern game, which had undergone a number of rule changes, the most far-reaching of which was the decision to reduce the number of players on the ice from seven to six. Frank Patrick had previously criticized this reduction in the number of players as a cost-saving ploy by the NHA owners – had no doubt a tactic also to convince some eastern players to consider going west – and he predicted that it would 'slow up the play.'[58] In this instance, the Vancouver club and the PCHA positioned themselves as defenders of hockey tradition. More likely, his criticism served as an appeal to the city's migrants from Central Canada, a potential group of customers who were familiar with the seven-man game. After the first game, the *Province* echoed Patrick's public accusation by printing a cartoon that depicted two hockey players smoking cigarettes while sitting on the bench. The caption said, 'The new rules in Eastern hockey have made the games there very tame.' Next to this derisive caricature of the NHA game was a sketch of the crowd cheering with wild excitement during the first game in the Vancouver's arena.[59] Ignoring the actual support at the turnstiles, the media was quite happy to adopt the Vancouver team and PCHA hockey as symbols of the exciting and dynamic nature of the city and the region.

In spite of the comparison between the new West and the lethargic East, the PCHA was a new league that had yet to prove the quality of its product. While the PCHA race was tight and exciting in the first season, the Patricks had to test their league against the NHA in order to confirm the PCHA's claim to major-league status, and so they proceeded to issue a challenge for the Stanley Cup. Due to an oversight in scheduling, however, the PCHA's inaugural season did not end until after 15

March. Since the tradition of the challenge gave home-ice advantage to the Cup holder, the earliest possible Stanley Cup game would not come until the end of March in Ottawa, home to the current defender of the trophy. By late March, however, most arenas in eastern Canada could not guarantee a playable ice surface, as none had artificial ice-making capability. Hence, the Stanley Cup challenge was out of the question.[60]

When it was clear that there would be no Stanley Cup challenge, the Patricks arranged for an NHA all-star team to come west to play a picked PCHA squad after the season was over. The all-star exhibition was important for several reasons. In place of the Stanley Cup challenge, it allowed West Coast patrons to gauge the calibre of PCHA players against the established league's. At the same time, the exhibition familiarized West Coast fans with eastern star players and would be good advertising for future Stanley Cup challenges. If the games were close or if the PCHA all-stars won, that would support the league's status as a major league. The series further functioned as a scouting exercise for next season's potential recruits; 'no expense will be spared to get the proper men' for the all-star team and an 'effort will be made to include Fred Taylor, the sensational coverpoint.'[61]

Indeed, the all-star series achieved what the Patricks had hoped for. As a spectacle, the series built enthusiasm for the sport. Out of the three-game series, Vancouver hosted the first and the third matches. Between six to seven thousand fans witnessed 'sensational hockey,' played under PCHA rules, in which the PCHA team won 10–4 in the first contest and the eastern all-stars edged out the locals 6–5 in the last contest of the series. With a victory in Victoria as well, 8–2, the PCHA squad won the series two games to one.[62] While the Vancouver attendance fell short of the arena's capacity, it would have almost filled the Montreal Arena, the next largest in Canada, which had a capacity of approximately seven thousand. Certainly, attendance the all-star series must have pleased Frank Patrick, as it was much better than for any of Vancouver's regular season games, which often had no more than two thousand.[63] In addition to increasing gate receipts, the series allowed the locals to assess the differences in rules that manifested in two distinct styles of play between the two leagues. Importantly also, the eastern press began to take the PCHA seriously, as the *Montreal Gazette* praised the quality of the series, 'the greatest hockey which, even those who have been accustomed to seeing the game in the East, have ever witnessed.'[64] Despite the success of the all-star series, however, the PCHA suffered a $9000 loss for the season.[65]

To improve attendance in the next season, Frank Patrick landed Fred 'Cyclone' Taylor, arguably the most famous player of the day. A teetotaler, Taylor represented the best that the professional game had to offer. Although not a big man, he was a tenacious, skilful, speedy, and flamboyant player who allegedly defied the powerful Ontario Hockey Association by joining the Houghton (Michigan) club of the International Hockey League as a professional. Like Wayne Gretzky in the late twentieth century, Taylor's fame and drawing power extended beyond Canada. After he left Houghton and returned to play in Canada, American promoters in New York and Boston insisted that Taylor be on one of the touring teams in post-season tournaments there. New York fans affectionately dubbed him little Jeff, after the former heavyweight boxing champion Jim Jeffries. Taylor was well aware of his value in the hockey market and used it to his advantage. When the bidding war between the NHA and the Canadian Hockey Association occurred in 1910, Taylor was able to negotiate a contract with the Renfrew Millionaires that made him the highest-paid player (on a per game basis) in all sports in North America. It was also in Renfrew that the Patricks, as team members, struck up a friendship with the entrepreneurial Taylor. Taylor had sat out the 1911–12 season because, once again, he stood up to the power establishment by refusing to report to the Montreal Wanderers club after the Renfrew team was disbanded. The Patricks had specifically asked for Taylor to be included in the all-star exhibition series at the end of the season, not only because of his abilities as a player and his potential as a marketing icon, but also as an opportunity for Taylor to visit the West Coast. They had tried to lure him there the previous winter. Now that he had been to Vancouver, Taylor was convinced that the West Coast was the place for a self-promoter and entrepreneur such as himself.[66]

Taylor's impact on the Vancouver club and the promotion of hockey to the city was almost immediate. Before the first home game, the press reminded Vancouver's consumers that 'Manager Frank Patrick has collected practically all of the stars worth taking from the N. H. A.' and that 'Fred Taylor, the most sensational player in the game ... is showing all of his old-time form.'[67] Whereas attendance was disappointing for the club the first season, Vancouver had the largest crowd in a regular season game in its first home game of the second season against New Westminster, nearly equalling those of the all-star series the previous season.[68] Taylor's presence created so much optimism that, amid early season successes, the press, in a moment of jubilation, averred that 'it would be hard to find a defence anywhere in Canada' better than the one in town.[69]

Early in the second season, the PCHA teams began adopting team nicknames similarly to the eastern teams. With the former highest-paid hockey player on the team, the Vancouver squad was called the Millionaires after the Renfrew team of 1910 that had signed players with little consideration of their asking price. The moniker perhaps also reflected the economic outlook of the city as the real estate market peaked in 1912. The value of building permits almost topped $20 million by the end of the year.[70] Indeed, the same rosy picture appeared in the 1912 year-end assessment of the team, based on the attendance of the two games already played and the talent on the squad: 'The defence is easily the best in the league, and for that matter, in Canada ... Frank Patrick is without doubt the best point player in the business ... Jack McDonald is the best left wing in this league,' and 'Fred Harris, the roughest and toughest boy in the league. Altogether [there] is not a weak spot anywhere in the Vancouver line-up, and ... they should make a straight dash to the championship.'[71] Unfortunately for the club, there would be no championship in the second season despite all the high praise. Even though the club's average attendance more than doubled the first season's, the Millionaires' dream of winning the league title and challenging for the Stanley Cup in 1913 dissipated, much the same as the Vancouver real estate market that had begun a five-year decline, bottoming out in 1917. The team's fortunes, however, recovered much faster than the real-estate market.[72]

Richard Gruneau and David Whitson posit that 'cultural symbols ... play an important role in representing communities and nations to outside world.'[73] By the 1910s, the Stanley Cup certainly qualified as such a symbol as towns clamoured to seek possession of it. As the media proclaimed hockey to be Canada's winter national pastime, the holder of the cup symbolized a community's strength and resolve to endure the struggle in achieving superiority. Of course, this transcendence over all others represented unspoken ideals of masculinity and labour–capital relations in a free-enterprise economy. If Vancouver had the 'best' player in Taylor, then Vancouver must also have possession of the Stanley Cup.[74]

Vancouver's chance at the Stanley Cup came in the 1914–15 season. For the first time since the league began, Vancouver became the PCHA champion. In the previous season the PCHA and the NHA had finally negotiated an agreement governing professional hockey after years of raiding each other's players. Among other terms, the agreement called for an annual best-three-out-of-five playoff series for the Stanley Cup between the champions of each league. As a sign of the growing status of the PCHA, the NHA also consented to play the annual series alternately in the East and West, with the home team having the advantage of its league's rules in the first, third, and, if necessary, fifth games. The differences in playing rules between the two leagues were quite significant by this time. While keeping the seven-man game, the PCHA had made a major change in the 1913–14 season by dividing the playing surface into three zones and allowing forward passing in the middle zone. Forward passing made the game flow more fluidly by cutting down on offside calls. Since the first such series between the two leagues had occurred in the East the previous season, Vancouver would have home-ice and rule advantages this time. What the Patricks had planned and hoped for finally came to fruition. Vancouver, the jewel of the PCHA, was going to host the country's most important sporting event and, in the process, demonstrate to the rest of the country that the city (and the PCHA) belonged to the larger Canadian hockey culture.[75]

The 1914–15 Stanley Cup challenge turned out to be a success even though the local media was cautious about the home team's chances before the first game of the series. A pre-tournament report in the *Vancouver Province* reminded readers that 'only four [of Vancouver's players] have ever played professional hockey before this winter.'[76] The *Vancouver World* warned that 'every member of the [Ottawa] team is an artist and, individually, they appear to have a shade on the homesters.'[77] When the Millionaires handily defeated the Ottawa Senators by a score of 6–2, however, the media let fly their exuberance. 'Vancouvers score brilliant win over eastern hockey champions,' exclaimed the *Vancouver Daily News-Advertiser.*[78] The *Vancouver World* lauded them, 'Coast champions play brilliant game and fans can't see Ottawa,'[79] and the *Vancouver Province* boasted, 'Millionaires skate rings round their rivals from eastern Canada and win handily.'[80] In spite of the praises of the visitors before the first match, seven thousand fans witnessed the failure of the Ottawa team to handle the speed of the Millionaires.[81] Vancouver went on to defeat Ottawa in the second game 8–3 and increased that margin with a 12–3 drubbing in the third to take the Cup in three straight games. Approximately twelve thousand attended the series. In four years, Frank Patrick had established a solid base of hockey fans in Vancouver.[82]

As a purveyor of culture, the media did not lack the enthusiasm to stress the historical significance of the Stanley Cup victory as well as its implications. The *Vancouver Province,* for example, told its readers that the trophy had never gone 'further west than Winnipeg ... Now British Columbia has come to the front through the enterprise of the Patricks and for the first time in history that a Coast team has tried for the historic silverware Vancouver has emerged successful.'[83] In the same mood of boosterism, the *Daily News-Advertiser* proudly reminded the citizenry that Vancouver now possessed three of the four major championship trophies in Canada and pointed out that it was 'only three [sic] years since ice hockey was introduced on the Pacific Coast.'[84] Crediting 'western methods of training and western style of play' as the reason for Vancouver's victory, the *Daily World* argued that 'the western or seven-man game is conducive to the better style of play and the cleanest game.'[85] Taking a more practical view, the *Vancouver Sun* commended Frank Patrick's 'exceptional managerial ability and a tenacity of purpose' that overcame 'many discouragements and many apparently insurmountable obstacles' to produce 'for the edification of Vancouver a hockey team.'[86] It suggested that the Stanley Cup victory gave the city free publicity and would help promote the tourist trade. These reports pointed at the values of persistence, industry, and entrepreneurship of the young and vibrant West Coast culture as the reasons for the team's success. Whereas criticisms had been levelled at hockey in the East as being violent, the product of the West Coast culture seemed to produce fairness and sportsmanship – very much in line with the values of the rising urban middle-class patrons.

Raymond Williams, in his discussion on culture, traces the etymological root of the word that indicates a process of cultivation.[87] Thus understood, culture then involves active interference from social agents who may or may not be conscious of the consequences of their actions. There is no reason to believe that the Patricks went into the professional hockey business with a grandiose plan to move Vancouver and the West Coast closer to the Canadian culture. Yet, as Gruneau and Whitson argue, 'culture and commerce are ... inextricably intertwined.'[88] It is undeniable that the Patricks' decisions and actions in providing professional hockey as entertainment for the growing populace in Vancouver also familiarized the West Coast's denizens with an important form of Canadian popular culture. In building a business in Vancouver, Frank Patrick built a clientele through the drama of sport and its concomitant cultural values. In the process, he created a cultural following for hockey.

Indeed, the cultural stature of the other Canadian national pastime, lacrosse, was declining by 1914 when professional hockey was staging an East-West Stanley Cup series for the first time.[89] While the First World War hampered the development of professional hockey in Canada as wartime difficulties limited its growth, Vancouver rebounded as a vibrant hockey town when the war was over. Vancouver would challenge for the Stanley Cup four more times: in 1918, 1921, 1922, and 1924. The city hosted the 1921 Cup challenge, when the Ottawas came west again, a series that went to the full five games. The first game had the largest crowd ever to attend a hockey match, as the arena sold out every seat.[90] In the fifth and deciding game, 12,000 fans watched the game, even though the arena's official capacity was only 10,500. Another 3000 were turned away at the gate. The press paid a compliment to Frank Patrick, the builder of the club, for cultivating fans who had developed 'a sincere appreciation of the class of contests delivered here [during the regular seasons].'[91] For his part, Frank Patrick must have been glad about the fruits of his entrepreneurship. In a letter to Frank Calder, his counterpart at the National Hockey League (which was formed in 1917 from the old NHA clubs, except Toronto), he expressed satisfaction for the way the series concluded, even though his team had lost.[92] Despite the general economic climate in the early 1920s, the Vancouver team was doing well and would go on to win the PCHA championship three more times.[93]

By 1926, however, the team and the league, which had now become the Western Hockey League, folded under the pressure of the NHL's expansion into the United States. Although the PCHA had included American franchises long before this expansion, the NHL's new teams all came from much larger population centres and their backers were millionaires and major corporations who either had built or were going to build bigger and more luxurious arenas than any of the West Coast league franchises had. Moreover, the expanded NHL also had deeper pockets when it came to player salaries. The West Coast franchises especially feared that the NHL would disregard the territorial arrangement between the two leagues and openly raid their players. Despite continuous support from Vancouver's fans, the Patricks did not believe they had any chances of keeping their players if a bidding war were to occur. Even if Vancouver could compete, others in the league surely would fold.[94]

Nonetheless, a hockey culture had already been firmly established on the West Coast of Canada by that time. While major-league hockey did not return to Vancouver until 1970, the Vancouver Arena, still under the ownership of the Patrick family, continued to host amateur league hockey games and those of the new minor league, the Pacific Coast Hockey League, until fire destroyed the facility in 1936. Indeed, Vancouver had become such an important hockey city that the Canadian Amateur Hockey Association chose Vancouver as the host for its senior championship, the Allan Cup, and of its annual meeting, in 1927.[95] Nor did major-league hockey entirely leave Vancouver. Local newspapers continued to report NHL news, and by the 1930s Vancouver hockey enthusiasts were able to follow major-league hockey when the Canadian Broadcasting Corporation began its coast-to-coast radio broadcasts of NHL play.[96]

NOTES

1 For a history of the International Hockey League, see Daniel Scott Mason, 'The Origins and Development of the International Hockey League and Its Effects on the Sport of Professional Ice Hockey in North America,' MA thesis (University of British Columbia, August 1994); Mason, 'The International Hockey League and the Professionalization of Ice Hockey, 1904–1907,' *Journal of Sport History* 25 (Spring 1998): 1017; and Mason and Barbara Schrodt, 'Hockey's First Professional Team: The Portage Lakes Hockey Club of Houghton, Michigan,' *Sport History Review* 27 (May 1996): 49–71. On the history of hockey as a commercial enterprise before the development of professional hockey, see John Chi-Kit Wong, *Lords of the Rinks: The Emergence of the National Hockey League, 1875–1936* (Toronto: University of Toronto Press, 2005), especially chapters 2, 3, and 4.

2 The PCHA joined the Western Canada Hockey League when its American franchises dropped out of the league, but in 1925 Seattle rejoined the league and the organization decided to drop 'Canada' from its name to reflect its membership.

3 Stephen Hardy, 'Entrepreneurs, Organizations, and the Sport Marketplace: Subjects in Search of Historians,' *Journal of Sport History* 13 (Spring 1986): 15.

4 Richard Gruneau and David Whitson, *Hockey Night in Canada: Sport, Identities and Cultural Politics* (Toronto: Garamond Press, 1993), 200–1.

5 Martin Robin, *The Rush for Spoils: The Company Province 1871–1933* (Toronto: McClelland and Stewart, 1972), 11–15 and n. 14. Quote is from R.E. Grosneil, *Sixty Years of Progress,* part 2 (Vancouver and Victoria: British

Columbia Historical Association, 1913), 8–9, who was talking about the
social life of the elite in Victoria in the late 1860s and early 1870s.

6 Eric Nicol, *Vancouver* (Toronto: Doubleday Canada, 1970), 12–15; Alan
Morley, *Vancouver: Milltown to Metropolis*, 3rd ed. (Vancouver: Mitchell
Press, 1974), 7–8. Captain James Cook had visited the area in 1778, but like
the first Spanish expedition he did not go ashore.

7 At the time of its creation, British Columbia was a separate entity from the
colony of Vancouver Island. However, its first governor, James Douglas,
ruled both colonies.

8 Morley, *Vancouver*, 19; Nicol, *Vancouver*, 16–18.

9 Morley, *Vancouver*, 20–6; quote on p. 25. Moberly and Burnaby also pros-
pected for coal allegedly found in the vicinity.

10 Morley, *Vancouver*, 36–7; Nicol, *Vancouver*, 31; Robert A.J. McDonald, *Making Vancouver: Class, Status, and Social Boundaries, 1863–1913* (Vancouver:
UBC Press, 1996), 7.

11 McDonald, *Making Vancouver*, 31.

12 After the government finished surveying the area, in 1870 it named the settlement outside the Hastings Mill Granville, which would form the basis
of the future city of Vancouver.

13 Nicol, *Vancouver*, 53.

14 The construction of social strata in Vancouver was much more complicated
and involved ethnic origin, education, religion, and profession besides
wealth and skin colour. Social separation as well as exchanges occurred
among groups. McDonald, *Making Vancouver*, 13, 23–31; Nicol, *Vancouver*,
35–8. See also Robert A.J. MacDonald, 'Vancouver's "Four Hundred": The
Quest for Wealth and Status in Canada's Urban West, 1886–1914,' *Journal
of Canadian Studies* 25 (1990): 55–73. For upper-class beliefs, see Robert A.J.
McDonald, '"He Thought He Was the Boss of Everything": Masculinity
and Power in a Vancouver Family,' *BC Studies* no. 132 (Winter 2001/2):
5–30.

15 Morley, *Vancouver*, 77–85; Nicol, *Vancouver*, 44–52.

16 Population figures are taken from Norbert MacDonald, 'Population
Growth and Change in Seattle and Vancouver, 1880–1960,' *Pacific Historical Review* 39 (1970): 301. For the importance of the CPR in Vancouver's
development, see Nobert MacDonald, 'The Canadian Pacific Railway and
Vancouver's Development to 1900,' *BC Studies* no. 35 (Autumn 1977): 3–35.
For the CPR's role in Vancouver's development and land speculation, see
also Robin, *The Rush for Spoils*, 46–8. The provincial government negotiated
the deal on behalf of Vancouver, which at the time was not an incorporated
entity. A contract was signed between the provincial government and the

CPR on 13 February 1886. Private businesses and citizens also agreed to give land to the CPR. Hastings Mill, for example, was to give up 4000 acres immediately.

17 Cordova Street, along the Granville townsite near the waterfront, was the major business centre at the time. Morley, *Vancouver*, 95; Nicol, *Vancouver*, 93–5; MacDonald, 'The Canadian Pacific Railway,' 16; McDonald, *Making Vancouver*, 37–9, 69.

18 British-born or British stock accounted for 88% of the Vancouver population in 1891. McDonald, *Making Vancouver*, 53–4, 58. See also MacDonald, 'Population Growth and Change in Seattle and Vancouver,' 297–321. For Vancouver city improvements, see Nicol, *Vancouver*, 95–6, 100–1; Morley, *Vancouver*, 100–12, 135–6; and MacDonald, 'The Canadian Pacific Railway,' 16.

19 Barbara Schrodt, 'Control of Sports Facilities in Early Vancouver: The Brockton Point Athletic Association at Stanley Park, 1888 to 1913,' *Canadian Journal of the History of Sport* (December 1992): 26–53. The author has kindly alerted me that the date in the article title is 1888, not 1880, which was a misprint. The Brockton Point Athletic Association was an interesting case. Supported by city council members and business leaders who wished to keep the property values near Stanley Park high, the Association acquired and developed land in the park to provide grounds and facilities for various sports clubs in the city on a rental basis. Some of the clubs renting the facilities were definitely not upper-class in nature. See also *News-Advertiser*, 10 May 1888, 6; 15 May 1888, 1 and 3; and 31 December 1889, 1, as cited in McDonald, *Making Vancouver*, 162.

20 McDonald, *Making Vancouver*, 162.

21 Ibid. The CPR began developing Shaughnessy Heights in earnest around 1910 as Vancouver's development pushed southward. See Morley, *Vancouver*, 156, and Nicol, *Vancouver*, 117.

22 Nicol, *Vancouver*, 82–5, 107; quote on p. 107. Morley, *Vancouver*, 144. See also Schrodt, 'Control of Sports Facilities in Early Vancouver,' 29.

23 See Morley, *Vancouver*, 134, for a sample of Vancouver's import/export trade.

24 As quoted in Nicol, *Vancouver*, 110.

25 Ibid.

26 It must be pointed out that there were few houses west of Denman Street that remained largely undeveloped in 1905. Nicol, *Vancouver*, 107; Morley, *Vancouver*, 149. Economic depressions impacted Vancouver between 1890 and the end of the century. Another depression occurred in 1907. For the

impact of the depressions on Vancouver, see Morley, *Vancouver*, 150–4, and Nicol, *Vancouver*, 105.

27 McDonald, *Making Vancouver*, 90–8.

28 Morley, *Vancouver*, 148, 155–6. Nicol, *Vancouver*, 130. Supposedly, $7 million came from Germany, backed by the Kaiser. For Vancouver's growth in this period, see Norbet MacDonald, 'A Critical Growth Cycle for Vancouver, 1900–1914,' *BC Studies*, no. 17 (Spring 1973): 26–42. Census figures are gleaned from p. 28, construction values from p. 31.

29 Nicole, *Vancouver*, 125.

30 Barbara Schrodt, 'Taking the Tram: Travelling to Sport and Recreation Activities on Greater Vancouver's Interurban Railway – 1890's to 1920's,' *Canadian Journal of the History of Sport* 19, 1 (May 1988): 52–62. Nicol, *Vancouver*, 129.

31 Barbara Schrodt, 'Sport in Emerging Urban Settings: Lacrosse in Early British Columbia Prior to World War I,' Proceedings of BC Studies Conference, Vancouver, November 1990. I am grateful to Professor Schrodt for a copy of this paper. For Con Jones, see also Donald M. Fisher, *Lacrosse: A History of the Game* (Baltimore and London: Johns Hopkins University Press, 2002), 49. For the middle class's rising influence in Vancouver municipal politics, see Robert A.J. McDonald, 'The Business Elite and Municipal Politics in Vancouver 1886–1914,' *Urban History Review / Revue d'histoire urbaine* 11, 3 (February 1983): 1–14. For wages in Vancouver, see Eleanor A. Bartlett, 'Real Wages and the Standard of Living in Vancouver, 1901–1929,' *BC Studies*, no. 51 Autumn 1981: 3–62; quote on p. 5.

32 Robin, *The Rush for Spoils*, 40–1.

33 Ibid., 91–2. For Joe Patrick's various career moves until his move to British Columbia, see Eric Whitehead, *The Patricks: Hockey's Royal Family* (Toronto: Doubleday, 1980), 10–14, 16, 23, 26, 39.

34 Whitehead, *The Patricks*, 90, 92–4. See also Vancouver City Archives, Joseph Patrick file, for various clippings on Joe Patrick's careers. It is of interest that one undated clipping notes that Joe's brother Louis drove the first CPR passenger train from Canmore, Alberta, to Donald, BC, in 1886 and that his wife, Minnie Elizabeth, became the CPR railway agent at Laggan (present-day Lake Louise) in 1885, 'and held the position when the first CPR came west.' In an interview with the Patricks' descendants, they could not recollect if Louis and Minnie had any influence on Joe's coming west. Robin, *The Rush for Spoils*, 107–24. See also British Columbia Archives, GR-1526, British Columbia, Registrar of Companies, Files of dissolved companies, societies and co-operatives, Patrick Lumber Company Limited, reel B04425, file QE0001861 (hereafter BCA, Patrick Lumber

Company), Johnson, McConnell & Allison, Bond and Investment Brokers, to D. Whiteside, Registrar of Joint-Stock Companies, 25 January 1912.

35 There were four shareholders in the company. As a majority shareholder, Joe Patrick's initial investment was $90,000 out of a total capitalization of $170,000. BCA, Patrick Lumber Company, Memorandum of Association of the Patrick Lumber Company, Limited. For the ways of entrepreneurs and innovations, see Joseph A. Schumpeter, *The Theory of Economic Development* (1934; repr. ed., Cambridge, MA: 1961), 66, as cited in Hardy, 'Entrepreneurs, Organizations, and the Sport Marketplace,' 20–1.

36 Schrodt, 'Sport in Emerging Urban Settings,' 4–7.

37 For the Renfrew team's tour of New York, see Whitehead, *The Patricks,* 81–7, and Frank Cosentino, *The Renfrew Millionaires: The Valley Boys of Winter 1910* (Burnstown, ON: General Store Publishing House Inc., 1990), 154–8. See also *New York Times,* 20 March 1910, 5. For a brief history of the refrigeration technology in ice hockey, see Donald M. Clark, 'Early Artificial Ice,' in *Total Hockey,* ed. Dan Diamond (Kansas City: Andrews McMeel Publishing, 1998), 564–5.

38 BCA, GR-1526, British Columbia, Registrar of Companies, Files of dissolved companies, societies and co-operatives, Vancouver Arena Company Limited, reel B05251, file BC0000519 (hereafter BCA, Vancouver Arena), Articles of Association of Vancouver Arena Company, Limited. Whitehead, *The Patricks,* 97. See also *Vancouver Province,* 30 December 1911, 8, for a review of Vancouver's economic prosperity. It is unclear if the Patricks purchased the land. There was no evidence to indicate they did so before 1926. Indeed, in the company's first annual report, filed in 1912, the balance sheet did not show land as part of the assets. Total liabilities amounted to $62,851, although the statement did not indicate their nature. BCA, Vancouver Arena, Balance Sheet, 30 April 1912. Further search into the title to the land revealed that the arena took title in 1926. All records relating to the five lots before 1926 were missing in the BC Land Title Office.

39 McDonald, *Making Vancouver,* 152–3; MacDonald, 'A Critical Growth Cycle,' 35.

40 BCA, Vancouver Arena, Statutory Report, 9 September 1911; see Notice of Registered Office, 12 July 1911, for the initial list of company directors. The two additional investors were Curtis W. Lester and Lewis C. Lester of Crescent Valley, BC, who bought their share some time between 12 September 1911 and 30 April 1912. See ibid., Return of Allotments, 25 February 1914. Whitehead has claimed that a small group of investors had invested $5000 and Joe Patrick returned their money (*The Patricks,* 97). The archival documents do not support that assertion.

41 BCA, Vancouver Arena, Balance Sheet, 30 April 1912. The final cost listed here excluded the cost of furniture, listed as $1,399.50. Whitehead's biography of the Patricks lists the final cost as $275,000. Thomas Picard gives $175,000 as the amount, although he does not specify whether the number was for the building alone or includes all work. His number was possibly taken from the report in the *Vancouver Province*, 22 November 1911, 10. See Whitehead, *The Patricks*, 109–10; and Thomas Picard, 'The Pacific Coast Hockey Association,' in *Total Hockey*, ed. Dan Diamond (Kansas City: Andrews McMeel Publishing, 1998), 35.

42 *Vancouver Province*, 22 November 1911, 10. Whitehead and Picard both give different dimensions: Whitehead, 90' × 220', and Picard, 200' × 85'. See Whitehead, *The Patricks*, 109; and Picard, 'The Pacific Coast Hockey Association,' 35.

43 *Vancouver Province*, 1 December 1911, 10.

44 Ibid., 21 December 1911, 10.

45 Bernard J. Mullin, Stephen Hardy, and William A. Sutton, *Sport Marketing*, 2nd ed. (Champlain, IL: Human Kinetics, 2000), 136.

46 Lalonde reported received a staggering sum of $6,500 for the 1911 season. See Alan Metcalfe, *Canada Learns to Play* (Toronto: McClelland & Stewart Inc., 1987), 217.

47 *Vancouver Province*, 6 April 1911, 11. The quote is from a letter to the paper's sport editor. While the two parts had been rearranged, they still conveyed the point about the writer's view on importing players in professional sports. For local media reporting on NHA affairs, see ibid., 10 February 1911, 22; and 7 March 1911, 14.

48 Frank Patrick was also a member of the Hockey Hall of Fame in the Builders category. Phillips and Griffis had been on winning Stanley Cup teams before coming to Vancouver. Lalonde was a prolific scorer in different professional leagues and would win the PCHA scoring title in his first season (http://www.legendsofhockey.net/html/legends.htm). The other members of the team were Allan Parr, goaltender, Fred Harris, Jack Ulrich, and Sibby Nichols. Charles L. Coleman, *Trail of the Stanley Cup*, 3 vols. (Sherbrooke, QC: Sherbrooke Daily Record Co., 1964), 1: 230. On Lester Patrick's trip east, see *Montreal Gazette*, 21 March and 4 April 1911, 10; and *Vancouver Province*, 7 April 1911, 11. See also Whitehead, *The Patricks*, 97–9; and Fisher, *Lacrosse*, 49. For the NHA salary cap, see Wong, *Lords of the Rinks*, 59–61. For Frank Patrick's recruitment of Newsy Lalonde, see *Vancouver Province*, 2 May 1911, 11.

49 Whitehead, *The Patricks*, 111. Ironically, the tight race produced charges of fixing the league standings to generate interest. For the Patricks' efforts

to pursue Edmonton and Calgary as part of the PCHA, see *Vancouver Province*, 25 July and 22 August 1911, 10; 26 September 1911, 11; and 12 October 1911, 10. See also *B.C. Saturday Sunset*, 18 November 1911, 19 and 16 December 1911, 6.

50 *Vancouver Province*, 5 January 1912, 10. Between 1892 and 1900, cross-ownership in major league baseball, wherein one owner controlled more than one team, became common practice. Often, an owner would move players from one of his controlled teams to another in order to manipulate team standings and financial return. See David Quentin Voigt, *The League That Failed* (Lanham, MD, London: Scarecrow Press, Inc., 1998), 187–226. See also Benjamin G. Rader, *Baseball: A History of America's Game*, 2nd ed. (Urbana and Chicago: University of Illinois Press, 2002), 85–6; and David Quentin Voigt, *American Baseball*, 3 vols. (University Park: Pennsylvania State University Press, 1983), 1: 228–9.

51 *Vancouver Province*, 9 November 1911, 10. For the organization of the city amateur league, see ibid., 15 November 1911, 10. The three rejected applicants were the Benge, the YMCA, and the Independents. See also ibid., 18 November 1911, 10 for its organization meeting.

52 Ibid., 20 December 1911, 10. While many of the Connaught skating club members or their spouses made their fame and fortune before they moved to Vancouver, some had entered the upper strata after they moved to Vancouver. Mr and Mrs Edward P. Davis, for example, had moved to Vancouver in 1893, but did not acquire upper-class status until the turn of the century. See McDonald, *Making Vancouver*, 151–2.

53 For the establishment of the Vancouver Curling Club, see *Vancouver Province*, 23 December 1911, 10. See also *B.C. Saturday Sunset*, 2 December 1911, 19.

54 The New Westminster franchise did have an executive board, but for all intents and purposes, the Patricks ran the league.

55 See *Vancouver Province*, 8 December 1911, 10; *Vancouver Daily News-Advertiser*, 8 December 1911, 8; and *Vancouver Daily World*, 8 December 1911, 14. Whitehead erred in saying that the meeting was held on 11 December. Whitehead, *The Patricks*, 106. To give the league more credibility and clear the air of nepotism, W.P. Irving, a former long-time executive of the Ontario Hockey Association, was elected president.

56 *Vancouver Province*, 5 January 1912, 10. Vancouver defeated New Westminster 8–3.

57 *B.C. Saturday Sunset*, 13 January 1912, 19. For attendance, see *Vancouver Province*, 6 January 1912, 8, which estimated about 5000 in attendance. Another newspaper put the number at 3500. See *Vancouver Daily News-Advertiser*, 6 January 1912, 8.

58 *Vancouver Province,* 14 October 1911, 10. For NHA rule changes, see Coleman, *Trail of the Stanley Cup,* 1: 219–20; *Montreal Gazette,* 12 October 1911, 11 and 4 December 1911, 13.

59 *Vancouver Province,* 6 January 1912, 8. Technically, the 5 January game was a home game for the New Westminster team, which played all its home games in the Vancouver arena that season.

60 For PCHA's Stanley Cup challenge, see *Vancouver Province,* 1 March 1912, 10. At the time when the Patricks issued the challenge, there were certain assumptions about the final league results. March 15 was an optimistic estimation.

61 *Vancouver Province,* 11 March 1912, 10.

62 For reports of the series, see ibid., 3, 5, and 7 April 1912, 10. It is doubtful that the seven-man PCHA rules had a significant influence on the outcome, since the NHA only changed to six-man hockey at the beginning of the 1911–12 season.

63 In terms of gate receipts, Vancouver's first season was a disaster. Only three of the reports on the eight Vancouver home games had attendance estimates. Three did not mention the crowd size whatsoever, and one, for 1 March, stated only that a small crowd attended. The last home game supposedly had the largest crowd of the season, but no estimate was provided. See *Vancouver Province,* 10, 20, and 27 January; 14 and 21 February; and 2, 6, and 20 March 1912, 10. In fact, the Vancouver Arena actually reduced admission for the 13 February match in order to attract customers, but to no avail. Only around 1800 attended.

64 *Montreal Gazette,* 8 April 1912, 12.

65 Whitehead, *The Patricks,* 114.

66 For Taylor's life and exploits, see Eric Whitehead, *Cyclone Taylor: A Hockey Legend* (Toronto: Doubleday Canada Ltd, 1977). For Taylor's fame in New York, see, for example, *New York Times,* 12 March 1911, S4 and 18 March 1911, 15.

67 *Vancouver Province,* 10 December 1912, 10.

68 Ibid. Whitehead gave Taylor credit for a sell-out crowd in Vancouver's second home game (*The Patricks,* 118). Yet, the newspaper report gives a figure of only 4500. Ibid., 22 January 1913, 10.

69 *Vancouver Province,* 19 December 1912, 14.

70 MacDonald, 'A Critical Growth Cycle,' 31, 34. The *Vancouver Province* first used the Millionaires moniker in a cartoon that appeared on 14 December 1912, 10.

71 *Vancouver Province,* 30 December 1912, 11.

72 MacDonald, 'A Critical Growth Cycle,' 31. Vancouver also experienced a period of economic depression between 1912 and 1915, during which

'there was at least 25 percent more labour in British Columbia than was needed.' Bartlett, 'Real Wages and the Standard of Living in Vancouver,' 59. Press estimates of Vancouver's attendance appeared for four (9 and 16 December 1912 and 5 and 21 January 1913) of the club's eight home games. The 28 January 1913 game was described as having a smaller crowd than on the other two times New Westminster visited town. The 4 February game was reported to have the largest crowd of the season, while the 16 February match had a 'good crowd.' See *Vancouver Province,* 10 and 17 December 1912, 10; 6, 22, and 29 January 1913, 10; and 5, 17, and 26 February 1913, 10.

73 Gruneau and Whitson, *Hockey Night in Canada,* 199.
74 For hockey and masculinity, see chapters 2 and 5. On the capital–labour relations of professional hockey, see Gruneau and Whitson, *Hockey Night in Canada,* 124–30; and Bruce Kidd, *The Struggle for Canadian Sport* (Toronto: University of Toronto Press, 1996), 224–31.
75 Coleman, *Trail of the Stanley Cup,* 1: 253–4, 258. The forward-pass rule in the central zone was adopted by the PCHA in the 1913–14 season. Traditionally, hockey had followed rugby's on-side rule: the puck could not be passed from the carrier to any player ahead.
76 *Vancouver Province,* 22 March 1915, 4. Lloyd Cook, Barney Stanley, and Mickey Mackay were playing their first season in the PCHA, and Stanley was a substitute when the veteran Si Griffis suffered a season-ending injury.
77 *Vancouver World,* 22 March, 1915, 8.
78 *Vancouver Daily News-Advertiser,* 23 March 1915, 6.
79 *Vancouver World,* 23 March 1915, 8.
80 *Vancouver Province,* 23 March 1915, 4.
81 The estimated attendance seemed to agree in two Vancouver newspapers. See *Vancouver World,* 23 March, 1915, 8 and *Vancouver Province,* 23 March 1915, 4.
82 For estimated attendance figures, see, for example, *Vancouver Province,* 27 March 1915, 10 and *Vancouver Daily News-Advertiser,* 27 March 1915, 6. The *Vancouver Sun* estimated that 18,000 attended the three games. *Vancouver Sun,* 27 March 1915, 7.
83 *Vancouver Province,* 27 March, 1915, 11.
84 *Vancouver Daily News-Advertiser,* 27 March 1915, 4.
85 *Vancouver Daily World,* 27 March 1915, 6.
86 *Vancouver Sun,* 29 March, 1915, 4.
87 Raymond Williams, *The Sociology of Culture* (New York: Schocken Books, 1982), 10.

88 David Whitson and Richard Gruneau, eds, *Artificial Ice: Hockey, Culture and Commerce* (Peterborough, ON: Broadview Press, 2006), 22.

89 For the problems and decline of lacrosse in Canada, see Metcalfe, *Canada Learns to Play*, 203–18 and Donald M. Fisher, *Lacrosse: A History of the Game:* (Baltimore: Johns Hopkins University Press, 2002), 43–52.

90 *Vancouver Sun*, 22 March 1922, 1. Although the official capacity of the arena was 10,500, a different source stated that 11,000 crammed into it. See Coleman, *Trail of the Stanley Cup*, 1: 387.

91 *Vancouver Sun*, 5 April 1922, 1 and 4; quote from p. 4.

92 Frank Patrick to Frank Calder, 6 April 1921, 1922–3, Vancouver Arena Company file, National Hockey League Archives (hereafter NHLA).

93 Frank Patrick to Frank Calder, 5 February 1921, 1922–3, Vancouver Arena Company file, NHLA.

94 The PCHA had not been a very stable league. With the exception of Vancouver, no franchises stayed with the league from the beginning until the end. In 1924, both Vancouver and Victoria joined the Western Canada Hockey League (WCHL) when Seattle, the only other franchise in the PCHL at that time, dropped out of the league. For its part, the WCHL also was not a very strong league in terms of market size and finances. All of its franchises were located in Canadian prairie cities without sizeable populations. And, the teams had to travel far for their scheduled games. When Portland rejoined professional hockey for the 1925–6 season, the WCHL dropped Canada from its title to reflect the new alignment.

95 *Vancouver Province*, 14 November 1926, 21. When an article from Fort William (Ontario) complained about Vancouver hosting the Allan Cup instead of having the finalists hosting the championship games, the *Province* replied that Vancouver had had strong support for amateur hockey for quite some time. If Fort William were to make the final, it could expect a 'very large crowd, which ... Fort William ... can scarcely hope for' due to the size of its home rink. Ibid., 16 November 1926, 19.

96 Kidd, *The Struggle for Canadian Sport*, 254–5.

Contributors

Carly Adams is an Assistant Professor in the Department of Kinesiology and Physical Education at the University of Lethbridge, Alberta. Her research interests include twentieth-century Canadian sport, oral, regional, and local histories, gender, and women's experiences in sport.

John Matthew Barlow is a goalie. He recently completed his PhD in history from Concordia University, Montreal. He currently teaches at John Abbott College, Montreal.

Robert S. Kossuth is currently a faculty member in the Department of Kinesiology and Physical Education at the University of Lethbridge, Alberta. He completed his doctoral studies in 2002 in the School of Kinesiology at the University of Western Ontario. Research interests include late-nineteenth- and early-twentieth-century Canadian sport, recreation, and leisure history, with a focus on local and regional experiences and masculine identity. Current research projects include historical investigations of sport and recreation practices in southern Alberta, including hockey, curling, baseball, and bicycling.

Stacy L. Lorenz is an Associate Professor of Physical Education at the University of Alberta, Augustana Campus, in Camrose, Alberta. He teaches in the fields of sport history, sport and social issues, and sport and popular culture. His research interests include Canadian newspaper coverage of sport, media experiences of sport, sport and local and national identities, and hockey and Canadian culture. He received the 1996 North American Society for Sport History Graduate Student Essay Award for his paper '"A Lively Interest on the Prairies": Western Canada, the Mass Media, and a "World of Sport," 1870–1939.'

Daniel MacDonald holds a PhD from the University of New Brunswick. He has taught sport, Canadian, and Atlantic Canadian history at Acadia University and Cape Breton University.

Geraint B. Osborne is an Associate Professor of Sociology at the University of Alberta, Augustana Campus, in Camrose, Alberta. His recent research interests include the social construction of deviance and crime, social control, and the politics of accommodation.

J. Andrew Ross completed his dissertation 'Hockey Capital: Commerce, Culture and the National Hockey League, 1917–1967' in the Department of History at the University of Western Ontario in 2008. He is currently a Postdoctoral Fellow in the Historical Data Research Unit at the University of Guelph.

John Chi-Kit Wong is an Assistant Professor of the Sport Management program at Washington State University. He is author of *Lords of the Rinks: The Emergence of the National Hockey League, 1875–1936*. His research interests include the business of hockey, sport in the Pacific Northwest, and power issues in sport.

Index